FROM ANCIENT ISRAEL TO MODERN JUDAISM
INTELLECT IN QUEST OF UNDERSTANDING

Number 174
FROM ANCIENT ISRAEL TO MODERN JUDAISM
INTELLECT IN QUEST OF UNDERSTANDING

Edited by
Jacob Neusner
Ernest S. Frerichs
Nahum M. Sarna

FROM ANCIENT ISRAEL TO MODERN JUDAISM

Intellect in Quest of Understanding

Essays in Honor of Marvin Fox

Volume Three

**Judaism in the Middle Ages:
Philosophers**

Hasidism. Messianism in Modern Times

**The Modern Age:
Philosophy**

Edited by
Jacob Neusner
Ernest S. Frerichs
Nahum M. Sarna

Managing Editor
Joshua Bell

Scholars Press
Atlanta, Georgia

FROM ANCIENT ISRAEL TO MODERN JUDAISM
Intellect in Quest of Understanding

© 1989
Brown University

The editors acknowledge with thanks the support of the
Tisch Family Foundation in the publication of this volume.

Library of Congress Cataloging in Publication Data

From ancient Israel to modern Judaism : intellect in quest of
understanding : essays in honor of Marvin Fox / edited by Jacob
Neusner, Ernest S. Frerichs, Nahum M. Sarna.
   p. cm. -- (Brown Judaic studies ; no. 159, 173-175)
   Contents: v. 1. What is at stake in the Judaic quest for
understanding. Judaic learning and the locus of education. Ancient
Israel. Formative Christianity. Judaism in the formative age:
religion -- v. 2. Judaism in the formative age: theology and
literature. Judaism in the Middle Ages: the encounter with
Christianity, the encounter with Scripture, philosophy, and theology
-- v. 3. Judaism in the Middle Ages: philosophers. Hasidism,
Messianism in modern times. The modern age: philosophy -- v. 4. The
modern age: theology, literature, history.
   ISBN 1-55540-342-5 (v. 3 : alk. paper)
   1. Judaism--History. 2. Philosophy, Jewish. 3. Fox, Marvin.
I. Fox, Marvin. II. Neusner, Jacob, 1932- . III. Frerichs,
Ernest S. IV. Sarna, Nahum M. V. Series: Brown Judaic studies ;
no. 159, etc.
BM157.F76 1989
296'.09--dc20   89-61111

Printed in the United States of America
on acid-free paper

TABLE OF CONTENTS

VOLUME ONE

VOLUME TWO

PART SIX:
FORMATIVE JUDAISM: THEOLOGY

PART SEVEN:
FORMATIVE JUDAISM: LITERATURE

PART EIGHT:
JUDAISM IN THE MIDDLE AGES:
THE ENCOUNTER WITH CHRISTIANITY

PART NINE:
JUDAISM IN THE MIDDLE AGES:
THE ENCOUNTER WITH SCRIPTURE

PART TEN:
JUDAISM IN THE MIDDLE AGES:
PHILOSOPHY AND THEOLOGY

VOLUME FOUR

Preface

In these essays, collected in four volumes, we honor as principal and leader of Judaic Studies in our generation Professor Marvin Fox, Philip W. Lown Professor of Jewish Philosophy and Director of the Lown School of Near Eastern and Judaic Studies at Brandeis University, because in our generation, Professor Fox has occupied the position of *doyen* of Judaic Studies in the academy. This position has come to him through force of character and conscience and is one that expresses the man's moral authority, as much as his acknowledged excellence as scholar and teacher. His scholarship is attested by the bibliography that follows, his teaching by the excellent contributions to this volume of many of his doctoral students. But while in learning and teaching he competes on equal terms with many, in stature and universal respect there is none anywhere in the world of Judaic Studies, at home or in the State of Israel, who compares. It is a simple fact that the scholars who contributed to these volumes, have nothing whatsoever in common save that they concur in expressing esteem for this remarkable colleague. This is a scholars' tribute to a great man; in paying this honor to Marvin Fox, we identify the kind of person we want as our representative and academic avatar. In our generation, this is the sort of scholar we have cherished.

The facts of his career do not account for the honor in which he is held, even though he has pursued, and now pursues, a splendid career in higher education. But the facts do explain something about the man. Professor Marvin Fox received his B.A. in philosophy in 1942 from Northwestern University, the M.A. in the same field in 1946, and the Ph.D. from the University of Chicago in 1950 in that field as well. His education in Judaic texts was certified by rabbinical ordination as Rabbi by the Hebrew Theological College of Chicago in 1942. He taught at Ohio State University from 1948 through 1974, rising from Instructor to Professor of Philosophy. During those years he served also as Visiting Professor of Philosophy at the Hebrew Theological College of Chicago (1955) and also at the Hebrew University of Jerusalem and Bar Ilan

University (1970-1971). In 1974 he came to Brandeis University as Appleman Professor of Jewish Thought, and from 1976 onward he has held the Lown Professorship. From 1975 through 1982 and from 1984 through 1987 he was Chairman of the Department of Near Eastern and Judaic Studies at Brandeis. From 1976 he has also served as Director of the Lown School of Near Eastern and Judaic Studies. In 1980-1981 he was Visiting Scholar in Jewish Philosophy at the Center for Jewish Studies of nearby Harvard University.

He has received numerous academic awards, a selected list of which includes the following: 1956-1957: Elizabeth Clay Howald Post-Doctoral Scholarship; 1962-1963, Fellow of the American Council of Learned Societies; 1975-1978, Director of the Association for Jewish Studies regional conferences, funded by the National Endowment for the Humanities; 1977-1980, Director of the project, "For the Strengthening of Judaic Studies at Brandeis and their Links to the General Humanities," also funded by the National Endowment for the Humanities. From 1979 he has been Fellow of the Academy of Jewish Philosophy; 1980-1981, Senior Faculty Fellow, National Endowment for the Humanities. He has served on the editorial boards of the *AJS Review*, *Daat*, *Judaism*, *Tradition*, *Journal for the History of Philosophy*, and other journals. He has lectured widely at universities and at national and international academic conferences and served as Member of the National Endowment for the Humanities National Board of Consultants for new programs at colleges and universities. Over the years he has counseled various universities and academic publishers as well.

His ties to institutions of Jewish learning under Jewish sponsorship are strong. He has served on the Advisory Committee of the Jewish Studies Adaptation Program of the International Center for University Teaching of Jewish Civilization (Israel), since 1982; International Planning Committee of the Institute for Contemporary Jewry of the Hebrew University since that same year; member of the governing council of the World Union of Jewish Studies since 1975; secretary, 1971-1972, vice president, from 1973-1975, and then president, from 1975-1978, of the Association for Jewish Studies; and he has been on the board of directors of that organization since 1970. From 1964 through 1968 he served on the Executive Committee of the Conference on Jewish Philosophy; from 1970 to the present on the Executive Committee of the Institute of Judaism and Contemporary Thought of Bar Ilan University; from 1972 as member of the Academic Board of the Melton Research Center of the Jewish Theological Seminary of America; member of the board of directors of the Institute for Jewish Life from 1972 through 1975; member of the board of directors of the Library of Living

Philosophers, from 1948; Associate of the Columbia University Seminar on Israel and Jewish Studies from 1968 through 1974; and many other organizations.

His committee service at Brandeis University has covered these committees: Graduate School Council; Philosophy Department Advisory Committee and Reappointment and Promotions Committee; University Tenure Panels; Academic Planning Committee (Chairman, 1982-1984); Faculty Committee for the Hiatt Institute; Tauber Institute Faculty Advisory Committee and its academic policy subcommittee; Committee on University Studies in the Humanities; Faculty representative on the Brandeis University Board of Trustees (1978-1980). His professional memberships include the American Philosophical Association, the Metaphysical Society of America, the Medieval Academy of America, as well as the Association for Jewish Studies, Conference on Jewish Philosophy, and American Academy for Jewish Research.

The editors of this volume bear special ties of collegiality and friendship with Professor Fox. In this project Professor Sarna represents Brandeis University and also has been a close and intimate colleague and friend for many years. Professors Frerichs and Neusner have called upon Professor Fox for counsel in the fifteen years since Professor Fox came to Brandeis University. And Professor Fox has responded, always giving his best judgment and his wisest counsel. Professor Fox has been a good neighbor, a constant counsellor, and valued friend. In the sequence of eight academic conferences, run annually at Brown University in the 1970s, Professor Fox played a leading role in the planning of the programs and in scholarly interchange. Through him and the editors of this volume Brown and Brandeis Universities held a conference at which graduate students in the respective graduate programs met and engaged in shared discussion of common interests. Professor Fox moreover has taken a position on numerous dissertation committees in Brown's graduate program in the History of Judaism. His conscientious and careful reading of these dissertations give to the students the benefit not only of his learning but also of his distinct and rich perspective on the problem of the dissertation. Consequently, among the many other universities besides Ohio State and Brandeis at which Professor Fox has made his contribution, Brown University stands out as particularly indebted to him for wisdom and learning.

The editors express their thanks to President Evelyn Handler of Brandeis University for sponsoring the public event at which the contributors to these volumes presented the books to Professor Fox and enjoyed the opportunity of expressing in person their esteem and affection for him; and to the Max Richter Foundation of Rhode Island

and the Program in Judaic Studies at Brown University for financial and other support in organizing and carrying out this project. Mr. Joshua Bell, Verbatim, of Providence, Rhode Island, produced the camera ready copy with the usual attention to aesthetic excellence and also accuracy of detail that have characterized all of his work for Brown Judaic Studies, Brown Studies in Jews and their Societies, Brown Studies in Religion (Scholars Press), and also Studies in Judaism (University Press of America). The staff of Scholars Press, particularly Dr. Dennis Ford, gave to this project their conscientious attention. Professors Frerichs and Neusner therefore express thanks to Verbatim, Scholars Press, and University Press of America, which in the past ten years have made Brown University's Judaic Studies Program the world's largest publisher of scholarly books and monographs in the field of Judaic Studies. All three editors thank the contributors to these volumes for their willingness to collaborate in what we believe is an important tribute to greatness in our field and in our time.

Jacob Neusner   Nahum M. Sarna
Ernest S. Frerichs   Department of Near Eastern
Program in Judaic Studies   and Judaic Studies
Brown University   Brandeis University
Providence, Rhode Island   Waltham, Massachusetts

Bibliography of Marvin Fox
1946-1989

1. "Three Approaches to the Jewish Problem," *Antioch Review*, 6(1), Spring 1946, pp. 54-68.

2. "Towards a Life of Joy: A Theological Critique," *Menorah Journal*, 36(2), Spring 1948, pp. 248-251.

3. "On Calling Women to the Reading of the Torah," *The Reconstructionist*, 13(19), January 1948. An exchange of letters with Robert Gordis. For Gordis' reply see *idem.*, 14(7), May 1948.

4. *Kant's Fundamental Principles of the Metaphysic of Morals,* edited with an introduction (Liberal Arts Press, 1949). Reprinted in numerous editions by the original publisher, then acquired by Bobbs-Merrill, and most recently by Macmillan.

5. Review of Chaim Weizmann, *Trial and Error,* in *Heritage*, Spring 1949, pp. 16-18.

6. Review of Morris R. Cohen, *Reason and Law,* in *Illinois Law Review*, 45(2), May 1950, pp. 305 -307.

7. *Moral Fact and Moral Theory: A Study of Some Methodological Problems in Contemporary Ethics.* Unpublished doctoral dissertation, University of Chicago, 1950.

8. Review of John A. Nicholson, *Philosophy of Religion,* in *Philosophy and Phenomenological Research,* 11(3), March 1951.

9. Review of Maxwell Silver, *The Way to God,* in *Philosophy and Phenomenological Research,* 11(4), June 1951.

10. "On the Diversity of Methods in Dewey's Ethical Theory," *Philosophy and Phenomenological Research,* 12(1), September 1951.

11. Review of Abraham Joshua Heschel, *Man is Not Alone,* in *Commentary*, 12(2), August 1951, pp. 193-195.

12. "Kierkegaard and Rabbinic Judaism," *Judaism*, 2(2), April 1953, pp. 160-169.

13. "Day Schools and the American Educational Pattern," *The Jewish Parent*, September 1953.

14. Review of J. Guttmann, *Maimonides' Guide of the Perplexed*, in *Judaism*, 2(4), October 1953, pp. 363-367.

15. "Moral Facts and Moral Theory," in *Perspectives* (Ohio State University Press, 1953), pp. 111-127.

16. Review of Martin Buber, *At the Turning*, New Mexico Quarterly, 24(2), Summer 1954, pp. 217-220.

17. "What Can the Modern Jew Believe?" Alfred Jospe, ed., *Judaism for the Modern Age* (B'nai B'rith Hillel Foundations, 1955).

18. "Our Missing Intellectuals: Another View," *National Jewish Monthly*, December 1954, pp. 10-13.

19. Review of Abraham Cronbach, *Judaism for Today*, in *Judaism*, 4(1), Winter 1955, pp. 82-84.

20. "Amicus Jacobus, sed Magis Amica Veritas," *Conservative Judaism*, 10(3), Spring 1956, pp. 9-17.

21. "The Trials of Socrates: An Analysis of the First Tetralogy," *Archiv fuer Philosophie*, 6(3/4), 1956, pp. 226-261.

22. "What's Wrong – and Right – with Deweyism," *The Jewish Parent*, December 1956.

23. Review of Abraham Joshua Heschel, *God in Search of Man: A Philosophy of Judaism*, in *Judaism*, 6(1), Winter 1957, pp. 77-81.

24. "Can Modern Man Believe in God," in Alfred Jospe, ed., *The Jewish Heritage and the Jewish Student* (New York, 1959), pp. 40-50.

25. "Who is Competent to Teach Religion," *Religious Education*, 54(2), March-April 1959, pp. 112-114.

26. "Torah Jews in the Making," *The Jewish Parent*, April 1960, pp. 4-5, 22.

27. "Heschel, Intuition, and the Halakhah," *Tradition*, 3(1), Fall 1960, pp. 5-15.

28. "Tillich's Ontology and God," *Anglican Theological Review*, 43(3), July 1961, pp. 260-267.

29. "Ve-al ha-Medinot Bo Ye'amer," *Panim el Panim*, No. 124-125, September 10, 1961, pp. 18-19. A symposium with Professor Salo Baron.

30. Review of Samuel Dresner, *The Zaddik*, in *Conservative Judaism*, 15(4), Summer 1961, pp. 39-42.

31. Review of Robert Gordis, *A Faith for Moderns*, in *Commentary*, 32(4), October 1961.

32. "Modern Faith," *Commentary,* 33(2), February 1962. An exchange of letters with Robert Gordis.

33. Review of Jakob Petuchowski, *Ever Since Sinai, Judaism,* 10(4), Fall 1961.

34. Review of Harry A. Wolfson, *Religious Philosophy: A Group of Essays,* in *The Classical Journal,* 58(2), November 1962.

35. "Einige Probleme in Buber's Moralphilosophie," in Paul A. Schilpp and Maurice Friedman, eds., *Philosophen des 20. Jahrhunderts: Martin Buber* (Kohlhammer, 1963), pp. 135-152. German translation of # 47.

36. "Theistic Bases of Ethics," in Robert Bartels, ed., *Ethics in Business* (Ohio State University Press, 1963).

37. Reviews of Joseph Blau, *The Story of Jewish Philosophy,* and Gerald Abrahams, *The Jewish Mind,* in *Commentary ,* 35(1), January 1963.

38. Review of Arthur A. Cohen, *The Natural and the Super-Natural Jew,* in *Commentary,* 35(4), April 1963.

39. Review of Ephraim Shmueli, *Bein Emunah Likfirah,* in *Commentary,* 36(2), August 1963.

40. "Religion and Human Nature in the Philosophy of David Hume," in William L. Reese and Eugene Freeman, eds., *Process and Divinity: Philosophical Essays Presented to Charles Hartshorne* (Open Court, 1964), pp. 561-577.

41. "Character Training and Environmental Pressures," in *The Jewish Parent,* October 1964.

42. Review of W. Gunther Plaut, *The Rise of Reform Judaism,* i n *Commentary,* 37(6), June 1964.

43. Review of Max Kadushin, *Worship and Ethics,* in *Commentary,* 38(6), December 1964.

44. Review of Israel Efros, *Ancient Jewish Philosophy,* in *Commentary,* 40(1), July 1965.

45. "Religion and the Public Schools – A Philosopher's Analysis," in *Theory into Practice,* 4(1), February 1965, pp. 40-44.

46. Review Essay on *Maimonides" Guide to the Perplexed,* Shlomo Pines, tr., with introductory essays by Leo Strauss and Shlomo Pines, in *Journal of the History of Philosophy,* 3(2), October 1965, pp. 265-274.

47. "Some Problems in Buber's Moral Philosophy," in Paul A. Schilpp and Maurice Friedman, eds., *The Philosophy of Martin Buber* (Open Court, 1966), pp. 151-170.

48.	"The Case for the Jewish Day School," in Judah Pilch and Meir Ben-Horin, eds., *Judaism and the Jewish School* (New York, 1966), pp. 207-213.

49.	"The State of Jewish Belief: A Symposium," *Commentary,* 42(2), August 1966, pp. 89-92.

50.	"Heschel's Theology of Man," *Tradition,* 8(3), Fall 1966, pp. 79-84.

51.	"Jewish Education in a Pluralistic Community," *Proceedings of the Rabbinical Assembly of America,* 30, 1966, pp. 31-40, 47-51.

52.	Review of Arnold Jacob Wolf, ed., *Rediscovering Judaism: Reflections on a New Theology, Commentary,* 41(2), February 1966.

53.	"Sakkanah Lishelemutah shel ha-Yahadut," *Hadoar,* 47(38), October 1967.

54.	Chapter in *The State of Jewish Belief* (Macmillan, 1967), pp. 59-69. Reprint of #49.

55.	"Heschel, Intuition, and the Halakhah," in Norman Lamm and Walter S. Wurzburger, eds., *A Treasury of Tradition* (New York, 1967), pp. 426-435. Reprint of #27.

56.	Review of *Harry Austryn Wolfson Jubilee Volumes,* in *Judaism,* 16(4), Fall 1967.

57.	"Prolegomenon" to A. Cohen, *The Teachings of Maimonides* (New York, 1968), pp. xv-xliv.

58.	"The Meaning of Theology Today," *Bulletin of the Central Ohio Academy of Theology,* January 1968.

59.	Review Article on Sidney Hook, in *Religion in a Free Society, The Journal of Value Inquiry,* 2(4), Winter 1968, pp. 308-314.

60.	"The Function of Religion," *Congress Bi-Weekly,* 36(3), February 1969, pp. 56-63.

61.	"La Teologia Dell'uomo Nel Pensiero di Abraham J. Heschel," *La Rassegna Mensile di Israel,* 25(4), April 1969. Italian translation of #50.

62.	Review of Zvi Adar, *Humanistic Values in the Bible,* in *Commentary* 47(1), January 1969.

63.	Review of Richard L. Rubenstein, *After Auschwitz* and *The Religious Imagination,* in *Commentary,* 47(6), June 1969.

64.	"Religion and the Public Schools," Kaoru Jamamotie, ed., *Teaching* (Houghton Mifflin, 1969), pp. 239-248. Reprint of #45.

65.	"The 'Commentary' Problem," *Judaism,* 18(1), Winter 1969, pp. 108-110.

66.	Review of Nathan Rotenstreich, *Jewish Philosophy in Modern Times,* in *Commentary,* 49(5), May 1970.

67. "Naturalism, Rationalism and Jewish Faith," *Tradition,* 11(3), Fall 1970, pp. 90-96.

68. "Day Schools and the American Educational Pattern," in Joseph Kaminetsky, ed., *Hebrew Day School Education: An Overview* (New York, 1970). Reprint of #13.

69. "Day Schools and the American Educational Pattern," in Lloyd P. Gartner, ed., *Jewish Education in the United States* (Teachers College, Columbia University Press, 1970), Classics in Education Series, No. 41. Reprint of #13.

70. "Continuity and Change in Jewish Theology," *Niv Hamidrashia,* Spring-Summer 1971, pp. 15-23.

71. Review of Mendell Lewittes, *The Light of Redemption,* in *The Jerusalem Post Magazine,* April 9, 1971.

72. "Moral Facts and Moral Theory," in Julius Weinberg and Keith Yandell, eds., *Problems in Philosophical Inquiry* (Holt Rinehart Winston, 1971), pp. 368-381. Reprint of #15.

73. "Freedom and Freedom of Thought," *Encyclopaedia Judaica,* Vol. 7, 119-121.

74. "God, Conceptions of," *Encyclopaedia Judaica,* Vol. 7, 670-673.

75. "God in Medieval Jewish Philosophy," *Encyclopaedia Judaica,* Vol. 7, 658-661.

76. "God in Modern Jewish Philosophy, " *Encyclopaedia Judaica,* Vol. 7, 662-664.

77. "God, Names of in Medieval Jewish Philosophy," *Encyclopaedia Judaica,* Vol. 7, 684-685.

78. "God, Names of in Modern Jewish Philosophy, *Encyclopaedia Judaica,* Vol. 7. 685.

79. "Maimonides and Aquinas on Natural Law," *Dine Israel: An Annual of Jewish Law, Tel-Aviv University,* Vol. 3, 1972, pp. 5-36.

80. "Kierkegaard and Rabbinic Judaism," in Robert Gordis and Ruth B. Waxman, eds., *Faith and Reason* (New York, 1972), pp. 115-124. Reprint of #12.

81. "Tillich's Ontology and God," in Keith Yandell, *God, Man and Religion* (McGraw-Hill, 1972). Reprint of #28.

82. Review of Nathan Rotenstreich, *Tradition and Reality,* in *Commentary,* 55(2), February 1973.

83. "Philosophy and Contemporary Jewish Studies," *American Jewish Historical Quarterly,* 53(4), June 1974, pp. 350-355.

84. "Berkovits on the Problem of Evil," *Tradition,* 14(3), Spring 1974, pp. 116-124.

85. "God in Modern Jewish Philosophy," *Jewish Values* (Keter, Jerusalem, 1974). Reprinted from #76.

86. "Conceptions of God," *Jewish Values* (Keter, Jerusalem, 1974). Reprinted from #74.

87. "The Future of Hillel from the Perspective of the University," in Alfred Jospe, ed., *The Test of Time* (Washington, 1974).

88. "Philosophy and Contemporary Jewish Studies," in Moshe Davis, ed., *Contemporary Jewish Civilization on the American Campus* (Jerusalem, 1974). Reprinted from # 83.

89. *Modern Jewish Ethics: Theory and Practice* (Ohio State University Press, 1975). Edited with introduction.

90. "Judaism, Secularism and Textual Interpretation," in M. Fox, ed., *Modern Jewish Ethics: Theory and Practice,* pp. 3-26.

91. "On the Rational Commandments in Saadia: A Re-examination," in M. Fox, ed., *Modern Jewish Ethics: Theory and Practice,* pp. 174-187.

92. "Philosophy and Religious Values in Modern Jewish Thought," in Jacob Katz, ed., *The Role of Religion in Modern Jewish History* (AJS, 1975), pp. 69-86.

93. Review of *The Code of Maimonides: Book IV, The Book of Women,* in *Journal of the American Academy of Religion,* March 1975.

94. "Maimonides and Aquinas on Natural Law," in Jacob I. Dienstag, ed., *Studies in Maimonides and St. Thomas Aquinas* (New York, 1975), pp. 75-106. Reprint of #79.

95. "Law and Ethics in Modern Jewish Philosophy: The Case of Moses Mendelssohn," *Proceedings of the American Academy for Jewish Research,* Vol. 43, 1976, pp. 1-13.

96. "Translating Jewish Thought into Curriculum," in Seymour Fox and Geraldine Rosenfeld, eds., *From the Scholar to the Classroom* (Jewish Theological Seminary, 1977), pp. 59-85.

97. Discussion on the "Centrality of Israel in the World Jewish Community," in Moshe Davis, ed., *World Jewry and the State of Israel* (New York, 1977).

98. "On the Rational Commandments in Saadia's Philosophy," *Proceedings of the Sixth World Congress of Jewish Studies,* Vol. 3 (Jerusalem, 1977), pp. 34-43. Slight revision of #91.

99. "Ha-Tefillah be-Mishnato shel ha-Rambam," in Gabriel Cohn, ed., *Ha-Tefillah Ha-Yehudit* (Jerusalem, 1978). pp. 142-167.

100. Review of Louis Jacobs, *Theology in the Responsa, AJS Newsletter*, No. 22, March 1978.

101. Review of Frank Talmage, *David Kimhi: The Man and his Commentaries, Speculum*, 53(3), July 1978.

102. "The Doctrine of the Mean in Aristotle and Maimonides: A Comparative Study," in S. Stern and R. Loewe, eds., *Studies in Jewish Intellectual and Religious History. Presented to Alexander Altmann* (Alabama, 1979), pp. 43-70.

103. Foreword to Abraham Chill, *The Minhagim* (New York, 1979).

104. *The Philosophical Foundations of Jewish Ethics: Some Initial Reflections*. The Second Annual Rabbi Louis Feinberg Memorial Lecture in Judaic Studies at the University of Cincinnati, 1979, pp. 1-24.

105. "Reflections on the Foundations of Jewish Ethics and their Relation to Public Policy," in Joseph L. Allen, ed., *The Society of Christian Ethics, 1980 Selected Papers* (Dallas, 1980), pp. 23-62. An expansion of #104.

106. Introduction to the *Collected Papers of Rabbi Harry Kaplan* (Columbus, 1980).

107. Review of Jacob Neusner, *A History of the Mishnaic Law of Women*, 5 Vols., in AJS Newsletter, No. 29, 1981.

108. "Human Suffering and Religious Faith: A Jewish Response to the Holocaust," *Questions of Jewish Survival* (University of Denver, 1980), pp. 8-22.

109. "The Role of Philosophy in Jewish Studies," in Raphael Jospe and Samuel Z. Fishman, eds., *Go and Study: Essays and Studies in Honor of Alfred Jospe* (Washington, D.C., 1980). pp. 125-142.

110. "Conservative Tendencies in the Halakhah," *Judaism*, 29(1), Winter 1980, pp. 12-18.

111. Review of Isadore Twersky, *Introduction to the Code of Maimonides, AJS Newsletter*, No. 31, 1982.

112. "The Moral Philosophy of MaHaRaL," in Bernard Cooperman, ed., *Jewish Thought in the Sixteenth Century* (Cambridge, 1983), pp. 167-185.

113. Review of Michael Wyschogrod, *The Body of Faith: Judaism as Corporeal Election*, in *The Journal of Religion*, 67(1), January 1987.

114. "Change is Not Modern in Jewish Law," *Sh'ma*, 13/257, September 16, 1983.

115. "Graduate Education in Jewish Philosophy," in Jacob Neusner, ed., *New Humanities and Academic Disciplines: The Case of Jewish Studies* (University of Wisconsin Press, 1984), pp. 121-134.

116. "Some Reflections on Jewish Studies in American Universities," *Judaism,* 35(2), Spring 1986, pp. 140-146.

117. "The Holiness of the Holy Land," Jonathan Sacks, ed., *Tradition and Transition: Essays Presented to Chief Rabbi Sir Immanuel Jakobovits* (London, 1986), pp. 155-170.

118. "The Jewish Educator: The Ideology of the Profession in Jewish Tradition and its Contemporary Meaning," in Joseph Reimer, ed., *To Build a Profession: Careers in Jewish Education* (Waltham, 1987).

119. "A New View of Maimonides' Method of Contradictions," in Moshe Hallamish, ed., *Bar-Ilan: Annual of Bar-Ilan University Studies in Judaica and the Humanities: Moshe Schwarcz Memorial Volume,* 22-23 (Ramat-Gan, 1987), pp. 19-43.

120. "Law and Morality in the Thought of Maimonides," in Nahum Rakover, ed., *Maimonides as Codifier of Jewish Law* (Jerusalem, 1987), pp. 105-120.

121. "Maimonides on the Foundations of Morality," *Proceedings of the Institute for Distinguished Community Leaders* (Brandeis University, 1987), pp. 15-19.

122. Foreword to Morris Weitz, *Theories of Concepts* (London & New York, 1988) pp. vii-xi.

123. "The Doctrine of the Mean in Aristotle and Maimonides: A Comparative Study," in Joseph A. Buijs, ed., *Maimonides: A Collection of Critical Essays* (University of Notre Dame Press, 1988), pp. 234-263. Reprint of #102.

124. "Nahmanides on the Status of Aggadot: Perspectives on the Disputation at Barcelona, 1263," *Journal of Jewish Studies,* 40(1), Spring 1989.

125. "The Holiness of the Holy Land," in Shubert Spero, ed., *Studies in Religious Zionism* (Jerusalem, 1989). Reprint of #117.

126. *Interpreting Maimonides: Studies in Methodology, Metaphysics and Moral Philosophy* (Jewish Publication Society, 1989).

127. "The Unity and Structure of Rav Joseph B. Soloveitchik's Thought," *Tradition,* 24(3), Fall 1989.

128. "Rav Kook: Neither Philosopher nor Kabbalist," in David Shatz and Lawrence Kaplan, eds., *Studies in the Thought of Rav Kook* (New York, 1989).

Part Eleven
JUDAISM IN THE MIDDLE AGES
PHILOSOPHERS: MAIMONIDES
AND HIS HEIRS

31

Aspects of Maimonides' Epistemology: Halakah and Science[1]

Isadore Twersky
Harvard University

I

A.

In contradistinction to the epistemology of classical philosophers or, more precisely, in a carefully premeditated expansion of the classical epistemological doctrine which recognized sense perception, primary premises (axioms), and scientific data (derivative knowledge) as sources of knowledge, the epistemology of medieval religious philosophers recognized not only these three but also tradition, true reliable tradition (received from the prophets or the wise men), as a supplementary source of knowledge. Maimonides writes in the Letter on Astrology – a document of particular importance for understanding the significance of science and philosophy in his thought and in which, as he himself emphasizes, statements elaborated elsewhere are reflected – as follows:

Know, my masters, that it is not proper for a man to accept as trustworthy anything other than one of these three things. The first is a thing for which there is a clear proof deriving from man's reasoning such as arithmetic, geometry, and astronomy. The second is a thing that a man perceives through one of the five senses such as when he knows with certainty that this is red and this is black. The third is a thing that a man receives from the prophets or from the righteous.[2]

Maimonides then goes on to urge his readers clearly to identify each of these sources and not to blur them:

Every reasonable man ought to distinguish in his mind and thought all the things that he accepts as trustworthy and say: 'This I accept as trustworthy because of tradition and this because of sense-perception and this on grounds of reason.'

Anyone who accepts as trustworthy anything that is not of these three species, of him it is said: 'The simple believes everything.' (Prov. 14:15).[3]

One consequence of this epistemological classification, emphasized by Maimonides, is that not everything written in a book is wisdom or truth; for a statement to be valid and trustworthy, it must be based on one or more of the sources of knowledge.[4]

In his study of the double-faith theory, Professor Wolfson summarized this epistemological development as follows: "revelation was a new immediate source of knowledge in addition to the sources enumerated by the Greek philosophers."[5] Apparent contradictions between these sources had to be resolved by meticulous re-examination

---

[2]"Letter on Astrology," in I. Twersky, ed., *A Maimonides Reader*, p. 464. Hebrew text edited by A. Marx, HUCA III (1926) 350. Note that this is a three-fold formulation in which immediate and derivative scientific knowledge are combined and treated as one category. See the antecedent classification in R. Saadya Gaon, *'Emunot ve-De 'ot*, introduction; VII, 2. Also, M. Zucker, *Perushe Rasag li-Bereshit*, p. 13, n. 9. See H. A. Wolfson, *Studies in the History of Philosophy and Religion*, v. I, p. 593. A representative later classification is found in R. Menahem ha-Meiri, *Perush Tehillim*, psalm 123.

[3]"Letter on Astrology," p. 465.

[4]*Ibid.*: "The great sickness and the 'grievous evil' (Eccles. 5:12, 15) consist in this: that all the things that man finds written in books, he presumes to think of as true and all the more so if the books are old." See also his "Epistle to Yemen" in *A Maimonides Reader*, p. 454: "Do not consider a statement true because you find it in a book, for the prevaricator is as little restrained with his pen as with his tongue. For the untutored and uninstructed are convinced of the veracity of a statement by the mere fact that it is written; nevertheless its accuracy must be demonstrated in another manner."

[5]H. A. Wolfson, "The Double Faith Theory," *JQR* XXXIII (1942) 222 and see 239. Note also in this connection Guide II, 33: knowledge of God is obtainable by demonstrative reasoning or by direct revelation.

of all data. Hence, I would submit that Maimonides' statement in a historical chapter of the *Guide* that the Andalusians – i.e., his Spanish predecessors – "cling to the affirmation of the philosophers and incline to their opinion insofar as these do not ruin the foundation of the Law."[6] reflects the dynamics of his epistemology which provides for the elimination of apparent contradictions between the various sources of knowledge by means of interpretation and re-interpretation. Not even Aristotle, the chief of the philosophers,[7] reigns supreme; philosophers who are opposed to religious principles may be faulty or shoddy and their teachings subject to correction (just as inaccurate sense perception or flawed scientific knowledge would be corrected). A medieval religious philosopher – and Maimonides was such a person – could not be a mindless follower of Aristotle; he had judiciously and rigorously to combine philosophic affirmations with religious foundations.

B.

The significance of this epistemological expansion for the realm of beliefs and opinions is well known, and the role of harmonization (which *eo ipso* entails the recognition of conflict) between philosophy and religion has received considerable scholarly attention. However, the question of whether there is a parallel process of confrontation and harmonization in the realm of halakah – juridical facts, beliefs, norms and assumptions – still awaits careful, judicious investigation. This paper proposes to outline an approach to the examination of the relationship between halakah and science in the Maimonidean corpus, with special attention to his great code of Jewish law. We are not dealing with the underlying logical, methodological, and ideological issue of faith and reason, not with such themes as the unity and incorporeality of God, creation, prophecy, miracles, divine foreknowledge, providence, ethical and political theory, nature of soul and spirit, attitude to death, immortality – all of which figure in the *Mishneh Torah*. Similarly, we need not concern ourselves with abstract views on science found in various parts of the Maimonidean corpus, with his attempt to formulate a comprehensive, unified physical theory (*Guide*, II, 13), with his comments on the problem of the incompatibility of Aristotelian physics and Ptolemaic astronomy (III, 14; II, 8) or with his ideas concerning progress in certain scientific disciplines (especially mathematics). In fact, we need not even concern ourselves directly with his few scientific opuscula (*Treatise on Logic*,

---

[6]*Guide*, I, 71.
[7]See *Guide*, I, 5; II, 23.

Treatise on Intercalation of the Calendar, assorted medical works). By turning to his halakic works – the *Mishneh Torah*, the Commentary on the Mishnah and, in some cases the *Sefer ha-Mizvot* – we get a sharply focused view of halakah and science. The *Mishneh Torah* – and the same is true for the Commentary on the Mishnah,[8] which Maimonides describes as containing all his explanations as well as whatever he attained from the study of science (*ilm*) – has an unmistakable scientific ambience, nurtured by such items as the identification of *ma'aseh bereshit* with natural science, thematic references to mathematics, geometry, astronomy and astrology, medicine, dietetics, psychology, and literary references to works on medicine, geometry, astronomy (and in the Commentary on the Mishnah, *Terumot* I, 2) to a *Quaestiones Naturales, She'elot Tiv'iyot*) as well as frequent scientific allusions and obiter dicta. The paramount importance of science, of comprehensive scientific knowledge, is perhaps most emphatically underscored by the dramatic recognition of its role as a conduit for knowledge and love of God.[9]

His proficiency in the exact sciences is amply demonstrated in the *Mishneh Torah*, especially in the presentation of an entire system of astronomical theory; the structure, comprehensiveness, and authoritativeness of this part of the code made it clear to all readers, admiring and critical alike, that Maimonides was a master of the field.[10] The late Professor Solomon Gandz has shown that the section entitled *Hilkot Kiddush ha-Hodesh* (Sanctification of the New Moon) is really a two-tiered construction. In chapters 1-10 the old Jewish laws concerning the regulation of the calendar on the basis of observation of astronomical phenomena and the additional Jewish methods relating to the regulation of the calendar on the basis of independent scientific calculation are analytically described, while the last nine chapters form a new section which deals with the astronomy of the visibility of the new moon, an extraneous matter taken from extraneous sources.[11] It is worth noting that Maimonides considered this material sufficiently important and sufficiently integral topics of law that he concluded this remarkable section with a resounding peroration:

---

[8]See my *Introduction to the Code of Maimonides*, pp. 365-367.
[9]e.g., *Hilkot Yesode ha-Torah*, II, 1, 2; *Teshuvah*, X, 6. Non-Maimonideans repudiate this by affirming that the Torah is far superior to natural science as a source of the knowledge of God. See, e.g., B. Septimus in I. Twersky, ed., *R. Moses Nahmanides*, p. 23, n. 42.
[10]See the comment of Rabad, *Hilkot Kiddush ha-Hodesh*, VII, 7.
[11]S. Gandz, *Studies in Hebrew Astronomy and Mathematics*, ed. S. Sternberg, pp. 113ff.

We have now expounded all the methods of calculation required for the determination of the visibility of the new moon and for the examination of witnesses, so that discerning students might be able to learn everything about it. Thus they shall not miss this particular branch of the many branches of the Law and will have no need to roam and ramble about in other books in search of information on matters set forth in this treatise. 'Seek out of the book of the Lord and read; none of these [truths] shall be missing.' (Is. 34:16).[12]

Astronomy of the visibility of the new moon is thus not really extraneous after all.

C.

We get a clear idea of his extensive, omnivorous reading from the scope of these extra-halakic references – i.e., they provide an oblique empirical substantiation of various personal-autobiographical statements. We should be attentive to the fact that, in various contexts, Maimonides mentions his reading interests and study habits: "When I studied the books of the Mutakallimun, as far as I had the opportunity and I have likewise studied the books of the philosophers as far as my capacity went."[13] Elsewhere we find "the excellent philosopher Abu Bakr ibn al-Saigh, under the guidance of one of whose pupils I have read texts...."[14] (In another context he mentions what he has heard about the astronomical system of Abu Bakr but qualifies it by adding "however, I have not heard this from his pupils.")[15] He says about his reading on astrology and idolatry "that it seems to me there does not remain in the world a composition on this subject, having been translated into Arabic from other languages, but that I have read it and have understood its subject matter and have plumbed the depths of its thought,"[16] and this ambitious pattern of exhaustive study is probably applicable to most other fields. His statement on medicine likewise underscores his commitment to know and analyze the sources of everything: "For you know how long and difficult this art is for a conscientious and exact man who does not want to state anything which he cannot support by argument and without knowing where it has been said and how it can be demonstrated."[17] Maimonides was

---

[12]*Kiddush ha-Ḥodesh*, XIX, 13.
[13]*Guide*, I, 71.
[14]*Op. cit.*, II, 9.
[15]*Op. cit.*, II, 24.
[16]"Letter on Astrology," pp. 465–466.
[17]*Iggerot ha-Rambam*, ed. D. Baneth, pp. 69–70. In an adjacent passage, Maimonides describes his hectic schedule; he complains that he has no time,

unquestionably a conscientious and exact man; he sought out and used all sources. I am, therefore, inclined to offer a friendly emendation to the comment of Professor S. Pines who, after noting Maimonides' references to "some Arabic scientists as distinct from the philosophers," offers this reserved, restrained summation: "Quite evidently, he had a knowledge of scientific literature that would have been regarded as adequate in the philosophic circles of his time."[18] It seems that, if we add to this the statements in the *Mishneh Torah,* and Commentary on the Mishnah and all the references scattered in his smaller treatises and letters – and what we now know about his mathematical writings as well[19] – we could say that he had a knowledge of scientific literature that would have been regarded as *impressive* if not encyclopedic.

To these references concerning his reading and study habits should be added the references concerning his teaching habits. He was a reader in the modern academic sense; he also *read* this literature with students and tutored them, either individually or in small groups. For example, he says to his student for whom he composed the *Guide:* "You know of astronomical matters what you have *read* under my guidance and understood from the contents of the *Almagest."*[20] This reminds us of Maimonides' more elaborate, emphatic statement in the *Dedicatory Epistle:* "When you came to me, having conceived the intention of journeying from the country farthest away in order *to read texts* under my guidance...." He proceeds to praise this young Joseph ben Judah by noting:

> When thereupon *you read under my guidance* texts dealing with the science of astronomy ant prior to that texts dealing with mathematics...my joy in you increases because of the excellence of your mind and the quickness of your grasp. I saw that your longing for mathematics was great and hence I let you train yourself in that science, knowing where you would end. When *thereupon you read*

---

other than on the Sabbath, to study Torah and has no time whatsoever for the other sciences.

[18]S. Pines, Translator's Introduction, *Guide of the Perplexed,* p. cxxxii. See F. Rosner, *Sex Ethics in the Writings of Moses Maimonides* (New York, 1974), p. 4:
    Maimonides must have been an avid reader, since his medical writings show a profound knowledge of Greek and Moslem medical works. Hippocrates Galen and Aristotle were his Greek medical inspiration and Rhazes of Persia, Alfarabi of Turkey, Ibn Zuho and Avenzoar are Moslem authors frequently quoted by Maimonides.

[19]See Y. Tzvi Langerman, "The Mathematical Writings of Maimonides," *JQR* LXXV (1984) 57-65.

[20]*Guide,* II, 24.

under my guidance texts dealing with the art of logic, my hopes fastened upon you.[21]

That this was not an isolated instance we may infer from the statement of Al-Qifti in his *History of Physicians* that "people studied philosophy under him"; this is the same Al-Qifti who reported that Maimonides had mastered mathematics.

It is well known that many of Maimonides' letters comment on or describe facets of his medical career.[22]

I would also note here the ease and naturalness, totally devoid of self-consciousness or the slightest twinge of apology, with which he refers to general scientific literature. Even in the heat of argument, when he had to rebut an uncongenial critic who mingled specific queries about the *Mishneh Torah* with sweeping accusations about its author, and generally in defending the legitimacy and usefulness of his Code, Maimonides refers nonchalantly to the fact that "any author who wrote a book dealing with Torah or with other sciences, whether the author was from among the ancient nations in possession of philosophy or from among the physicians, would necessarily adopt one of two opinions."[23] I find this rather striking. The candor and spontaneity underscore the fact that the universality of reference, and of perception, was completely routine and unrehearsed; this was Maimonides' natural, indispensable mode of writing and thinking.

It is significant – and especially so for our purposes – that in the long, carefully-crafted answer to the question about astrology (what to believe and what not to believe), Maimonides says that, had the respected scholars of southern France already received the *Mishneh Torah*, they would not have raised the question they did, because everything is clarified by his formulations in that work. The *Mishneh Torah*, in other words, reflects his positions and attitudes on epistemology and science, on reason, tradition, and unacceptable notions.[24] Analogously, in the Treatise on Resurrection he observes that only people of religion and science (*al-din* and *al-ilm*)[25] will appreciate the excellence of the *Mishneh Torah* for, obviously, it contains more than just an ordinary summation of positive law, and special sensibilities are required to appraise its excellence. It is a good barometer of his attitudes and positions, it reflects his methodology

---

[21]*Guide*, Dedicatory Epistle.
[22]See, e.g, my *Introduction*, p. 366, n. 28.
[23]*Kovez Teshuvot ha-Rambam*, I, 25b.
[24]See above, n. 1.
[25]*Ma'amar Tehiyyat ha-Metim*, ed. J. Finkle, p. 4. Even in *Sefer ha-Mizvot*, negative commandment 179, Maimonides says that only the vulgus without knowledge of natural sciences will marvel at his statement.

and philosophy, and therefore only properly qualified readers will properly gauge its achievement.

D.

Leo Strauss, the great lover of paradox, commented in his "Notes on Maimonides' Book of Knowledge": "This would seem to mean that in an important respect Maimonides' *fiqh* (talmud) books are more 'philosophic' than the Guide."[26]

In light of this, I seek to determine Maimonides' attitudes to science, or the impact of science on the normative formulations of halakah. The primary source material will be drawn from his halakic works. What will emerge is that there is a meticulous attempt to integrate science, to relate scientific vocabulary and axiology to rabbinic law and lore, to acknowledge its normativeness and regulative autonomy, but not to superimpose it forcibly on the structure and fabric of halakah. Certain areas must remain independent of science while some areas transcend it. Maimonides, I shall suggest, provides a blueprint for a three-tiered structure: unification, separation, transcendence.

II

A.

Maimonides' philosophical-scientific posture was perceptively described by R. Moses Nahmanides when he said: "he diminishes miracles and augments nature."[27] This epigrammatic characterization, although submitted by Nahmanides in criticism of Maimonides, may actually echo Maimonides' own statements; in the Letter on Resurrection,[28] e.g., he sharply contrasts the masses who delight in setting up Torah and reason as contradictory poles and shun seeing any phenomenon as natural (*davar 'al minhag ha-teva'*), either in descriptions of the past, observations of the present, or promises of the future, with himself and his like who try to harmonize Torah and reason and regard all things as following a possible natural order. Similar statements – with such perception or self-perception – are found elsewhere as well. Maimonides may have said it all very tersely and epigrammatically when he described the purpose of the *Mishneh*

---

[26]L. Strauss, "Notes on Maimonides' Book of Knowledge," *Studies in Mysticism and Religion Presented to G. Scholem*, p. 269.

[27]R. Moses Nahmanides, *Torat ha-Shem Temimah*, in H. Chavel, ed., *Kitve ha-Ramban*, v. I, p. 154.

[28]*Ma'amar Tehiyyat ha-Metim*, p. 22.

Torah as "lekarev ha-devarim el ha-sekel 'o el derek ha-rov."[29] There has been abundant discussion and little consensus in recent scholarly literature about the second part of this statement (*derek ha-rov*), but the very suggestive first part should not be overlooked. It is a clear and distinct declaration of purpose and procedure. Moreover, while Nahmanides addressed himself, in the first instance, to the issue of natural law versus miracles – the philosophic preoccupation with the permanence and stability of the universe and the fear of any disruptive phenomena or destabilizing possibilities – Maimonides' own statements are more general in intent and are, in fact, accurate markers of his essential scientific temper. The fact that they are applied to the *Mishneh Torah* is especially significant for us.

If we had to, as we must because of time constraints, isolate one issue, Maimonides' attitude to magic and medicine is most emblematic. Medicine, of course, plays a great role in his life and writing; Galen is a major influence.[30] Maimonides' writings show that he is fully aware of the relevance and importance of medicine, is indeed a firm believer in medicine and hygiene.[31] While mindful of the differences between medicine and religion,[32] he is a genuine enthusiast of medicine. He has no reservations whatsoever, religious or otherwise, theoretical or practical, about its permissibility; it is, to be sure, obligatory.[33] Medical perspective may even have led him to explain the details of a certain law about visiting the sick differently than in the Talmud; this was, in any event, the opinion of R. David ibn Zimra.[34]

Most important, his writing is a good illustration of the empiricist and experimentalist temper in the development of medieval medicine. Maimonides' attitude is similar to that formulated by his contemporary Abu'l Barakat: "medicine derives for the greater part

---

[29]*Teshuvot ha-Rambam*, n. 252 (p. 460). See Commentary on Mishnah, *Kelim*, II, 1.

[30]When he is apparently scornful of "mere doctors" (e.g., Isaac Israeli or Razi), it is because they were not at the same time philosophers and were nevertheless dabbling in philosophy.

[31]*Hilkot De'ot*, IV, 20, 21.

[32]See especially the medical tract published in *Transactions of American Philosophical Society* 54 (1964), p. 40. Revealed religion commands that which is useful in the world-to-come while the physician informs his patient concerning that which is useful to the body in this world.

[33]See especially Commentary on the Mishnah, *Pesaḥim*, IV, 10; *Guide*, III, 37. Just as idolatrous practices are religiously useless, so they are also medically useless.

[34]*Hilkot Avel*, IV, 5 and Radbaz, *ad loc.*

from experiments and inferences based on the principles of physics."[35]
Medical procedures should be as scientific as possible; the
determination whether or not a particular drug has curative properties
should follow from reason or experience. Indeed only such procedures
and the use of such drugs warrant the violation of the Sabbath in an
effort to save or prolong life.[36] If not for the concept of medicine, the
idea of a reasonable and effective therapeutic procedure, there would
be no concept of *piku'ah nefesh*. In the *Mishneh Torah* (*Hilkot Shabbat*
II, 1) Maimonides formulates the halakah simply and forcefully: "The
Commandment of the Sabbath, like all other commandments, may be
set aside if human life is in danger. Accordingly, if a person is
dangerously ill, *whatever a skilled local physician considers necessary*
may be done for him on the Sabbath." According to the Maimonidean
explanation put forth in the Mishnah Commentary on *Pesaḥim*, the
Book of Remedies which King Hezekiah destroyed contained magical
procedures and astrological cures; his act was *not* a demonstration of
skepticism of or antagonism toward medical science and practice. It was
an affirmation of medicine and a negation of magic.

B.

Maimonides' unconditionally negative attitude to assorted magical
practices – e.g., incantations – is neatly correlated with an
uncompromisingly positive attitude toward genuine medical practices.
His scientific temper the empiricist-experimentalist one is
dramatically underscored by the fact that not only does he condemn
magical procedures but he also rules out the therapeutic-practical use
of sacred objects, lest they be converted into amulets. Note this
resounding formulation:

> One who whispers a spell over a wound, at the same time reciting a
> verse from the Torah, one who recites a verse over a child to save it
> from terrors, and one who places a Scroll or phylacteries on an infant
> to induce it to sleep are not in the category of sorcerers and
> soothsayers, but they are included among those who repudiate the
> Torah; for they use its words to cure the body whereas these are only

---

[35]See S. Pines, *Collected Works*, v. II, p. 329; also, *ibid.*, p. 191 and 361. R.
McKeon, "The Empiricist and Experimentalist Temper in the Middle Ages,"
Essays in Honor of John Dewey (New York, 1929), pp. 216-234. See L. Demaitre
in *Speculum* 63 (1988) 118. Galenism meant "medicine was to be taught from a
philosophical basis, with reason governing theory and theory guiding practice;
the regula rationis distinguished it as an art...."
[36]Commentary on the Mishnah, *Yoma*, VIII, 4; see *Hilkot Shabbat*, XIX, 13.
Rabbi Solomon ibn Adret, *Teshubot*, 414, contends that Maimonides' position
is inconsistent and untenable.

medicine for the soul, as it is said, 'They shall be life to your soul' (Prov. 3:23).[37]

Kedushah (holiness) generally is interpreted to mean transcendence; it is not an intrinsic quality which can be transferred from the sacred object to its users or admirers. One may say that Maimonides' concept of the sacred and the resultant spiritualization of laws (which I have dealt with elsewhere)[38] serves, inter alia, a scientific purpose: to neutralize magical procedures and/or magical consequences. The Torah, while interested in the well-being of the body (*tikkun ha-guf*, and prescribing laws which are conducive to it), is medicine for the soul (*refu'at ha-nefesh*).[39] There is no need to attempt, or be tempted, to rely upon supernatural effects flowing from sacred objects inasmuch as the Torah commands and commends natural science. Natural-scientific procedures are congruent with the Torah's goals for individual welfare. The Torah has its distinct, spiritual, other-worldly teleology of life, but it yields completely to the imperative to prolong life in this world; in this context, it endorses the best empirical results in the field of medicine, to the exclusion of magical procedures as well as improper use of sacred objects.

There is much that is novel in this position; it is established and sustained by sharp exegesis, innovative interpretation and unrelenting

---

[37]*Hilkot 'Akum,* XI:12; for the coupling of "Scroll or phylacteries," see *Hilkot Shevu'ot,* XI:11. This entire halakah should be correlated with *Hilkot Mezuzah,* V:4:

> It is a universal custom to write the word *Shad-dai* (Almighty) on the other side of the *mezuzah,* opposite the blank space between the two sections. As this word is written on the outside, the practice is unobjectionable. They, however, who write names of angels, holy names, a Biblical text, or inscriptions usual on seals within the *mezuzah,* are among those who have no portion in the world to come. For these fools not only fail to fulfill the commandment but they treat an important precept that expresses the Unity of God, the love of Him, and His worship, as if it were an amulet to promote their own personal interests; for, according to their foolish minds, the *mezuzah* is something that will secure for them advantage in the vanities of the world.

[38]See my *Introduction,* pp. 418ff.

[39]This is completely congruent with what Maimonides says in his medical treatises see, e.g., above, n. 31. The teleology is all-important in understanding the differences between religion and medicine. The Torah, while not intending "its words to cure the body," is concerned with the well-being of the body (note in this context *Guide,* III, 27); it delegated the means to the science of medicine. To put it differently, the Torah allows for its suspension in order to prolong life, but the teleology of life in turn is completely subordinate to the Torah.

polemics. As we shall see, here as elsewhere, he had to balance naturalism with supernaturalism. He had, for example, to demolish the widespread view which, for misguided religious reasons, condemned the reliance upon medicine as if medicine was an unwarranted, even arrogant, naturalistic intrusion upon, or attenuation of religious belief. An indication of how novel his position was is the history of its reception and rejection: it was periodically disavowed throughout the generations; his demolition was demolished, a kind of *tahafut 'al-tahafut*. As recently as a generation ago the great R. Abraham Karelitz, the Hazon Ish, affirms that the view, angrily and disdainfully characterized by Maimonides as empty, foolish, and fanciful and resoundingly rejected by him, is in truth a profound, impregnable tradition; it is Maimonides' alternate proposal which is problematic and difficult to sustain.[40]

The whole issue demanded concerted effort and considerable ingenuity. Many Talmudic passages had to be presented in new perspectives or transposed to new contexts or conceptualized in new ways. Demonology was derailed; belief in talismans and amulets was undermined. The transcendental purity of sacral objects was preserved.

This process of interpretation and conceptualization, which could be and was frequently challenged and criticized (Nahmanides could say, e.g., after referring to *Hilkot 'Akum* XI, 9 that "the texts are against it"),[41] was particularly crucial in this context. Magical acts were not buttressed by logical considerations or propositions of natural causality. There is no scientific-rational connection between whispering a spell over a wound and restoration of good health. The only epistemological support and justification would consequently have to come from religious tradition. It is, therefore, incumbent upon Maimonides to demonstrate that tradition does not legitimize any of these magical procedures or astrological beliefs. If, as I cited earlier, "every reasonable man ought to distinguish in his mind and thought all the things that he accepts as trustworthy and say 'this I accept as trustworthy because of tradition, and this because of sense-perception and this on grounds of reason,'" he will realize that he has no support from any of the recognized sources of knowledge. Identification of the sources of knowledge will help filter out untrustworthy and unworthy beliefs. Hence, Maimonides' sweeping program of interpretation was mandated by epistemology. Sharp and, in his opinion, compelling interpretation was his incontestable prerogative. Rabbi Abraham ben David said in another context: this author possesses great

---

[40]See R. Abraham Karelitz, *'Inyene Emunah u-Bittahon*, ch. v.
[41]See *Kitve Ramban*, I, p. 380.

(interpretive) powers and is thus able to interpret matters as he sees fit.[42] The critical intent of the remark does not invalidate the insightfulness of the characterization which underscores the central importance of the interpretive process.

III

A.

Constraints of time prevent us from discussing in detail other areas in which scientific data are paramount. Suffice it to mention, without elaboration for the moment, that the introduction of the concept *tevah*, signifying nature of physical properties as well as nature of human beings, is very repercussive. *Tevah* is apparently a neologism[43] suggesting necessity, compulsion, inexorable causality – often synonymous or interchangeable with *minhag* or *minhago shel 'olam*; the latter denotes nature and natural law as distinct from miracle, i.e., something which challenges the regularity and immutability of nature.[44]

Hilkot Temurah IV, 13 is an important example of *tevah* applied to human nature, i.e., to the area of psychological explanations. It is man's nature (*tevah shel 'adam*) to increase his possessions and to be sparing of his wealth. The Torah is concerned with the tendency of human nature which places a premium on material self-interest and cultivates excessive parsimony. This may even lead one who dedicates an object to God to yield to fickleness and fluidity of motive, and try to shortchange Him. Hence, the Torah intervenes in order to channel and qualify this natural propensity; it does not change the fact of human nature but disciplines and curtails certain traits.[45]

---

[42]*Hilkot Avadim*, I, 5.

[43]See *Teshuvot Ḥakam Zevi*, 18. (The Talmud does, of course, refer to *tiv'ah*.) See, generally, W. J. Courtenay, *Covenant and Causality in Medieval Thought* (esp. ch. III, "Nature and the Natural in Twelfth-Century Thought"). J. A. Weisheiph, "Aristotle's Concept of Nature: Avicenna and Aquinas," in L. D. Roberts, ed., *Approaches to Nature in the Middle Ages.*

[44]See *Hilkot Roze'ah*, I, 9. Birth changes the role of the embryo. The fetus no longer poses a threat to the mother; that one of two people may die is within the realm of nature (*tiv'o shel 'olam*). Note also *Teshuvah*, VI, 5; *Hilkot Avel*, XIII, 11, and *Ta'aniyot*, I, 3; Commentary on Mishnah, *Niddah*, III, 2.

[45]As we shall soon see, there is a symmetry in the attitudes to and attempted changes of nature; physical nature may be changed temporarily by divine miraculous acts whereas human nature may be disciplined and directed by divine laws. For other examples of psychological explanation, see also *Hilkot Shabbat*, X, 10; *'Issure Bi'ah*, I, 9; *Gerushin*, II, 20; *Sanhedrin*, XVIII, 6; Commentary on Mishnah, *Shabbat*, II, 5, *Sanhedrin*, VI, 1, 2; *Guide*, III, 46.

We should also call attention to an intriguing halakic formulation in which scientific knowledge determines the applicability of the juridical norm.

> It is well known to wise men endowed with understanding and knowledge that the sun is 170 times larger than the earth. If an ordinary person swears that the sun is larger than the earth, he is not liable to flogging because of a false oath. For although the fact is as stated, this is not commonly known to any but the most eminent scholars, and no person is liable unless he swears about a thing well known to at least three ordinary persons, e.g., that a man is a man, or a stone a stone. Similarly, if he swears that the sun is smaller than the earth, even though this is not so, he is not liable to a flogging. For this subject is not familiar to all men, and it is therefore not like swearing that a man is a woman, as he is merely swearing about the way the sun appears to him, and he does indeed see it small. This holds good in all similar cases connected with calculations dealing with astronomical cycles, constellations, and geometrical measurements, and other scientific matters which are known only to some men.[46]

B.

In light of this, Maimonides' statement on *terefah* (organic disease which is deemed fatal) in animals, with its unequivocal pronouncement that scientific-medical opinion is irrelevant to this halakic complex, is striking. The passage in *Hilkot Shehitah*,[47] based on tractate Hullin, with some stylistic-substantive additions, deserves exceedingly careful study. The sharp Maimonidean formulation is even more noteworthy if we recall that in a subsequent chapter Maimonides re-affirms unequivocally the decisive role of doctors in determining and defining *terefah* in human beings.[48] Maimonides is telling us that the list of seventy kinds of *terefah* is traditional, matter-of-fact, and therefore he extricated it from the constraints of science. Tradition is the exclusive determinant. There was no room or possibility in this context for re-interpretation, so he removed the matter from the orbit of science. He would not allow scientific data or assumptions to change the halakah. By so doing, he is in fact free of apologetics. Comparison with the position of Rashbah puts the significance of this into sharp focus.

---

[46]*Hilkot Shevu'ot*, V, 22. We may surmise that this halakah becomes elitist inasmuch as knowledge of the relevant facts depends on general scientific sources (see *Hilkot Yesode ha-Torah*, III, 6; *Kiddush ha-Ḥodesh*, XVII, 25). Only one sensitive to the importance of science will seek to acquire such knowledge. See also Commentary on the Mishnah, *Introduction*, p. 37: Ptolemy's *Almagest* is the source of this information.

[47]*Hilkot Sheḥiṭah*, X, 12-13.

[48]*Hilkot Roze'ah*, II, 8. See *Min ḥat Ḥinnuk* on *Sefer ha-Ḥinnuk*, mizvah 34.

R. Solomon ibn Adret[49] tried to reconcile medicine and halakah and insisted on their complete compatibility by positing the fallibility of medical diagnosis. He refused to recognize any exceptions to the Talmudic rule of *terefah 'enah hayyah* and therefore argued for complete congruence of halakic prescription and scientific reality. The list of seventy kinds of *terefah* is not only traditional but is also scientifically sound. Maimonides, per contra, by positing the extra-scientific character of this halakah, spares himself this agonizing confrontation and forced harmonization. Maimonides does not invoke the doctrine of the limitations of human knowledge (see *Guide* I, 31) nor does he discredit medicine; he merely posits that it is not relevant in this context.

I would summarize it as follows. The medicine-magic complex, which is multi-dimensional, has an interpretive infrastructure and that provides flexibility. The invitation, indeed the need, to interpret unifies all those related issues.

Now, when interpretation was relevant, even with regard to *terefah,* Maimonides was not timid or apologetic. Note the following. *Hilkot Shehitah*[50] contains a provocative halakic formulation: "removal of the upper jaw" (*lehi 'elyon*) is mentioned as an incidence of *terefah*. When asked by the Lunel scholars about this unprecedented and, consequently, challenging formulation – the Talmudic list, which is presumed to be complete, does not contain this distinction and hence does not mention this case of *terefah* ("removal of the upper jaw") – Maimonides confidently replied that originality of interpretation was a fact of scholarly life. An author particularly attuned to certain problems may discern a nuance or *novum* in well-known texts which his predecessors had missed completely. Much depends on the author's perception of the material as well as his halakic-conceptual mass of apperceptions, in the light of which traditional texts are made to yield their meaning. An apparent addition may be merely a compelling interpretation or deduction. He defends his formulation as an unimpeachable inference supported by scientific reasoning. His answer to the Lunel rabbis is that he merely interpreted the Talmudic texts and reached a different conclusion. He was not changing the halakah because of scientific data he could bring to bear, but eliciting an intended even if hitherto unnoticed conclusion. To be sure, science could

---

[49]*Teshuvot,* I, n. 98. See also R. Isaac b. Sheshet, *Teshuvot,* n. 45. There is a very interesting discussion in the work of a great-grandson of the Hatam Sofer: R. Moshe S. Glazner, *Dor Revi'i,* introduction p. 4. Rashbah, he says, wants to "deny reality."

[50]*Shehitah,* VIII, 16, 23 and X, 9. *Teshuvot,* n. 315 (p. 585).

be a guiding principle in interpretation but it was not empowered to alter the list of *terefah*. Maimonides seems to be zealous to preserve the universality and immutability of halakah, just as more generally he emphasizes the permanence and stability of religion.[51]

C.

We may turn our attention to an analogous halakah which substantiates this conclusion. A complicated law concerning vows of Naziriteship includes the following:[52]

> If several persons, while walking along the road, see a *koy* in the distance and disagree about it, in this wise: A says, 'I undertake to become a Nazirite if that is a beast of chase'; B says, 'I undertake to become a Nazirite if that is a domestic animal'; C says, 'I undertake to become a Nazirite if that is not a beast of chase'; D says 'I undertake to become a Nazirite if that is not a domestic animal'; E says, 'I undertake to become a Nazirite if that is neither a beast of chase nor a domestic animal'; F says, 'I undertake to become a Nazirite if that is both a domestic animal and a beast of chase' all of them become Nazirites. For the koy resembles a beast of chase in some respects, and a domestic animal in others. In some respects, it resembles both beasts of chase and domestic animals, and in others neither. The same would hold good if they saw a hermaphrodite and fell to disputing whether he was a man or a woman, all of them vowing in the same way they did about the koy they would all become Nazirites. For the hermaphrodite resembles a man in some respects and a woman in others. In some respects, he resembles neither man or woman, and in others he resembles both.
>
> All these resemblances refer to Scriptural commandments and not to the object's nature or heredity (*beṭṭiv'o vetoladeto*).

Halakic reality is autonomous *vis-à-vis* scientific status. The nature, anatomy or genetic structure of the androgynous being are one thing; the reality which governs halakic procedures is another.

A statement of Maimonides in his Commentary on the Mishnah, dealing with the formula giving the circumference and area of a circle, may also illumine this approach; the halakic calculation is not contingent upon the scientific query.

> You should know the ratio of the diameter of a circle to its circumference is not known, that is, it is impossible to express it exactly. This is not a lack of knowledge on our part, as the uneducated think, but this thing is intrinsically unknowable (*mizad tiv'o bilti nodah*) and cannot be known. However, it is possible to approximate it closely, and the expert geometers have written works on this subject, that is to approximate the ratio of the diameter to its circumference,

---

[51]*Guide*, III, 34: "governance of the law ought to be absolute and universal."
[52]*Hilkot Nazir*, II, 10, 11.

and various proofs of the approximations. The approximation that the scientists use is that of the ratio of one to three and one-seventh....Since this [ratio of circumference to diameter] took the round figure and said that all that have a circumference of three handbreadths have a diameter of one handbreadth. They were satisfied with this [approximation] in all the measurements that they needed throughout the Torah.[53]

IV

The next point, which we shall treat in compressed form, is to underscore the parallelism between Maimonides' attitude to rationalism and his attitude to science. Just as his acceptance of the permanence and stability of the universe, and of the living species it contains,[54] as a cardinal philosophic principle or fundamental postulate did not eliminate the miracles – they are, as is generally known, restricted, some are based on the immanent natural order (i.e., included in the original order of the universe) and, above all, are not seen as permanent changes in nature[55] – similarly, and this may serve as a mirror of or paradigm for the entire theme, the central role assigned to science in halakah does not eliminate miracles. Maimonides' statement on leprosy establishes this clearly.

> Leprosy is a comprehensive term (i.e., a homonym or amphibolous term) covering sundry incompatible matters. Thus, whiteness in a man's skin is called leprosy; the falling off of some of his hair on the head or the chin is called leprosy; and a change of color in garments or in houses is called leprosy.

> Now this change in garments and in houses which Scripture includes under the general term leprosy was no normal happening (*minhago shel 'olam*) but was a portent and a wonder (*'ot u-feleh*) among the Israelites to warn them against slanderous speaking.[56]

The contrapuntal use of *minhago shel 'olam* and *'ot u-feleh* is precise and expressive.[57] If this phenomenon (leprosy of garments and houses) were presented or perceived as *minhago shel 'olam*, it would be

---

[53]Commentary on the Mishnah, *'Eruvin*, I, 5. See. S. Sternberg's introduction to S. Gandz, *Studies*, p. xxxiii. As S. Sternberg put it: "Maimonides explains that since it is an irrational number, we have to be satisfied with some approximation. The acceptable degree of approximation then becomes a legal matter." In other words, the halakah creates a reality which may differ from purely scientific reality; in any event, the halakah is not stumped by a scientific impasse.

[54]See S. Pines, *Collected Works*, p. 189.

[55]It was this cautious, restrictive approach to miracles which irked R. Moses Naḥmanides.

[56]*Hilkot Ṭume'at Ẓara'at*, XVI, 10.

[57]See, e.g., *Hilkot Roze'ah*, VI, 12.

problematic and demand harmonization; however, inasmuch as it is unmistakably labeled as *'ot u-feleh*, the need for allegory or reductionism is obviated. Whereas Philo says that leprosy is to be interpreted allegorically[58] and R. Judah Halevi says that the sages had profound knowledge of leprosy which surpasses our understanding,[59] Maimonides suggests that leprosy does not need to be explained away, does not need to be allied with scientific categories, nor should it be denied by omission or reformulation. It is a miraculous phenomenon – Maimonides mentions in *Guide* III, 47 "This is a miracle that was perpetuated in the religious community like that of the waters of the woman suspected of adultery" – and is unapologetically recognized for what it is; it is philosophically and halakically viable.[60]

We should interject here that this point is most important historically, for the prolonged and heated debate which crystallized in Jewish thought in the wake of Maimonidean philosophy centered on the question of the natural versus supernatural. Would Aristotelian naturalism reign supreme and displace the supernaturalism which undergirds traditional religion? Would the philosophic tendency to recognize fixed principles and laws of nature that could be analyzed and understood result in a complete desacralization of nature? Maimonides, in fact, did *not* eliminate the supernatural but his critics thought that he did not give it ample recognition, that he let it be overshadowed and drastically reduced its importance. Already R. Judah Alfakar, and he would be followed by Nahmanides, Rashbah, R. Joseph ibn Shushan and a host of others, sounded this refrain: "His intention was [to explain the Bible such] that the laws of nature not be abrogated, so that the Torah might be at one with Greek philosophy."[61] What was a distinct virtue for Maimonides was a serious shortcoming for the Spanish anti-Aristotelians.

Maimonides' doctrine of providence also illustrates the essential difference between science and scientism. In many contexts Maimonides repeats that divine providence transcends the law of nature. Its influence is not bound by natural causality.

---

[58]See H. A. Wolfson, *Philo*, I, p. 137.
[59]Judah Halevi, *Cuzari*, IV, 31.
[60]The formulation in *Ṭume 'at Ẓaraᴐat*, XVI, 10 is fully congruent with Commentary on the Mishnah, *Neg'aim*, XII, 5 and *Guide*, III, 47. Note that in *Ṭume'at Ẓaraᴐat*, X, 7 the isolation of the leper is not because "leprosy is contagious and that almost by nature all men find it disgusting," but is rather a punishment which makes the repetition of slander impossible.
[61]See the lucid comments of B. Septimus, *Hispano-Jewish Culture in Transition*, p. 91.

One clear example of this is the Maimonidean critique of Sabianism. In the *Guide* and elsewhere, Maimonides painstakingly reproduces the Sabian denial of natural causality which led them to posit a universe governed by myth:

> When you consider these ancient and unhealthy opinions, it will become clear to you that among all men it was an accepted view that through the worship of stars the earth becomes populated and the soil fertile. Their men of knowledge, as well as the ascetics and the men of piety among them, preached this to the people and taught them that agriculture, on which the existence of man depends, can only be perfected and succeed according to wish if you worship the sun and the stars; if you anger them through disobedience, the land will become barren and devastated....Inasmuch as these opinions were generally accepted, (the idolaters) connected idolatry with agriculture, the latter being necessary for the subsistence of man and of most animals. Accordingly, the priests of idolatry preached to the people during their assemblies in the temples and fortified in their minds the notion that through practices of this cult, rains would fall, the trees would bear fruit, and the land would become fertile and populous.

The conclusion pointedly contrasts Sabian mythology with Biblical belief.

> Now inasmuch as these notions were generally accepted so that they were regarded as certain, and as God, may He be exalted, wished in His pity for us to efface this error from our minds and to take away fatigue from our bodies through the abolition of these tiring and useless practices and to give us Laws through their instrumentality of Moses our Teacher, the latter informed us in His name, may He be exalted, that if the stars and the planets were worshiped, their worship would be a cause for the rain ceasing to fall, for the land being devastated and producing nothing, for the fruit of the trees falling off, for misfortunes attending circumstances, for infirmities befalling the bodies, and for a shortening of lives. These are the intentions of the words of the covenant, which the Lord made. You will find that this intention is reiterated in the whole of the Torah: I mean that it is a necessary consequence of the worship of the stars that rains will cease to fall, that the land will be devastated, that circumstances will become bad, that the bodies will suffer from diseases, and that lives will be short; whereas a necessary consequence of the abandonment of their worship and the adoption of the worship of God will be rainfall, the fertility of the land, good circumstances, health of the body, and length of life. This is the contrary of what was preached by the idolaters to the people in order that they worship idols. For the foundation of the Law consists in putting an end to this opinion and effacing its traces, as we have explained.[62]

---

[62]*Guide*, III, 30. *Guide*, III, 51, suggests that providence protects one from evil; the lack or absence of providence leaves one exposed to the impartial law of nature. Note also that in the "Letter on Astrology" *Maimonides* emphasizes the

The alternative to this pagan mythology is not the scientific postulate that good crops depend on rainfall and related climactic phenomena but that true belief and proper worship of God will ward off adversity. Idolatry is in no way related to agriculture, but God may work through nature and above nature.

This is also the rationale which Maimonides finds in the institution of fasting. His morphology of fasting relates it to the experience of prayer while the teleology of fasting is repentance. The entire conceptualization reflects the essential theory concerning the relation between nature and providence.

> This procedure is one of the roads to repentance, for as the community cries out in prayer and sounds an alarm when overtaken by trouble, everyone is bound to realize that evil has come upon him as a consequence of his own evil deeds, as it is written, 'Your iniquities have turned away these things, and your sins have withheld good from you' (Jer. 5:25), and that his repentance will cause the trouble to be removed.

> If, on the other hand, the people do not cry out in prayer and do not sound an alarm, but merely say that it is the way of the world for such a thing to happen to them, and that their trouble is a matter of pure chance, they have chosen a cruel path which will cause them to persevere in their evil deeds and thus bring additional troubles upon them. For when the Scripture says, 'But walk contrary to Me; then I will walk contrary to you in fury' (Lev. 26:27-28), the meaning is: If, when I bring trouble upon you in order to cause you to repent, you say that the trouble is purely accidental, then I will add to your trouble the fury appropriate to such an 'accident.'[63]

V

Professor S. Pines, in a short article entitled "Introduction to Medieval Science," contributed to Professor S. Sambursky's book *Physical Thought from the Presocratics to the Quantum Physicists* (London, 1974), writes:

> While Maimonides has an implicit belief in the correctness of Aristotelian physics as an explanation of the phenomena of the sublunar world, he wishes to point out that Aristotle's views concerning celestial physics are subject to doubt. Like Kant, he is interested in showing that some of the so-called verities and certainties of science are unfounded; as a consequence room can be left for faith.[64]

---

total lack of utility in mythological-astrological belief; true belief is naturally linked to usefulness (*to 'elet*).
[63]*Hilkot Taœaniyot*, I, 2, 3.
[64]S. Pines, *Collected Works*, p. 355.

For our purposes we may simply say that our study of halakah and science suggests the following: as a consequence room can be left for non-scientific or extra-scientific phenomena the credibility of which rests on that additional source of knowledge, namely tradition.

32

Intellectual Perfection and the Role of the Law in the Philosophy of Maimonides

Howard Kreisel
Ben-Gurion University of the Negev

I

Maimonides views human perfection primarily as the perfection of the intellect. In *The Guide of the Perplexed*, III. 54, he defines perfection as, "the acquisition of the rational virtues – I refer to the conception of the intelligibles *(ma'aqulāt)*, which teach true opinions *(ārā' saḥīḥāt)* concerning the divine things."[1] Knowledge of the intelligibles related to God is possible only after one masters all of the sciences, or apprehends the whole of existence to the extent of human capability.[2] It is this apprehension alone which leads to human immortality.[3]

---

[1]The *Guide of the Perplexed*, trans. S. Pines (Chicago, 1963), 635. Arabic readings are taken from J. Kafih's edition of *Moreh haNevukhim*, (Jerusalem, 1972), 692.

[2]See *Guide*, Introduction; I. 34; III. 27; 28; 51.

[3]*Guide*, I. 30; 70; 72; III. 8; 27; 51; 54; *Mishneh Torah, Laws of the Principles of the Torah*, IV. 8-9; *Laws of Repentance*, VIII. 2-3; *Mishnah 'im Perush Rabbenu Moshe ben Maimon: Seder Nezikin*, ed. J. Kafih (Jerusalem, 1975), 205 (*Introduction to Pereq Ḥeleq*). For a discussion of the intellect and the relationship between intellect and immortality in Maimonides' thought, see A. Altmann, "Maimonides on the Intellect and the Scope of Metaphysics," in his *Von der mittelalterlichen zur modernen Aufklaerung*, (Tubingen, 1987), 60-129. See also S. Klein-Braslavy, *Maimonides' Interpretation of the Adam Stories in Genesis* (Heb.), (Jerusalem, 1986).

25

Maimonides' view raises numerous difficulties, both from a traditional Jewish standpoint and a philosophical one. Neither the sages of the Talmud nor subsequent religious authorities regard immortality as consequent upon intellectual perfection. Maimonides' profound departure from his Jewish sources suggests that he was motivated by compelling philosophical considerations. Man *qua* corporeal creature is subject to both generation and corruption. The soul of man is intrinsically tied to matter and thus it too is subject to corruption.[4] It appears that the philosophical principle underlying the connection Maimonides draws between knowledge and immortality is the Aristotelian identity between thinker, thought, and object of thought.[5] It follows from this principle that only in man's apprehension of the Active Intellect, which is an intellect that is separate from all matter and incorruptible, does man turn into an incorruptible 'separate' intellect. Maimonides terms this intellect, the acquired intellect *(al-'aql al-mustafād)*.[6] This position can be found in the early writings of Alfarabi.[7] It is questionable, however, whether the human intellect, which is generated and tied to matter, is capable of apprehending that which is divorced from matter, thereby conjoining with the Active Intellect and transforming man from a mortal being into an immortal one. These apparently were among the considerations which led Alfarabi to retract from his earlier position and deny any form of human immortality.[8] Moreover, it is unclear what

---

[4]This is the view of Alfarabi. Maimonides alludes to it in the *Guide*, I. 41; 70; *Laws of the Principles of the Torah*, IV. 9; *Introduction to Pereq Heleq* (Kafih, p. 205).

[5]See Aristotle, *De Anima*, Book III, chap. 5. Maimonides' acceptance of this principle can be seen from the *Guide*, I. 68. See also *Eight Chapters*, VIII; *Laws of the Principles of the Torah*, II. 10.

[6]*Guide*, I. 72. For a study of Maimonides' view and its sources, see A. Altmann, *op. cit.* (note 3), 60-85. Maimonides alludes to the apprehension of the Active Intellect in I. 34; 43; 49; 62; II. 12. Maimonides consistently uses the root *d-r-k* to indicate apprehension, while the roots '-*l-m* and '-*q-l* are used to designate God's Self-knowledge. What, if any, are the differences between these terms is the pivotal problem. It should be noted that in I. 62 he terms the apprehension of the Active Intellect, a "science" (*'ilm*), while in I. 68 he appears to use the roots *d-r-k* and '-*q-l* interchangeably.

[7]For a study of the acquired intellect, as well as the other forms of human intellect, in the philosophy of Alfarabi, see F. Rahman, *Prophecy in Islam*, (London, 1958), 11-14; H. Davidson, "Alfarabi and Avicenna on the Active Intellect," Viator, 3 (1972), 109-154.

[8]Alfarabi presents this position in his lost commentary to *Nichomachean Ethics*, which is known to us by a number of citations in the works of Islamic and Jewish philosophers. For a discussion of Alfarabi's revised view, see H. Davidson, *op. cit.*, 152ff; S. Pines, "The Limitations of Human Knowledge

is the connection in Maimonides' thought between man's apprehension of the Active Intellect and his knowledge of God, the latter being treated as the pinnacle of knowledge. According to Maimonides, man can not attain any positive knowledge of God Himself, but can know only His 'negative' attributes.[9] How such knowledge, which is not the apprehension of being and identification with the object of apprehension, can lead or even contribute to the immortality of the intellect calls for an explanation. Maimonides, unfortunately, fails to enter into any details concerning these matters.

Maimonides' acceptance of the possibility of apprehending the Active Intellect is not, however, without ambiguity, particularly in light of the limits he places on human knowledge of the physical, in addition to the incorporeal, world. The apparently contradictory positions he presents regarding human knowledge and the ability to apprehend the Active Intellect may be interpreted as a subtle hint to his ultimate rejection of the possibility of the transformation of man into an eternal being.[10] This interpretation is further buttressed by the philosophical problems that an acceptance of the possibility of human immortality entails, as well as by the fact of Maimonides' awareness of Alfarabi's retraction from his earlier position. Without doubt, this interpretation, if correct, dictates a radical reevaluation of Maimonides' philosophy. It is not my purpose, however, to deal here with this issue, an issue which has engaged some of the leading Maimonidean authorities of the generation. The present study is based upon the supposition that this interpretation, for all the solid arguments advanced in its support, is incorrect.[11] Maimonides' position, notwithstanding all the problems that it entails, is that the metaphysical knowledge which the perfect individual is capable of attaining leads to the immortality of the intellect, and there is no other way of attaining immortality. Therefore, he who does not intellectually apprehend the existence and unity of God to the limits of man's capacity, together with the whole of existence which flows from God, is not perfect, and his soul will pass away with the corruption of his body.

---

according to Al-Farabi, Ibn Bajja, and Maimonides," *Studies in Medieval Jewish History and Literature*, I, ed. I. Twersky, (Massachusetts, 1979), 82ff.
[9]*Guide*, I. 52-60.
[10]The leading exponent of this interpretation is S. Pines. See *op. cit.* (note 8), 82-109. See also his recent study, "The Philosophical Purport of Maimonides' Halachic Works and the Purport of *The Guide of the Perplexed*," in *Maimonides and Philosophy*, eds. S. Pines and Y. Yovel (Dordrecht, 1986), 1-14.
[11]Pines' interpretation has been challenged in detail by Altmann, *op. cit.* (note 3), 60-129.

II

Maimonides' approach to the Torah derives from his conception of human perfection. Maimonides has no doubt that the ultimate end of the Torah is the same as that of man *qua* man – i.e., the perfection of the intellect. The Jews for him do not constitute a separate species, as they did for Halevi before him and many of the mystics after him.[12] Furthermore, the road to intellectual perfection is the same for all of mankind, and that is by way of study of the sciences. Given these assumptions, the problem with which Maimonides grapples is how does the Torah in practice contribute to the attainment of this end, in addition to the end of a well organized society which is common to most legislations. In the *Guide*, III. 27 (p. 510), Maimonides stresses,

> The Law as a whole aims at two things: the welfare of the soul and the welfare of the body. As for the welfare of the soul, it consists in the multitude's acquiring correct opinions *(ārā' saḥīḥāt)* corresponding to their respective capacity. Therefore some of them are set forth explicitly and some of them are set forth in parables. For it is not within the nature of the common multitude that its capacity should suffice for apprehending *(idrāk)* the subject matter as is.

Significantly, Maimonides in this chapter distinguishes between the "welfare of the soul" and the "perfection of the soul."[13] The perfection of the soul is defined as having, "an intellect in actu *('aql bi-l-fi'l)*; this would consist in his knowing everything concerning all the beings that it is within the capacity of man to know in accordance with his ultimate perfection" (p. 511). The connection between "welfare" and "perfection" is summarized by Maimonides in the continuation of his remarks. He describes the role of the Torah as imparting "sound beliefs" *(ṣalāḥ al-'itiqādāt)* and "correct opinions through which ultimate perfection is achieved." That is to say, the Torah transmits correct opinions in a non-scientific manner in order that they be understood by all, and in this way directs its adherents to perfection. Perfection, however, is attained only after intellectually grasping the whole of existence in a scientific manner. Maimonides is explicit on the point that it is the attainment of ultimate perfection which is, "the only cause of permanent preservation." In the following chapter, Maimonides indicates that the Torah communicates correct opinions in a sketchy and general manner, and that a detailed apprehension of them in fact requires knowledge of all of the theoretical sciences. It is

---

[12]See, for example, *Kuzari*, I. 95; II. 50; III. 1; IV. 3.
[13]See M. Galston, "The Purpose of the Law according to Maimonides," *JQR*, 69 (1978), 35ff.

precisely Maimonides' attempt to bridge the gap between the correct opinions imparted by the Torah on one hand, and the knowledge which leads to ultimate perfection on the other, that underscores the depth of this gap in his thought. There is a profound difference between the acquisition of correct opinions in parable form and the intellectual apprehension of all which they denote. Thus the study of the Torah and its observance do not in themselves confer perfection upon the individual. At best they create the ideal environment both from a social standpoint and more important, an intellectual one, in which the capable individual can strive for perfection. They also help transmit to the individual the moral traits without which intellectual perfection is unattainable. Maimonides further attempts to bridge the gap between the Torah and perfection by incorporating knowledge of physics and especially metaphysics into one's religious obligations.[14] This knowledge forms an integral part of the commandments to know the existence of God, that there is no other god besides Him, to unify Him, to love Him and to be in awe of Him. Maimonides rules that the last two commandments are observed only by contemplating God's activities and creatures.[15]

The role of the Torah and its limits are graphically illustrated by Maimonides in his parable of the king in his palace (*Guide*, III. 51). One who holds an incorrect opinion, either because of faulty speculation or an erroneous tradition – and it is clear that Maimonides is dealing with errors in beliefs pertaining to the Deity – is within the polis, but with his back to the palace. The masses of Jews, on the other hand, face the palace but are so far away that they do not even catch a glimpse of it. Maimonides indicates that they observe the Torah, but he does not mention anything in regard to their opinions. Those who circle the

---

[14]For a detailed analysis of this point, see I. Twersky, *Introduction to the Code of Maimonides*, (New Haven, 1980), 488-507; W. Harvey, "Political Philosophy and Halakhah in Maimonides (Heb.)," *Iyyun*, 29 (1980), 198-212. See also H. Kasher, "Talmud Torah as a Means of Apprehending God in Maimonides' Teachings (Heb.)," *Jerusalem Studies in Jewish Thought*, V (1986), 71-82; *idem*, "Does 'Ought' Imply 'Can' in Maimonides (Heb.)," *Iyyun*, 36 (1987), 13-34.

[15]*Laws of the Principles of the Torah*, I-IV. Cf. *Guide*, III. 28. Maimonides' formulation of the commandment to love God in the *Mishneh Torah* reflects a subtle but crucial change from his prior formulation in *The Book of the Commandments*, positive commandment #3. In the latter work, he includes contemplation of the divine commandments as part of the commandment to love God, thereby more closely adhering to his source in *Sifre, va-ethḥanan*. No explicit mention of contemplation of the commandments, however, is made in the former work. See W. Harvey, *op. cit.* (note 14), 206. An explicit connection between rational contemplation of God and love of Him already appears in Saadya, *The Book of Beliefs and Opinions*, II. 13.

palace and search for the gate are the scholars, "who believe true opinions *(ārā' saḥīḥāt)* on the basis of traditional authority and study the Torah concerning the practices of divine service, but do not engage in speculation *(naẓra)* concerning the fundamental principles of religion and make no inquiry whatever regarding the rectification of belief *(taṣḥiḥ al-'itiqād)* (p. 619)." Only speculation in the principles of religion,[16] according to Maimonides, gains a person entrance to the antechambers, and only knowledge of all that man is capable of knowing in physical and metaphysical matters allows him entry to the inner court. The role of the Torah, in this parable, is confined to turning its adherents in the right direction, and at best directing them to the outer wall of the palace. Speculation, however, is the key to the gate. Maimonides is explicit in his view that perfection is confined to a small group of individuals,[17] and one should in no way equate adherence to correct opinions on the basis of tradition with the acquisition of intellectual perfection.[18] Thus while Maimonides uses the phrase, "correct opinions" *(ārā' saḥīḥāt)* to characterize the knowledge of the masses, the scholars and the perfect, he leaves no doubt to the difference between possessing these opinions in a non-scientific manner in accordance with the masses' limited capacity, or based solely on tradition, and intellectually apprehending these opinions based on a thorough scientific knowledge of all that exists. It should be noted that the parable of the king and the palace not only underscores the limits of the Torah's capacity to guide its adherents to perfection, but how far the vast majority of its adherents remain from perfection.

---

[16]Maimonides may be referring to the thirteen principles he presents in his *Commentary on the Mishnah: Sanhedrin, X (Introduction to Pereq Ḥeleq),* most of them having no basis in theoretical philosophy. At the very least the fundamental principles include the existence and unity of God (together with His incorporeality and eternity), which do belong to the science of metaphysics. The speculation concerning the other principles may well belong to political philosophy in Maimonides' view. For an in depth analysis of the notion of "principles" in Maimonides' thought, together with a discussion of all the important scholarly literature on the subject, see M. Kellner, *Dogma in Medieval Jewish Thought,* (Oxford, 1986), 10-65.

[17]This point is already stressed by Maimonides in the introduction to his *Commentary on the Mishnah.*

[18]In the concluding chapter of the *Guide,* Maimonides distinguishes between knowledge of the Torah and knowledge of "wisdom" (or philosophy). Knowledge of the Torah is knowledge of correct opinions on the basis of tradition, while knowledge of philosophy is knowledge of the proofs of the correct opinions on the basis of speculative reasoning. Maimonides leaves no doubt that the latter knowledge is superior to the former, though one must acquire knowledge of the Torah prior to engaging in speculation.

In most cases, the Torah succeeds only in turning them in the right direction, and little more.

III

Maimonides' essentially negative attitude regarding the acceptance of belief *solely* on the basis of tradition is even more extreme than appears at first glance. In matters directly pertaining to the theoretical intellect, most notably metaphysics, not only does belief solely on the basis of tradition not lead directly to a person's perfection,[19] but from a philosophical standpoint such belief is generally false due to the improper way in which it is grasped. The belief in the unity of God serves as a good example of this point. In I. 50 of the *Guide,* Maimonides maintains that, "if someone believes that He is one, but possesses a certain number of essential attributes, he says in his words that He is one, but believes Him in his thought to be many" (p. 111). Maimonides opens this chapter by defining belief (*'itiqād*), "not the notion that is uttered, but the notion that is represented in the soul when it has been averred of it that it is in fact just as it has been represented."[20] The conclusion presented in the continuation of Maimonides' discussion of divine attributes is exceptionally far reaching.

> I shall not say that he who affirms that God, may He be exalted, has positive attributes either falls short of apprehending Him or is an associator or has an apprehension of Him that is different from what He really is, but I shall say that he has abolished his belief in the existence of the deity without being aware of it.
>
> I. 60, p. 145

Implicit in these remarks is the notion that anyone who ascribes to God anger, mercy, or any of the other emotions, in a positive manner,

---

[19]It is true that in certain matters Maimonides counsels, at least on the exoteric level, adhering to traditional teaching when no demonstration to the contrary exists – belief in the creation of the world being a prime example (*Guide,* II. 16; 25). Yet it is questionable how a person's beliefs in these matters add anything to the perfection of his theoretical intellect. Furthermore, a number of scholars, both medieval and modern, have raised serious objections to regarding belief in creation as Maimonides' real view.

[20]For a discussion of "belief" in the thought of Maimonides, see A. Nuriel, "Maimonides and the Concept of Faith (Heb.)," *Daat,* 2-3 (1979), 43-47; idem, "Remarks on Maimonides' Epistemology," in *Maimonides and Philosophy,* 36-51; S. Rosenberg, "The Concept of 'Emunah in Post-Maimonidean Jewish Philosophy," *Studies in Medieval Jewish History and Literature,* II, ed. I. Twersky (Massachusetts, 1984), 273-307.

essentially denies the existence of God.[21] He believes in something which does not exist in reality – an emotional deity – while the real deity is not the object of his belief. Needless to say, the same is the case with one who ascribes to God any corporeal attributes. Thus from a philosophical perspective, most Jews deny the existence of God. While many may affirm His non-corporeality, few conceive of Him as lacking all emotions, and fewer still do not regard Him as possessing knowledge and will as diverse essential attributes. Only through an apprehension of the sciences can one represent to oneself correct notions about God which provide the real basis for true belief.

IV

Maimonides' view of the Torah primarily as a pedagogical device, yet severely limited by nature in the extent of its effectiveness, is a fundamental point for understanding his philosophy. The final end of the Torah is the perfection of the intellect. The Torah at best, however, can inculcate true beliefs only in a popular manner to society at large, beliefs which the vast majority will improperly grasp, while it encourages the perfect *in potentia* to strive for final perfection. The fact that the Torah was framed for a community at a certain point of historical development made the challenge all the more acute. It had to address the masses leaving Egypt in the idiom that they were capable of understanding and willing to accept, at the same time that it subtly pointed out to the elite of that generation, and all subsequent generations, the direction that they were to follow.

Insofar as the Torah is concerned with the *process* of bringing people closer to the truth, after insuring their social well-being, it evaluates beliefs in a different way than does theoretical philosophy. The Torah must take into consideration what are the beliefs to which people are accustomed and what are the beliefs closer to the truth which they can be persuaded to accept; which false beliefs are more harmful than others; what are the influences of specific beliefs on people's actions and how do specific activities influence their beliefs. The method whereby the beliefs of the various strata of society are molded so that benefit accrues to each of the strata is a primary concern of the Torah.[22] Clearly, such an approach to belief must be dynamic, changing in accordance with the circumstances. The question of truth and falsity is not in itself sufficient to determine how a belief is to be

---

[21]The various categories of attributes which are to be negated of God is presented by Maimonides in *Guide*, I. 52.
[22]Maimonides mentions many of these points in *Guide*, Introduction; I. 33; II. 31; III. 28-30; 32.

evaluated. Furthermore, given the natural limitations of the masses to grasp properly the truth, the Torah must often rest content with formal allegiance being paid to a certain belief even though it is grasped in an inaccurate manner.

How these considerations lie at the foundation of Maimonides' approach to the Torah is illustrated by his treatment of the belief in the corporeality of God. The negation of the corporeality of God is brought by Maimonides as one of the principles of Judaism.[23] His attack on the belief in a corporeal deity occurs frequently in his writings and is severe to the extreme.[24] What motivated Maimonides to adopt this stance, and what if any halakhic sources support it, are crucial problems which his position raises. Yet equally significant is the question of Maimonides' approach to the relation between the belief in a corporeal deity and the Torah. Maimonides is well aware that the text of the Torah itself, when read literally, teaches the belief in a corporeal deity. In other words, the Torah, whose primary intent is the inculcation of true beliefs, conveys a false belief in the most important area of knowledge. From the standpoint of Maimonides' philosophy, this fact demands an explanation. Why does not the Torah teach in a literal manner that God is incorporeal, instead of misleading its followers? Maimonides addresses this problem, but his answer is far from being the one that we anticipate hearing. He does not claim that there existed an exoteric tradition how to understand the corporeal descriptions of God – a tradition which was lost with the dispersion of the Jews. Such an explanation, based on the integral connection between the written text and the oral tradition, would allow Maimonides to maintain that the Torah always taught true beliefs. False beliefs were never taught intentionally, but came about as a result of a historical tragedy. While Maimonides at times employs the "exile" to account for ignorance and lack of perfection among the Jews,[25] he adopts a far different stance when dealing with the problem posed by the Torah's corporeal descriptions of God.

> ...A similar thing has occurred with regard to the knowledge of God...given to the multitude in the books of the prophets and also in the Torah. For necessity required that all of them be given guidance to the belief in the existence of God...and in His possessing all the perfections....The minds of the multitude were accordingly guided to the belief that He exists by imagining that He is corporeal, and to the belief that He is living by imagining that He is capable of motion. For

---

[23]*Introduction* to *Pereq Ḥeleq*, principle 3.
[24]See, for example, *Laws of the Principles of the Torah*, I. 7-12; *Laws of Repentance*, III. 7; *Guide*, I. 35-36.
[25]*Guide*, I. 71; II. 32; 36.

the multitude perceive nothing other than bodies as having a firmly
established existence and as being indubitably true....That, however,
which is neither a body nor in a body is not an existent thing in any
respect, according to man's initial representation, particularly from
the point of view of the imagination.

Guide, I. 46, p. 98[26]

It follows from Maimonides' remarks that the Torah deliberately
misleads the people in the matter of the corporeality of God. The
choice facing the Torah was either in educating the masses in the belief
in a single, corporeal deity, or educating them in the belief in a single,
incorporeal deity. If it had chosen the latter course, the result would
have been a complete rejection in the belief in God, for the masses were
incapable of accepting the existence of such a deity. Consequently, they
would have accepted the belief in many gods, such as the belief that
the celestial bodies are gods, which was the prevailing belief in that
period.[27] From a conceptual standpoint, belief in a single, corporeal
deity is equivalent to the belief in the non-existence of God, just as is
the case with a belief in many corporeal gods. From a pedagogical
standpoint, however, there is a profound difference between these two
beliefs. One who believes in a single, corporeal deity is closer to the
true belief than one who believes in many gods. It is precisely with the
belief in a single deity, as opposed to the belief in many gods or in no
god, that one turns to the direction of the palace in Maimonides'
parable of the king. The Torah has no choice but to compromise with
reality in order to educate the people effectively. For the elite, it can
offer only hints that God is in fact incorporeal, and the descriptions
should not be interpreted in a literal manner. Maimonides indicates
that the sages of the Talmud did understand how to interpret the
corporeal descriptions, while they continued to employ them in their
own parables.[28] Thus the true religion, according to Maimonides,
teaches false beliefs in regard to God not only to improve the moral
behavior of the masses – a position Maimonides explicitly presents
when dealing with the notion of necessary beliefs –[29] but also in order
to inculcate true beliefs in a preliminary manner. The truth which is
possible to convey to the masses must be conveyed in stages. In this
manner, the beliefs of the masses are refined, without precipitating a
regression. From a conceptual standpoint, there is no belief in the
existence of God without the belief in His absolute unity, and there is

---

[26]Cf. I. 26.

[27]*Guide*, III. 29; *Laws of Idolatry*, I. 1-2.

[28]*Guide*, I. 46.

[29]*Guide*, III. 28. An example of a necessary belief is that God is angry with the
disobedient. Such beliefs help insure obedience to the Law.

no belief in His absolute unity without belief in His incorporeality.[30] From a pedagogical standpoint, however, these beliefs must be divided and transmitted one at a time.

V

In light of Maimonides' comments in the *Guide*, it is clear that he is well aware of the innovation he introduces in his halakhic works when he labels as heretics those who express a belief in a single, but corporeal, deity.[31] Not only does Maimonides lack any clear basis in Jewish law for his ruling,[32] but it appears to negate the stance of the Torah which intentionally chooses to describe God as corporeal. The reason that Maimonides adopts this position is that the circumstances had changed. The situation in his period permitted the further refinement of the beliefs of the masses. The greatest change was the decisive victory of the belief in a single God vs. the belief in many gods. In the period of Abraham, as well as Moses, the beliefs of the Sabians, according to Maimonides, were dominant. The Sabians worshipped the stars, recognizing no deity beyond the celestial bodies. Abraham began to challenge this belief, and teach that there is a single deity who is the Lord of the world. The Law of Moses continued in the path of Abraham, but employed a more effective pedagogical device in conveying the belief in a single deity to the masses – commandments rather than rational arguments. The fact that the vast majority of the world now glorify Abraham attests to the extent of his victory.[33] Maimonides considers the reason for many of the commandments to be the effacement of the beliefs of the Sabians, by means of rejecting the forms of worship which were associated with those beliefs. The fact that the specific reasons for a good number of the commandments are no longer known is due to our present day ignorance of the Sabians' beliefs.[34] In other words, our ignorance of the reasons for many of the commandments is the result of the Torah's singular victory in effacing the beliefs of the Sabians and their practices.

---

[30]*Guide*, I. 35; 60.
[31]*Introduction to Pereq Ḥeleq; Laws of Repentance*, III. 7. This innovation drew the ire of the Rabad who remarks in his *Hassagot* on III. 7, "...greater and better than he [Maimonides] held this view [God's corporeality] according to what they saw in the Scriptures." For an enumeration of the terms for heresy in the writings of Maimonides, see M. Kellner, *op. cit.* (note 16), 19-21.
[32]See, however, J. Kafih's commentary to *Sefer Mishneh Torah: Sefer ha-Madda'*, (Jerusalem, 1984), 609 n. 34.
[33]*Guide*, III. 29. See L. Kaplan, "Maimonides on the Singularity of the Jewish People," *Daat*, 15 (1985), V-XXVI.
[34]*Guide*, III. 48. Cf. III. 29.

With the victory of the belief in a single deity, there is no longer any danger in publicly teaching the belief in an incorporeal deity. In the period of the Torah, such teaching would have resulted in the acceptance of many corporeal gods. This belief, however, no longer exists, at least not in its vulgar form.[35] Thus there is no reason not to emphasize in public that which the Torah could only hint. The time was ripe to transfer the teaching of the incorporeality of the Deity from the "secrets of the Torah" that needed to be conveyed in the form of parables hidden from the understanding of the masses, to a teaching that was to be conveyed to all. The masses could now be habituated to think of God in a more profound manner.[36] The corporeal descriptions of God, serving by Maimonides' time more as a stumbling block to the welfare of the soul rather than an aid, could be designated for what they were – figurative representations which were not to be interpreted literally.[37] The spread of Islam, with its proclamation of the

---

[35]Maimonides does classify the Christians as idolaters, without indicating the reason for his ruling. In the *Guide*, I. 50, he mentions that they affirm the unity of God, though their belief in the Trinity entails a belief in multiplicity. As H. Wolfson has shown, Maimonides in this passage *compares* belief in the Trinity with belief in essential attributes, but does not *equate* the two. From a logical standpoint, both beliefs violate the Law of Contradiction and entail multiplicity. From a religious standpoint, however, Maimonides does not consider the affirmation of essential attributes as polytheism, but does consider affirmation of the three persons of the Trinity to be such. See, "Maimonides on the Unity and Incorporeality of God," *JQR*, 56 (1965), 124-134 [repr. *Studies in the History of Philosophy and Religion*, II, eds. I. Twersky and G. Williams (Massachusetts, 1977), 445-455]. There is also a hint in one of his responsa that the deification of Jesus is the basis for his ruling. See *Teshuvot ha-Rambam*, ed. J. Blau (Jerusalem, 1961), no. 448. In any case, Maimonides does not regard Christianity as negatively as the idolatrous religion of the Sabians, in large part because the Christians acknowledge the divinity of the Torah. For an analysis of Maimonides' view both of Christianity and Islam, see D. Novak, "The Treatment of Islam and Muslims in the Legal Writings of Maimonides," *Studies in Islamic and Judaic Traditions*, eds. W. Brinner and S. Ricks (Atlanta, 1986), 233-250.

[36]In I. 31 of the *Guide*, Maimonides adds "habit and upbringing" to Alexander of Aphrodisias' list of causes of disagreement (and error). He brings as an example the multitude's belief in the corporeality of God on the basis of a literal reading of Scripture. Maimonides' discussion in this passage raises a series of difficult problems which I cannot deal with in the present context. Suffice it to say, Maimonides endeavors to break this habit inasmuch as it no longer serves any positive purpose, though it did so in the past.

[37]See *Guide*, Introduction; I. 26; 31; 35; 46. Maimonides' discussion of parables in the introduction to his treatise is particularly significant. True understanding of a text requires first knowing whether the text is a parable. Maimonides is not the first of the great rabbinic scholars to adopt this approach to Scripture. He was preceded by Saadya in this matter (*The Book of Beliefs and Opinions*, II),

incorporeality of God, made the public teaching of this belief within Judaism both easier and more incumbent.[38] Maimonides saw no problem in bringing to his aid the full authority of the Torah in this matter, and designating as a heretic one who professes belief in a corporeal deity, with all the legal consequences such a designation entails.[39] The rectification of belief is, in the final analysis, the ultimate purpose of the Torah in Maimonides' view. Thus there is no incongruity between the Torah's choice to hide the view of God's incorporeality in order to safeguard the view of His existence and perfection, and Maimonides' insistence that the masses, "should be made to accept on traditional authority the belief that God is not a body (*Guide*, I. 35, p. 80)." It is clear that the vast majority will continue to hold beliefs which from a conceptual standpoint entail the corporealization, and hence the non-existence, of God. Significantly, Maimonides does not include among the heretics those who affirm essential attributes, though such affirmation logically entails corporeality.[40] He is sensitive to the degree that a proper belief in divine incorporeality can be impressed upon the masses. Maimonides rests content with incorporating the denial of positive attributes as part of the commandment to unify God (*Laws of the Principles of the Torah*, I. 11). In the prolonged process of refining people's beliefs, it is sufficient that at this stage the explicit, publicly proclaimed belief in a corporeal deity join the explicit, publicly

---

as well as by many of the subsequent Jewish thinkers. To what extent does this approach have its roots in the midrash of the Sages requires a separate study.

[38]Maimonides rules that the Moslems are not idolaters. Moreover, they believe in a correct manner in the unity of God (*Teshuvot ha-Rambam*, no. 448). Yet this point proved to be somewhat of an embarrassment as well, inasmuch as Maimonides distinguishes the divine religion from the others by the fact that it inculcates correct beliefs leading to the welfare of the soul. Islam, which at best was regarded by Maimonides as a poor imitation of Judaism, nonetheless was far more explicit than Judaism in its teaching of the incorporeality of God. Thus on one level, it appears to satisfy better the criteria of a divine religion. By making the incorporeality of God a principle of the faith, Maimonides also safeguards the inherent superiority of Judaism as he understands it.

[39]For the practical legal consequences of heresy, see M. Kellner, *op. cit.* (note 16), 18-21.

[40]See H. Wolfson, *op. cit.* (note 35), 120ff. It should be stressed that while Maimonides appears to consider the fulfillment of the commandments involving a knowledge of God to be purely mental acts (and on this point I disagree with Wolfson), the same is not the case with heresy. A heretic is one who states certain false beliefs out loud. This point, however, is hardly surprising. As is the case with all acts which carry with it practical legal consequences, the act of heresy must be a public act.

proclaimed belief in the existence of many gods, and vanish from the world.

VI

Maimonides' attempt to continue in the path laid down by the Torah, as he understood it, and rectify people's beliefs, finds its most blatant expression in the first part of *The Book of Knowledge, the Laws of the Principles of the Torah*.[41] The opening of his great legal compendium, the *Mishneh Torah*, with the commandments to know the existence of God and His unity, and the viewing of the commandments to love and fear God as intrinsically dependent upon the extent of one's knowledge of Him and His world, attest to the importance this matter held for him. Yet it is hard to overlook the problems raised by the manner in which Maimonides formulates these commandments, not the greatest being the absence of explicit legal sources for his rulings. On one hand, these commandments are incumbent upon everyone. On the other hand, Maimonides indicates,

> The things which I have said in these two chapters are like a drop in the ocean compared to what has to be elucidated on this subject. The exposition of all the principles in these two chapters is what is called *ma'aseh merkavah* (The Account of the Chariot)....The early sages commanded not to expound these matters except to a solitary individual who is wise and understands by means of his own reasoning....
>
> II. 11-12

In light of Maimonides' remarks, the question arises why he treats these commandments as incumbent upon everyone if he identifies their subject matter with the esoteric topics *ma'aseh merkavah* and *ma'aseh bereishith* (The Account of the Beginning) – topics which he equates with metaphysics and physics?[42] Even more puzzling, if Maimonides thinks that the teaching of these topics is to be withheld from the masses, following the ruling of the Sages, why does he open his legal

---

[41]A number of important philosophical studies have been devoted to exploring aspects of this work. See especially, L. Strauss, "Notes on Maimonides' Book of Knowledge," *Studies in Mysticism and Religion Presented to Gershom Scholem*, ed. E. Urbach (Jerusalem, 1967), 269-283; S. Rawidowicz, *Iyyunim Bemahshevet Yisrael*, I, (Jerusalem, 1969), 381-415; I. Twersky, *op. cit.* (note 14), 488-507; L. Berman, "Maimonides, the Disciple of Alfarabi," *Israel Oriental Studies*, IV (1974), 154-178; J. Kraemer, "Alfarabi's *Opinions of the Virtuous City* and Maimonides' Foundations of the Law," in *Studia Orientalia Memoriae D. H. Baneth Dedicata*, (Jerusalem, 1979), 107-153; W. Harvey, *op. cit.* (note 14), 198-212; H. Kasher, "Does 'Ought' Imply 'Can'...." (note 14), 13-34.

[42]See also *Guide*, Introduction; *Commentary to Mishnah: Hagigah*, II. 1.

compendium with a detailed outline of them. Maimonides appears to demand from the masses what is not in their capacity to fulfill and at the same time reveals to them matters which he himself indicates that the Sages commanded to conceal.

Part of the answer to this problem is found in Maimonides' *Guide*. The commandment to "know" (*da '*) which opens the *Laws of the Principles of the Torah* does not imply detailed scientific knowledge. Rather it refers to the acceptance of correct opinions, rendering the Arabic *'itiqad*.[43] These are precisely the opinions which Maimonides indicates in the *Guide* are to be communicated to everyone. It is the scientific explication of these principles which belongs to the domain of philosophy and is to be restricted to the elite. Therefore, Maimonides in fact does not demand from the masses what they are incapable of fulfilling on a simple level, though they are incapable of fulfilling the full dimensions of these commandments. Nor does Maimonides reveal what the Sages command to conceal, for it is only the full explication of these commandments which belong to the secrets of the Torah.

While this answer resolves the apparent contradiction in Maimonides' stance, it does not, however, explain the enigmatic nature of Maimonides' formulation. In the *Guide* Maimonides draws a sharp line between that which is to be taught to the masses, and that which is to remain secret. In the *Laws of the Principles of the Torah* he deliberately blurs the distinction. No clear enumeration of topics which are to remain hidden from the masses is to be found there, in contradistinction to the *Guide*.[44] Rather, he appears to encourage the study of esoteric topics by incorporating them as such into the commandments and providing their salient details. This tendency reemerges in the *Laws of the Study of the Torah* where Maimonides prominently includes the study of *pardes* (metaphysics and physics) in the study of Talmud, to which a person is obligated to devote at least a third of his study time.[45] His reiteration of the warning of the Sages regarding the study of these topics thus appears to run counter to the dominant trend of his entire presentation.

---

[43]This point has been argued by S. Rawidowicz, "On Maimonides' *Sefer ha-Madda*," in *Essays in Honour of the Very Rev. Dr. J. H. Hertz*, eds. I. Epstein, E. Levine, and C. Roth (London, 1942), 331-339 [repr. S. Rawidowicz, *Studies in Jewish Thought*, ed. N. Glatzer (Philadelphia, 1974), 317-323]. See also A. Nuriel, "Maimonides and the Concept of Faith" (note 20), 43-47.

[44]See *Guide*, I. 35.

[45]I. 11-12; cf. *Laws of the Principles of the Torah*, IV. 13. For an analysis of this point, see I. Twersky, *op. cit.*, 489ff; H. Kasher, "Talmud Torah...." (note 14), 75ff.

Maimonides' approach becomes clearer if we consider the first chapters of the *Laws of the Principles of the Torah* as primarily intended for the potential elite, rather than for the masses. These are the individuals who have the capability of achieving perfection, but lack knowledge of the proper path. This group is particularly worthy of attention for only in them is the ultimate purpose of Judaism realized. This group is not to be completely identified with the ideal readers of the *Guide*. They are not yet prepared for Maimonides' discourse in the *Guide*, for they have not yet attained philosophic knowledge. The challenge facing Maimonides is to reach these individuals when they are scattered around the world and when it is not easy to identify them.

The social and political circumstances of the Jews in the period of Maimonides made the educational model presented by Alfarabi, and rooted in Plato, inapplicable. No enlightened centralized leadership could organize and implement an educational system which divided people according to their potential and placed each group in its own tract of learning.[46] The primary means at Maimonides' disposal was the written word. Maimonides could only hope that in reaching the largest possible audience through his legal works, he would be able to prod the potential elite in the right direction. It is for this reason that at times Maimonides' philosophic positions are much more explicit in the *Laws of the Principles of the Torah* than they are in the *Guide*. The *Guide* is intended for a limited audience who are well versed both in Jewish tradition and philosophy. The danger in the writing of the *Guide* is that the work may fall into the hands of those who do not belong to this group. For this reason, the truth concerning certain topics is revealed by means of hints which only the ideal reader is capable of understanding. The *Mishneh Torah*, on the other hand, is intended for everyone, especially the potential elite at the beginning of their path. Subtle hints would not prove sufficient in reaching this group, inasmuch as they had not yet attained philosophic knowledge and may well have been educated in an environment which was hostile to philosophy. It was incumbent upon Maimonides to reveal his positions

---

[46]See M. Mahdi, *Alfarabi's Philosophy of Plato and Aristotle*, (Glencoe, 1962), 34-41. Cf. Plato, *Republic*, II. 376e-412b; IV. 421c-427c; VI-VII. 509d-541b. To what degree did Alfarabi feel that the practical implementation of his model was possible is a difficult problem. As for the application of this model to Jewish society, no institution equivalent to the caliphate in power and authority existed in Judaism in Maimonides' time which would make this even a theoretical possibility. Maimonides, however, still was strongly influenced by Alfarabi's views on the virtuous religion in framing his "principles." See J. Kramer, *op. cit.* (note 41).

in a more explicit manner, and from the very beginning of his work, in order to set this group upon the right path.[47]

The essential message which emerges from Maimonides' discussion of the commandments to know God and love Him is that one who desires to reach perfection as a Jew, which is in fact human perfection, and to attain immortality, must devote himself to the study of philosophy. By describing God as the First Existent and Mover of the Sphere, and by introducing other philosophic conceptions, Maimonides points to the knowledge which is necessary for the true fulfillment of the first commandment. By presenting an outline of *ma'aseh merkavah* and *ma'aseh bereishith*, and identifying the angels with the Separate Intellects, he indicates his rejection of other conceptions of these topics, conceptions which may attract the potential elite and lead them astray. By labeling knowledge of the other commandments "a small matter," in comparison to the commandments to know God, fulfilled by a mastery of *ma'aseh merkavah* which is "a great matter,"[48] Maimonides leaves no doubt to which studies a person must dedicate himself. His reiteration of the warning of the Sages regarding the study of these topics in this context serves more as a stimulus to the potential elite rather than a deterrent. Maimonides certainly would not have revealed what he did in the *Laws of the Principles of the Torah* if he felt that this would cause damage to the faith of the masses. He judged that they would not appreciate the full significance of his position, and only the elite would understand and turn to the right path in their studies. At any rate, he saw no alternative but to set down these commandments at the beginning of his work, with all the transparent "hints" to his true view on the subject of perfection, despite the dangers involved. Otherwise the Torah would be for nought, since it would not attain its ultimate objective.

---

[47]The view that Maimonides' theological positions in his halakhic works are no less philosophical than the positions he presents in the *Guide*, has been argued by S. Pines, "The Philosophical Purport...." (note 10), 2ff.

[48]Laws of the *Principles of the Torah*, IV. 13. See I. Twersky, *op. cit.*, 493ff. Twersky points to Maimonides' novel, yet very literal, interpretation of "great" (*gadol*) and "small" (*katan*) in terms of nobility. Yet perhaps of greater moment is Maimonides' novel and non-literal interpretation of knowledge of the "discussions (*havvayot*) of Abbaye and Raba" as referring to knowledge of the "forbidden and permitted and their like from the rest of the commandments." That is to say, Maimonides equates the talmudic deliberations of Abaye and Raba with most of the Oral Law (excluding the commandments involving the study of physics and metaphysics), as the context of his remarks makes clear. See also W. Harvey, *op. cit.* (note 14), 207.

VII

It would be wrong to conclude from all that was stated till now that
Maimonides believes in historical progress regarding the most
important area – man's knowledge of God – and he acts primarily from
this optimistic evaluation of the situation. Maimonides does discern
progress in popular universal beliefs, and consequently what is possible
to teach the masses. He also notes the progress made in knowledge of
scientific matters, most notably astronomy.[49] Yet at the same time he
believes there was a great regression in regard to the attainment of
intellectual perfection. This regression, perhaps even more than the
progress which was made, prodded him to compose his treatises. The
regression was most evident in the Jewish leaders or scholars of his
generation, the group in which were to be found most of the perfect *in
potentia*. The contempt with which Maimonides holds the scholars of
his generation emerges clearly and repeatedly from his writings.
Maimonides is of the opinion that most of the perfect lived towards the
beginning of Jewish history. On the highest level stand Moses and the
forefathers. Beneath them stand the prophets, followed by the sages of
the Mishnah and Talmud. This is, of course, the traditional conception.
Thus it is hardly surprising that it finds an explicit expression in
Maimonides' works. Yet it appears that this is not simply Maimonides'
"exoteric" opinion, but his real opinion as well. His view of the
prophetic visions and Talmudic midrashim as philosophic parables is
not an attempt to create a new myth by means of which he can justify
and encourage the study of philosophy. He actually understands their
words in this manner.[50] For this reason, the ignorance of philosophy
displayed by the Jewish scholars of his generation distressed him
greatly. In his view, they were educating the generation to view the
subordinate as primary, and not to recognize the primary at all. No
longer were those who attained intellectual perfection leading the
people and guiding each to the perfection of which he was capable, as
advocated by Plato and had been to a large degree the case in the
past.[51] Instead, the Jewish people were being led by those who shared

---

[49]*Guide*, II. 24.
[50]For a detailed analysis of the conflict among the Maimonidean scholars on
this issue, see A. Ravitzky, "The Secrets of the *Guide of the Perplexed*: Between
the Thirteenth and the Twentieth Centuries (Heb.)," *Jerusalem Studies in
Jewish Thought*, V (1986), 23-70.
[51]Moses was the philosopher-king *par excellence*, in Maimonides' view, while
the subsequent prophets and Talmudic sages served as "princes of the law."
These are leaders who understand and implement the intention of the law, but

with the masses the same false conceptions of the truth and guided them accordingly.[52]

What caused this regression, with a narrowing of the gap between the Sages and masses, was the loss of the esoteric oral tradition transmitted by the sages to the elite of their students. Maimonides opens the third part of the *Guide* (p. 415), which deals with *ma'aseh merkavah*, with the comment,

> They have already made it clear how secret the *Account of the Chariot* was and how foreign to the mind of the multitude. And it has been made clear that even that portion of it that becomes clear to him who has been given access to the understanding of it, is subject to a legal prohibition against its being taught and explained except orally to one man having certain stated qualities, and even to that one only the *chapter headings* may be mentioned. This is the reason why the knowledge of this matter has ceased to exist in the entire religious community, so that nothing great or small remains of it.

Maimonides' remark should not be treated simply as a typical, and even formalistic, rationale for writing down matters whose transmission is supposed to be in oral form. Maimonides sincerely believes that knowledge of metaphysics was once part of Jewish tradition, and it is incumbent upon him to rediscover and transmit what was known to the sages of old. The exile and dispersal of the Jewish people led to the loss of this knowledge.[53] Conceptions far from the truth, in Maimonides' view, supplanted the lost tradition. If Judaism is to retain its essential meaning, this regression must be halted and the scholars must be directed to a proper understanding of the non-corporeal world and what constitutes human perfection.[54]

---

do not frame new legislations. See Alfarabi, *The Political Regime*, ed. F. Najjar (Beyrouth, 1964), 81.

[52]See in particular Maimonides' remarks towards the beginning of his *Treatise on Resurrection* ('*Iggerot ha-Rambam*, ed. I. Shailat (Maaleh Adumim, 1987), 319-321; 339-343).

[53]*Guide*, I. 71. Cf. I. Introduction; 33; 34. For a discussion of Maimonides' reconstruction of history, see I. Twersky, *op. cit.*, 370, 496ff.; L. Berman, *op. cit.* (note 41), 165ff.

[54]Certainly, even if Maimonides *did not* in fact believe that the prophets attained a level of metaphysical knowledge greater than that of the Aristotelian philosophers, and the sages of the Talmud attained at least the same level, he would have had to express this opinion in order to justify his radical approach from the standpoint of Jewish tradition. Yet the impression that Maimonides conveys, in my reading of the texts, is that he believes in his reconstruction of history. He did not consciously seek to redefine the essence of Judaism in order to make it conform to the philosophic truths which he accepted. Rather, he sought to rediscover the essence of Judaism, as intended by the Lawgiver and known to the prophets and sages of old. Judaism, in his view, in fact

From this evaluation of the situation of the Jewish people Maimonides acted. In order to reach the perfect *in potentia* and to guide them to perfection, Maimonides first had to write works directed to the entire people. He had to refine the beliefs of the masses, thereby raising the intellectual level of society, at the same time that he directed the elite to the proper path. His goal was to mold a new group of scholars, who like the sages of old would be teachers of truth and ideal leaders. With no single center for Jewish learning and with the potential elite scattered throughout the world, no longer could the esoteric tradition be renewed orally.[55] There appears to be some type of master plan in Maimonides' main literary activities, a plan which receives a vague formulation already in his *Commentary on the Mishnah*.[56] The *Guide* could only be written towards the end of his life, after his previous efforts bore fruit and helped in creating a group of scholars intellectually prepared for this composition.

VIII

In summary, Maimonides ascribes to the Torah a pedagogical role in the bringing about of intellectual perfection and sees in this role the superiority of the Torah over all legislations. Maimonides' own compositions are designed to continue in the path of the Torah. Yet the relation between the pedagogical role of the Torah and Maimonides' compositions on one hand, and the acquisition of metaphysical knowledge and intellectual perfection on the other hand, is complex. A profound gap separates the acceptance of the opinions of the Torah, or the principles formulated by Maimonides, and the grasping of the realm of metaphysics. The study of philosophy alone can bridge this gap.

In the final analysis, however, there is no great gap between the Jewish masses and those who hold false conceptions of God. Both groups are far from grasping the truth, and as a result do not attain immortality. The final destiny of those whose back is to the palace of the king, those who face in the direction of the palace but do not see it,

---

conformed to those truths, and only the loss of knowledge among the leaders led to its inability to achieve its ultimate purpose.

[55]See Maimonides' dedicatory epistle to his pupil, R. Joseph b. Judah, at the beginning of the *Guide*.

[56]Maimonides, in the introduction to his commentary, announces his plan to write books explaining the prophetic parables and the midrashim of the sages. In the introduction to the *Guide*, he indicates his decision to revise his original plan and write the present work instead. Nor is it a coincidence that between these two works he wrote the *Mishneh Torah*, which begins with the principles of the religion.

and those who search for the entrance is the same. A failure to apprehend that which is separate from matter and to conceive God as non-corporeal characterizes the thought of the masses, no matter how much they may affirm the existence of God and His unity, or observe the commandments. It is evident from Maimonides' approach that all of Israel does not have a portion in the World to Come, with the exception of a few individuals. The importance of instruction regarding the World to Come is to insure obedience to the Torah.

Thus for the vast majority of the people, philosophy confers no benefit, for they are incapable by nature of attaining perfection. The study of philosophy may even bring harm to their life in this world by undermining their faith and obedience to the Torah, thereby destroying the fabric of Jewish social life. The study of philosophy must be restricted to the elite. The purpose of the opinions inculcated by the Torah is not to serve as a substitute for the study of philosophy or even to supplement the scientific knowledge attained by way of philosophy. Maimonides' dedication to the rectification of Jewish belief, and his view that in this area lies the essential superiority of the Torah over all other legislations, do not stem from a conviction that the inculcation of correct opinions has any ultimate significance for the masses. Nor does it add to the intellectual perfection of those who have mastered all of the sciences. The importance of such instruction lies in the type of society it helps mold, with the ideal society being the one providing the best environment, both physically and spiritually, for those with the potential for attaining perfection. Maimonides is explicit in his view that society exists for the perfect.[57] Different "official" beliefs lead to the molding of societies which differ in their intellectual orientation and moral climate. A society in which its inhabitants affirm the unity of God, albeit in accordance with their false conceptions of divine unity, fundamentally differs from a society of idolaters. The former provides an environment far more conducive to the attainment of perfection by the elite than does the latter. The Torah, in Maimonides' thought, addresses itself to everyone, but it is those who are perfect *in potentia* who are its primary concern. The Torah, however, can address this group directly only by means of hints, in order to avoid bringing harm to the others. The hints also serve as a test to determine who really belong to the elite, at the same time that it guides them in the right direction. Though the precise manner in which beliefs are rectified must be determined in light of the social situation, the goal remains forever the same – to bring to intellectual

---

[57]See the introduction to his *Commentary on the Mishnah*.

perfection all those with the proper potential, while at the same time insuring the preservation of society.

Maimonides' legal corpus is framed with this end in mind. In determining how to continue in the path laid down by the Torah, Maimonides discerned in his period two fundamental differences from the Biblical and Talmudic periods. The first was a change for the better. In his day the possibility existed to teach the masses beliefs in the realm of metaphysics to which the Torah could only hint. There no longer was need to fear that the teaching of the incorporeality of God would lead to a weakening of faith in Judaism. The second was a change for the worse. The esoteric oral tradition was lost as a result of the dispersal of the Jews. Maimonides felt that he rediscovered this tradition through the study of philosophy. It was incumbent upon him to transmit this knowledge to the worthy among a dispersed nation. Moreover, he had first to help create a group from which the worthy would emerge, at the same time that he devoted himself to the well-being and continuity of Jewish society as a whole. This task called for an exceptionally subtle pedagogical strategy which finds its expression in Maimonides' various compositions.

33

Maimonides and the Alternatives Concerning the World's Being Everlasting

Keith E. Yandell
University of Wisconsin

All passages that you find in the Scriptures, in which it is predicated of Him, may He be exalted, that He is *the First and the Last* are analogous to those in which it is predicated of Him that He has an eye or an ear. The purpose of this is to indicate that He, may He be exalted, is not subject to change and that no motion is produced in Him anew. It is not meant to indicate that God, may He be exalted, falls under time, so that there would be some analogy between Him and that which is other than He and is in time, so that He would be *the First and the Last*. All these words as applied to Him are *according to the language of the sons of men*.[1]

The Law has given us knowledge of a matter the grasp of which is not within our power, and the miracle attests to the correctness of our claims.[2]

Introduction

It is, in a way, the height of folly for a professor of philosophy, trained in Midwestern state universities, innocent of Hebrew language and culture, and bred upon twentieth century analytic philosophy, to write on Maimonides in homage to an eminent Maimonides scholar. Yet, however great Maimonides' prestige in his own community, he is hardly mentioned in contemporary analytic philosophy, including

---

[1]Maimonides, *The Guide of the Perplexed* (Chicago: The University of Chicago Press, 1983), tr. Shlomo Pines, p. 133. Hereafter cited as *Guide*.
[2]*Guide*, 329.

47

contemporary philosophy of religion. This remains the case even though philosophical theology has recently come out of retirement in analytic philosophical circles.[3] Perhaps, then, even a modest contribution to Maimonides studies, shaped in the methodology and terminology of contemporary analytic philosophy, may give evidence of the relevance of Maimonides' thought to contemporary philosophy of religion.

Given this purpose, there are many topics that one might choose to pursue. The topic explored here concerns Maimonides' views on the issue as to whether the world enjoys an unbeginning past.[4] The discussion, following Maimonides' lead, considers the implications for this question of the existence of God.[5] Assume that God exists – not some pale imitation but an omnipotent, omniscient, perfectly good Creator. What consequences follow regarding the existence of the world; how are we to understand this term "Creator?" My purpose in what follows is to consider certain answers to this question as they arise in the history of philosophical theology, and particularly as they arise in Maimonides' *The Guide of the Perplexed*.

There is, of course, the objection that Maimonides is a theologian, not a philosopher, and there is something to this suggestion.[6] His philosophy, or his use of philosophy, is cast in the role of servant to the Law and the Prophets. These considerations have to do with his overall world-view and his motives. Even if someone does philosophy for plainly wicked reasons, he may do it well and one may learn from it. The same holds if one trims one's philosophical cloth to the shape of one's theology; what goes into the pattern of the cloth may be highly instructive, even for those whose perspective has different contours. After all, materialism may currently play a role for many

---

[3]See, for example, Thomas V. Morris, *Divine and Human Action: Essays in the Metaphysics of Theism* (Ithaca: Cornell University Press, 1988) and Thomas V. Morris, The Concept of God (New York and Oxford: Oxford University Press, 1987). Maimonides is referred to once in each volume.

[4]Herbert A. Davidson, *Proofs for Eternity, Creation, and the Existence of God in Medieval Islamic and Jewish Philosophy* (Oxford: Oxford University Press, 1987) provides a superb study of subjects to which its title refers.

[5]Maimonides' discussion of the everlastingness of the world is predicated on the assumption that God exists, and his claim is that "the existence of the deity has already been demonstrated." *Guide*, 285. Cf. Sections I, 71-II,2.

[6]Strictly, "The first purpose of this Treatise is to explain the meanings of certain terms occuring in books of prophecy....Or rather its purpose is to give indications to a religious man for whom the vitality of the law has become established in his belief, such a man being perfect in his religion and character, and having studied the sciences of the philosophers and come to know what they signify." *Guide*, 5.

contemporary philosophers not very different from that which the current suggestion worries that theology plays for Maimonides.

It is true that even if Maimonides, to use the traditional terms, views philosophy as handmaiden to theology, his philosophizing may be highly instructive. Nonetheless, it is worth asking exactly how Maimonides does use philosophy. Objections are better faced than deflected.

The paper that follows, then, falls into two general sections. One concerns some of Maimonides' philosophical reflections concerning creation. The other concerns his own understanding of the proper role of such reflections.

I. Maimonides on the Creation of the World

The Content of the World

Let "the world" refer to whatever depends for its existence on something other than itself. There now exist such things, so there is a world. Let a series of things that, whether it has a beginning or not, exists without there being any temporal gaps in it, be a "temporally unbroken" series. Perhaps there could be a sequence of times at which there are dependently existing things, and then one or more moments when no such things exist, and then another sequence of times at which there are such things again (the same ones, if that is possible, or else others). But suppose, for the sake of simplicity, that the current existence of dependently existing things comes as the most recent installment in a temporally unbroken series. Then the world is viewed as having a continuous history. The question remains as to whether its history has a beginning.

Standard Monotheism and the World

Let us call the set of beliefs shared by some important monotheistic traditions – Judaism, Christianity, and Islam, but also the monotheistic varieties of Hindu Vedanta, for example – "standard monotheism." Standard monotheism conceives of God as an omnicompetent being that exists independently. It is standard monotheism that there is a world that exists dependent on God. If one accepts this standard monotheism, that does not settle the question as to whether the world has an infinitely long past. The world might always have depended for its existence upon God, and then it would have an infinitely long past; or it might have been brought into existence without having previously existed. The Indian Vsistadvaita and Dvaita Vedanta philosopher-theologians typically have held that God has always sustained the world in existence. They do not hold that God created time. They do believe that the world depends for its existence upon God. For example, referring to things other than God, Ramanuja represents Brahman or God as asserting "Know that they all originated from me. They abide in me; they are my body, but I am not in them, which is to say, *I do not depend on them*."[7] He also represents Brahman or God as saying "I pervade the universe as its Inner Controller, in order to support it, and by virtue of being its owner...I am the supporter of finite beings, but I derive no benefit from them."[8] Jewish and Christian theologians have tended to hold that the world's past is finitely long. The truth of standard theism leaves both possibilities open.

Eternal versus Everlasting

There is a distinction between *being eternal* and *being everlasting;* an eternal being has no temporal properties, and so has no past and no present and no future. If God is eternal, it is false of Him that He exists *now*, not because it is false that He exists, but because it is false that He has has any temporal properties at all, including the property *existing now*. (If the popular but strikingly weakly argued view that *existence* is not a property is correct, then what is false is that God has any property now, and to exist now something now must have some property or other.) If God is everlasting, then He does have a past, a present, and a future; He exists now and exists without beginning or end.[9]

Whether or not God is eternal, the world is not; even if it is beginningless, or even beginningless and endless, it is everlasting rather than eternal. One alternative regarding its past is that God has always sustained the world in existence. Another alternative is that time, so to say, predates the world, and that the world was created by God at some time before which the world did not exist and before which much time elapsed. That these are the *only* alternatives will be strongly denied by anyone who takes the position that God is eternal and that time cannot be empty; one who holds this view (as do Augustine and Maimonides) will insist that another alternative (in fact the correct one) is that God created time and the world together.

---

[7]Cited in John Carman, *The Theology of Ramanuja* (New Haven and London: Yale University Press, 1974), p. 128; the passage is from Ramanuja's *Gita Bhaysa*, 7.12; my italics.

[8]Cited in Eric Lott, *Vedantic Approaches to God* (London and Basingstoke: The Macmillan Press, 1980), p. 52; the passage is from Ramanuja's *Gita Bhaysa* 9.4, 5; 14.

[9]A good exposition of this view is Nicholas Wolterstorff, "God Everlasting," in Clifton J. Orlebeke and Lewis B. Smedes, eds., *God and the Good* (Grand Rapids: William B. Eerdmans Publishing Co., 1975), pp. 181-203.

Time itself is viewed as one of "the created things." A curious feature of Maimonides' discussion of the question as to whether the world has an infinitely long past is that, strictly speaking, the apparently obvious alternative of God creating the world *at* a time finitely long ago preceded by times at which no world existed is not offered as an alternative – a fact that will require some explanation and comment.

All of the alternatives we have mentioned are alleged to be possibilities and each has been thought true by one or another intelligent and reflective monotheist.

Some Preliminary Arguments

Arguments for, and counter-arguments against, any one of these alternatives are easy to come by. For example, here is an argument that the world is everlasting.[10] Any reason that God ever has for creating the world, He always has; no matter how time is divided, and whether time is continuous or discrete, no one time-slot cries out more to be occupied by dependent entities than does any other. But God is rational and what a rational God does, He does for a reason. If the world exists, it exists dependently, and what exists dependently depends for its existence on God. A world will exist only if God creates it, and there is a world. So God created the world, and did so for a reason. Since He always has that reason, He has always been creating the world; so the world is everlasting.

One could reply, however, that since God is eternal, He has no reason at any time at all; time exists only when there are things in existence that change, and God does not change.[11] So a crucial premise of the argument that the world is everlasting is false, namely the one that says that any reason that God ever has, He always has. Time exists only if the world exists; for God to create the world is also for Him to create time. Thus no time precedes creation, and so no matter how good it is that the world exists, no value is lost if the world does not 'yet' exist since if the world does not exist, no time exists to be wasted until creation occurs.

This reply to the argument that the world is everlasting assumes that time does not exist prior to the creation of the world. Another reply can be made that does not make that assumption. If God always has whatever reason He ever has to create the universe, then at any time He has the same reason to bring it into existence that He has at

---

[10]Compare *Guide*, 288.
[11]Compare *Guide*, 300, 301. Maimonides argues that God, being omnicompetent and eternal, needs no incentives, has no needs, and faces no impediments.

any other time. He then has no better reason to create the world at any one time than at any other, though He has sufficient reason to create it at some time or other. A rational agent who has sufficient reason to do something at some time or other, but no better reason to do it at one time rather than another, does that thing at some arbitrarily selected time; the only rational way to choose when to do something that you have sufficient reason to do but no reason for doing at one time rather than another is arbitrarily. So whenever God brings the world into existence, He has sufficient reason for doing so, and His doing so at one time rather than another is no objection to His goodness or His rationality.

If one replies that on this view an infinite amount of time is lost when there might have been a world, the response comes in two parts. One part is that the world can still exist for an infinite amount of time; if it is not everlastingly past, it can be everlastingly future. The other part is that since the notion of a best possible world is inconsistent, there is no *best* that God can do – there can be no action that maximally manifests or exhausts divine omnicompetence; so for anything God does, He could always do something better. Thus even if it is better that God create a world that is everlastingly past as well as everlastingly future, He could always create a still better world – *whatever* He does, no matter how good, He could always do something better. But then all that is reasonable to expect is that, being perfectly good, what He does is something that it is good that He do. Some worlds that are not everlastingly past can be good to create, and if He creates a world that is not everlastingly past, He will create one of them. His doing so is perfectly compatible with His omnibenevolence.

Obviously, then, things quickly become complicated. Questions of metaphysics (*is* the notion of a "best possible world" inconsistent, as was suggested in one of the replies?) and of ethics (what sort of world is better created than not?) join questions concerning the longevity of the world. But that is the nature of philosophy generally, and of philosophical theology. Save by refusing to ask the questions, one cannot escape dealing with complexities in attempting a serious answer. Perhaps enough has been said initially to indicate how it is possible that reflective and articulate monotheists might differ in their approaches to our topic.

Maimonides' Account of Three Positions

Maimonides begins Chapter 13 of Part II of *The Guide of the Perplexed* by saying that "There are three opinions of human beings, namely of all those who believe that there is an existent deity, with regard to the eternity of the world or its production in time."[12] "The eternity of the world" here refers to its being everlasting, and particularly its being infinite in its past history; regarding that matter, Maimonides says, monotheists take one or another of three lines. One line is that the world and time were created together; both are "created things." A second line is that the world exists everlastingly dependent upon God. More specifically, "they believe that there is a certain matter that is eternal [i.e., everlasting]; and that He does not exist without it, nor does it exist without Him. They do not believe that it has the same rank in what exists as He, may He be exalted, but that He is the cause of its existence...and that He creates in it whatever He wishes. Thus sometimes He forms out of it a heaven and an earth, and sometimes He forms out of it something else. The people holding this opinion believe that the heaven too is subject to generation and passing-away but that it is not generated out of nothing and does not pass away into nothing." [13] The third line differs from the second essentially in the status that it assigns to the heaven, which it views as a "permanent thing not subject to generation and passing-away." The first line is Maimonides' own, "and it is undoubtedly a basis of the Law of *Moses our Master*, peace be on him. And it is second to the basis that is the belief in the unity [of God]."[14] Line two is Plato's, and the third line is Aristotle's.

A Fourth Position?

We have noted another alternative that a monotheist might take; one might easily have expected that this would have been one of Maimonides' three alternatives and that the second and third of his actual alternatives would have been presented as variations on a single theme or else that the alternatives presented would have been four in number. The other alternative is that time, so to say, predates the world, and the world is created *in* time rather than *along with* time, so that perhaps (indeed, presumably) an infinite amount of time will have elapsed before the world was created by God. But this other alternative is not one of Maimonides' three alternatives. Why?

Maimonides on Time

One reason is obvious. Maimonides himself has a view of time on which this apparent alternative is not an option. The view of time that he briefly offers goes like this: "[God] brought into existence out of

---

[12]*Guide*, 281.
[13]*Guide*, 283.
[14]*Guide*, 282.

nothing all the beings as they are, time itself being one of the created things. For time is consequent upon motion, and motion is an accident in what is moved."[15] This view is amplified in the following remarks: "What caused the nature of time to be hidden from the majority of the men of knowledge so that that notion perplexed them – like Galen and others – and made them wonder whether or not time had a reality in that which exists, is the fact that time is an accident subsisting in an accident. For the accidents that have a primary existence in bodies, as for instance colors and tastes, can be understood at the outset and a mental representation can be had of their notions. But the nature of the accidents whose substrata are other accidents, as for instance the glint of a color and the curve and circularity of a line, is most hidden – more particularly if, in addition, the accident that serves as a substratum has no permanent state, but passes from one state to another."[16]

On this view of time, time is a second-order accident, a property of a property with each property depending for its existence on what it is a property of. Thus time is viewed as an epiphenomenon of creation, a second-order property caused by the creation of dependent things that have first-order properties. It is a pervasive sort of epiphenomenon, of course, in that (unlike such things as life and consciousness and self-consciousness which are also sometimes viewed as epiphenomena) one cannot create any dependent things without creating it. If there are non-material dependent things, then time is a more pervasive phenomenon than even space. On this view of time, the apparent alternative of a world created in time after some time has elapsed is not possible. Second-order properties cannot exist without first-order properties, and first-order properties require substances. So there is no time without substance. Eternal substance is independent and timeless, but the world consists of dependently existing substances that change, and if such substances exist, the world exists. So if there is time, the world exists. But then there cannot be time without there being a world.

There are two elements in Maimonides' view of time. One might describe one of these elements as Aristotelian (time as the measure of change and impossible without change) and the other as added by Maimonides (time as a created thing). Maimonides' acceptance of this two-element view of time provides one explanation of why the apparent fourth alternative is not listed. But since the correctness of his view of time has been asserted but not demonstrated, one who is inclined toward the fourth position, or merely wishes to consider it, has

---

[15]*Guide*, 281.
[16]*Guide*, 281, 282.

not been shown more than this: the first alternative is not compatible with the fourth.

The Shape of the Fourth Alternative

The fourth alternative branches into two lines. On one line, God is eternal and time uncreated, and the world was created only after time had passed. It agrees with Aristotle that time is uncreated and agrees with Maimonides that the world was created. It holds that time can be empty; there being time does not require that there be a world. In this respect, it disagrees with Aristotle and Maimonides. In these respects, it is about the same distance from Aristotle's view as is Maimonides' own view. Maimonides agrees with Aristotle that time cannot be empty, but holds that time and the world were created. The fourth view, then, developed along line one, denies both elements of Maimonides' view of time; it holds that time is uncreated and that time can be empty and thus denies that time is impossible without change. Still, none of these views – Aristotle's, Maimonides', or this version of the fourth alternative – denies that anything that is in time must be generated and be subject to change and to corruption.

On the other line, God is everlasting and the world is created. This perspective differs from Maimonides and agrees with Aristotle that time is uncreated. It need not hold that time can be empty, for according to it God exists at whatever time you like. But it breaks the Aristotelian link between *being temporal* and *being generated,* for it holds that God is temporal but ungenerated. Thus it also breaks the Aristotelian link between *being temporal* on the one hand and *being subject to corruption* on the other. It need not break the link between *being temporal* and *being subject to change* if it allows that God can undergo non-essential change, and one could trace another branching of the fourth position in terms of whether it did, or did not, allow for this possibility. So this perspective, in one of its varieties, can accept the other element of Maimonides' view of time, namely that time is impossible without change. Still, Maimonides' view is much closer to Aristotle's than is this second line of the fourth alternative (in either of its branches). Maimonides does not break the Aristotelian links between temporality, generability, and corruptibility. These links are important elements in a metaphysical perspective, and Maimonides does not challenge them whereas the fourth alternative, in both branches of its second line, does.

Maimonides and the Fourth Position

We have noted that one reason why Maimonides does not think that there is a fourth possibility of the sort described is that on his view of time, that possibility is not an option. He writes: "Consider this matter thoroughly. For thus you will not be necessarily attached to objections from which there is no escape for him who does not know it. For if you affirm as true the existence of time prior to the world, you are necessarily bound to believe in the eternity [i.e., everlastingness] [of the world]. For time is also an accident which necessarily must have a substratum. Accordingly it follows necessarily that there existed some thing prior to the existence of this world existing now. But this notion must be avoided."[17] The suggestion here is that one who holds that time predates the world cannot escape, in all consistency, embracing the view that the world has no beginning. If one thinks that time cannot be empty of dependent, changing substances, one indeed will agree with this assessment. Since that view is highly challengeable, it is appropriate to ask whether Maimonides has any other reason for thinking that one who does not accept both elements of Maimonides' view of time must suppose that the world is beginningless.

That There Is Something Not Produced In Time

Maimonides writes that "It is clear that everything produced in time has of necessity an efficient cause that causes it to be produced after not having been existent."[18] He adds that "This cannot, however, go on to infinity...if there is a thing that is produced in time, we must finally come to something eternal and not produced in time that has caused that thing to be produced in time."[19] These remarks suggest the following argument:

1. Necessarily, everything produced in time has a cause that brought it into existence after its not having been existent.
2. There cannot be an infinitely past series of things produced in time producing other things produced in time.

Therefore:

3. Something produced in time is produced by something that is not produced in time.

This argument is intended to rule out the view that the world is a *self-explanatory* series of dependently-existing things that is everlastingly past. Assuming that its premises are true, it does rule that out. On the same assumption, does it rule out the fourth alternative?

---

[17]*Guide*, 282.
[18]*Guide*, 277.
[19]*Guide*, 277.

It does not. It is consistent with an Aristotelianism for which there is a beginningless sequence of things in time, where things in time depend on something that is eternal and that therefore is not produced in time. It is consistent with a Maimonidean perspective for which there is a series of things produced in time, with both the things produced in time and time itself produced by something that is eternal. It is also consistent with there being a series of things produced in time, after time has passed, that is produced by something that is *in* time but is not *produced* in time – by something temporal but not dependent for its existence on something else, or by some independently-existing eternal being (the fourth alternative).

A monotheist of course will take the unproduced producer of the argument's conclusion to be God. Nothing in the argument rules out time predating the world, and presumably by itself it was not meant to do that. But perhaps it can be combined with something else in order to provide grounds for rejecting what seems to be a fourth option besides the three that Maimonides mentions.

One might try to discover this something further along the following lines. Maimonides ascribes to Aristotle these propositions: "Everything that is subject to generation is subject to passing-away. Everything that is subject to passing-away is subject to generation. Everything that has not been generated will not pass away. Everything that will not pass away has not been generated."[20] While of course he does not agree that these propositions establish the everlastingness of the world, Maimonides does not question their truth. Add to these propositions the proposition that everything temporal is generated. A monotheist who accepts these propositions will deny that God is temporal, since a temporal God, if these propositions are true, would pass away. Such a monotheist will not embrace the second line of the fourth alternative.

One could, of course, deny that anything in time must be produced, but embrace the argument in question and assent to one or another of the versions of the Principle of Sufficient Reason, which lies behind it, all the time holding that God is everlasting. But the important point here is that one could view God as eternal, accept the argument expressed in (1-3), *and* embrace the four explicit and the one implicit propositions, and without inconsistency go on to accept the fourth alternative in its *first* line. So not even all of this would rule out the fourth alternative. Equally, one could accept all of this and join with Ramanuja in holding that the world is everlastingly, and so beginninglessly, sustained in existence by God, who nonetheless creates freely.

---

[20]*Guide*, 286, 287.

The propositions entail that what is generated will pass away. The world is generated, produced, dependent, and temporal. If one takes "the world" distributively in the sentence "The world will pass away," then what follows from the proposition that this sentence expresses is that each dependent thing, at some time or other, passes away, but this is compatible with there always being some dependent thing or other. If one takes "the world" collectively in the sentence "The world will pass away," then what follows from the proposition that sentence expresses is that there not being any dependent things is a possibility that comes to pass. If one thinks that time cannot be empty, then one must conclude that the sentence, read the second way, expresses a false proposition, or else must hold that time is a created thing. If one thinks that time can be empty of dependent things, then one holds a view on which, so far, both propositions can be true. In sum: neither the soundness and validity of the argument expressed by (1-3), nor that argument plus the truth of the explicit and implicit Aristotelian propositions, is inconsistent with the fourth alternative being the correct one. I do not suggest that Maimonides thought otherwise.

Maimonides Against Plato and Aristotle

Maimonides, of course, considers the sort of reasons that Platonists and Aristotelians offer for their views. One reason that they can both accept as an argument against the view Maimonides favors is this: "It is absurd that God would bring a thing into existence out of nothing....To predicate of God that He is able to do this is, according to them, like predicating of Him that He is able to bring together two contraries in one instant of time, or that He is able to create something that is like Himself, may He be exalted, or to make Himself corporeal, or to create a square whose diagonal is equal to its side, and similar impossibilities."[21] In sum, *God creates the world from nothing* is a contradiction. In one sense of the sentence in question, it does indeed express a contradiction: "God takes nothing and makes the world out of it." But in another it does not: "God causes a world to exist that did not previously exist and that is not made from previously existent material." If this latter sentence is true, there is nothing (including nothing) *out of which* the world is made. Maimonides' view is that the sentence "Something is caused to exist that did not exist previously, and is not made of anything that did exist previously" is not a contradiction. Strictly speaking, there is nothing properly called *proving that a proposition is not contradictory*. A proof that a

---

21*Guide*, 283.

proposition is true of course would also prove that it was not contradictory; a way of stating a proposition that translated it without logical inelegance into a model granted not to be contradictory can be useful in exhibiting the consistency of that proposition. But one who insisted that the proposition in question really was contradictory could always maintain that the proof could not be sound and valid, because contradictions are false and any alleged proof of a contradiction must either have a false premise or be invalid. And one who insisted that the proposition in question really was contradictory could hold that its expressibility in a model previously thought consistent in fact revealed the latent contradictoriness of the model. But *creation ex nihilo*, as Maimonides (and much of his tradition, and of the Christian and Islamic traditions) understand it in fact does not seem contradictory. David Hume plausibly claimed that it is not even contradictory that something come to exist that was not around previously or made of anything that previously existed, and that it not be caused to have done so. Maimonides' claim requires that at least the first half of Hume's thesis be true – that it is not a contradiction that something come to be that was not made from something else.

Maimonides, of course, is joined in this view by one who holds the alternative that Maimonides does not mention, for that alternative no more requires that God do something that is logically impossible in bringing the world into existence than does Maimonides' own view. On this issue, the first and fourth positions agree. They both hold that "God causes a world to exist that did not previously exist and is not made from previously existent materials" is perfectly consistent. One who disagrees should be prepared to exhibit the contradiction involved. Once that claim is distinguished from "God takes nothing and makes the world out of it," it is hard to see what contradiction there is in Maimonides' claim.

Of course, Maimonides means by the claim something different from what a proponent of the fourth position means by it. Maimonides means: "God makes a world that did not exist previously and that is not made from anything that previously existed" in the sense that, before the world, there is nothing that exists save God, and that without a world all reference to time, including to "previous" time, is empty. The proponent of the fourth position means: "God makes a world that did not previously exist and that is not made from anything that previously existed" in the sense that, before the world was made, nothing but God existed, but that, even without a world, reference to time, including to "previous" time, is perfectly in order.

Maimonides on Some Aristotelian Considerations

Early in Part II, Chapter Fourteen, of the *Guide,* Maimonides informs us that "I shall pay no attention to anyone who besides Aristotle has engaged in speculative discourse, for it is his opinions that ought to be considered. And if there are good grounds for refuting him or raising doubt with regard to these opinions as to some point on which we make a refutation or raise doubts, these grounds will be even firmer and stronger with respect to all the others who disagreed with the fundamental principles of the Law."[22] Paying attention only to Aristotle, it turns out, allows one to consider certain Aristotelian themes as they were developed in the tradition that bears Aristotle's name.

This too has an obvious relevance to the question as to why the fourth alternative is neglected. Historically, it is not an alternative one need refer to in order to responsibly discuss Aristotle; it is certainly not Aristotle's position (or Plato's, for that matter). Methodologically, as it is not the only position one can take as an alternative to Aristotle, one need not refer to it in order to have some position one can take if one finds Aristotle's position problematic.

Aristotle's position is that the world is everlasting, and in particular that it is beginningless. Maimonides considers four Aristotelian "methods" or lines of argument for this position which I shall blend here. One prominent theme is that "There is no motion except in time" and "time cannot be intellectually conceived save through motion," where of course "motion" means "change."[23] This, as we saw, is half of Maimonides' own view.

Another important theme is that some sort of matter or other "must not be generated from some thing"; otherwise every sort of matter is generated from another to infinity, and this is impossible. But whatever is ungenerated escapes passing away and so is everlasting. So some sort of matter at least (the specific candidate is first matter, common to all four elements) is everlasting. One could escape from this conclusion by accepting a doctrine of creation *ex nihilo,* with or without accepting the view that time is a created thing.

Even without considering other parts of the Aristotelian argumentation, to which we return in a moment, one can see another reason for Maimonides not to deal with the fourth alternative. The fourth alternative is *deeply* foreign to Aristotle's position, more deeply even than is Maimonides' own. As we saw, the fourth position itself

---

[22]*Guide,* 285, 286.
[23]*Guide,* 286.

breaks into two alternatives. One involves God being eternal and creating the world in time after it has gone uncreated for some period. The other involves God Himself being a temporal being, albeit a being incapable of change, or at least incapable of a change in His essential properties. Once the alleged necessary linkage between temporality and change, and so between temporality and corruptibility, has been broken, the possibility arises that God Himself be temporal. If one wishes to show that there are alternatives to a position that do not have certain consequences that the position itself has and that one finds objectionable, it may be good strategy to wander no further from the position in question than is required in order to establish what one wishes to establish. Maimonides seems to have followed this strategy. He accepts the Aristotelian links but insists that the chain of dependent being and time itself are created *ex nihilo*.

A third central theme in the Aristotelian argumentation that Maimonides describes is that even the *possibility* of change requires an underlying substratum. Thus Maimonides refers to Aristotle's later followers who said: "Before the world came into being, its production in time must have been either possible or necessary or impossible. Now if it was necessary, the world could not have been nonexistent. If its production in time was impossible, it could not be true that it ever would exist. And if it was possible, what was the substratum for this possibility? For there indubitably must be an existent thing that is the substratum of this possibility and in virtue of which it is said of the thing that it is possible."[24] Maimonides rejects the Mutakallimun reply that the substratum of the possibility that there be a world does not lie in the world but in an agent that can make the world, for he thinks that "there are two possibilities. For with respect to everything produced in time, the possibility of its being produced precedes in time the thing itself. And similarly in the agent that produced it, there is the possibility to produce that which it has produced before it has done so. There are indubitably two possibilities: a possibility in the matter to become that particular thing, and a possibility in the agent to produce that particular thing."[25] One can argue, then, that a change at a given time must be produced by another change at an earlier time which in turn must be produced by another change at a time yet earlier, and so on to infinity, but one can also argue that the possibility of a change at a time must be accompanied by that in which the change is possible, and that therefore if a certain change regarding a certain

---

[24]*Guide*, 287.
[25]*Guide*, 287.

thing is always possible, then the thing in which that change is possible must always exist.

Obviously these considerations count against time predating the world; if they are sound, they show that empty (and so pre-world) time is impossible, that change and time are necessarily coexistent, and that even the possibility of change and the possibility of time are coexistent.

A Brief Preliminary to Considering Aristotle: The Modalities

The logical modalities are *necessity, contingency,* and *possibility.* They are properties of propositions, not sentences, where a proposition is what is asserted by a standard use of a declarative sentence. The same proposition can be asserted by the use of various sentences in various languages. The proposition expressed by *Bob both is, and is not, six feet tall* is *contradictory* and so *necessarily false.* Its opposite, expressed by *Bob is not both six feet, and not six feet, tall,* is *necessarily true.* Thus *necessity* has two varieties: necessary truth and necessary falsehood. A proposition is *contingent* if neither it nor its opposite is necessarily false. Thus the proposition expressed by *Bob is six feet tall* is contingent, as is the proposition expressed by *Bob is not six feet tall.* "Contingent" in this sense does not mean "dependent on." A proposition is *possible* if it is not necessarily false; a proposition that is not contradictory is possible. Thus the proposition expressed by the sentence *Bob is six feet tall or he is not* is possible, as is the proposition expressed by the sentence *Bob is six feet tall.*

Philosophers disagree over the issue as to whether a given proposition has its modal properties with necessity; a proposition has its modal properties with necessity if and only if it is logically impossible that its modal properties change. I shall assume here that it is logically impossible that any modal property of a proposition change. This seems to me the truth of the matter; the proposition expressed by the sentence *Bob is six foot tall* has, and cannot not have, the modalities *contingent* and *possible.* Convention has nothing to do with this. Of course convention does decide what proposition a particular sentence expresses, but that is another (and here an irrelevant) matter. That propositions have their modal properties with necessity is also assumed by the "followers of Aristotle" whom Maimonides describes as affirming that "if its [the world's] production in time was impossible, it could not be true that it ever would exist."[26]

Now one could hold that propositions have modalities, and that they have their modalities with necessity, and go on to deny that

---

[26]*Guide,* 287.

anything has an essence. But it is charitable in discussing Aristotle, as well as plausible in itself, to hold that there are natural essences. If so, there are only certain changes that (say) an alligator can undergo and remain an alligator, and similarly for mushrooms and oak trees and human beings, for there are certain properties that a thing must have in order for it to be an alligator, a mushroom, an oak, or a human. If something is an alligator only if it has certain properties, then it cannot be an alligator and change in such a way as to lose any of those properties; the properties in question constitute an essence. I shall assume here that there are essences.

Neither the assumption that a proposition has its modalities with necessity nor the assumption that there are essences (nor, for that matter, the assumption that there are propositions) is essential to what I shall argue here. They do provide a convenient context for making the relevant distinctions. Aristotle certainly shares the assumption about essences, and he is not a conventionalist about modalities.

One might object that this way of discussing the modalities is hopelessly anachronistic, and of no use in discussing the Aristotelian tradition. The terminology is contemporary; but the ideas are not foreign to the tradition. Al-Farabi, for example, writes: "Everything that exists belongs to one of two kinds. In the case of beings of the first kind, existence is not involved in their essence. These are called 'of possible existence.' In the case of a being of the second kind, its essence does involve existence. This is called 'necessary existent.'"[27] Given the perspective on modality sketched above, one would expect that *X is a necessary being* be explained as *It is logically impossible that X not exist* and *X is a contingent being* be expounded as *It is logically possible that X exist and it is logically possible that X not exist.* Al-Farabi's "possible" is our "contingent." The passage from Al-Farabi continues: "To suppose that which is of possible existence as being non-existent involves no contradiction; for in order to exist this being requires a cause other than itself. And if it *is* necessary, it has become necessarily existent through something outside itself."[28] Setting aside the last sentence for a moment, "possible existence" is defined exactly as suspected: something is possibly existent if its existence involves no contradiction and its non-existence involves no contradiction. Consider

---

[27]Cited in Emil L. Fackenheim, "The Possibility of the Universe in Al-Farabi, Ibn Sina, and Maimonides," in Arthur Hyman, ed., *Essays in Medieval Jewish and Islamic Philosophy* (New York: KTAV Publishing House, 1977), p. 303. Cited from *Philosophiche Abhandlungen*, ed. F. Dieterici (Leiden 1890), p. 57.
[28]*Ibid.*, p. 303.

now a passage from Ibn Sina: "The necessary being is that which, if assumed to be non-existent, involves a contradiction. The possible is that which may be assumed to be non-existent or existent without involving a contradiction."[29] That is, *"X exists" is necessarily true* if and only if *It is logically impossible that X not exist* and *"X exists" is contingent* if and only if *Neither "X exists" nor "X does not exist" is contradictory*. The passage continues: "The necessary being may either be *per se* or not *per se*. In the former case, a contradiction is involved if it is assumed to be non-existent....As for the being which is necessary but not *per se*, this is a being which is necessary, provided a certain being other than it is given....Everything that is necessarily existent *ab alio* is possibly existent *per se*....Considered in its essence it is possible; considered in actual relation to that other being it is necessary, and the relation to that other being considered as removed, it is impossible."[30] It is plain that, allowing that our "contingent" is Al-Farabi's and Ibn Sina's "possible," things regarding *necessity per se* and *possibility per se* are as we would expect if we approached their writings with our perspective.

The matter is complicated by the notion of *necessity ab alio*, the concept of a type of thing the existence of which is not logically necessary though its existence is in some sense necessary given the existence of some *necessary per se* being. Such beings are said to be possible (=contingent) in themselves but necessary when considered in relation to a *necessary per se* being.

It is not obvious how to understand this notion of a being that is *necessary ab alio*. Suppose that X is *necessary per se*, that Y is *possible per se*, and that *X exists* entails *Y exists*. If X is *necessary per se*, *X exists* is necessarily true. Whatever a necessary truth entails is necessarily true; a necessary truth cannot be possibly false, and so it cannot entail anything that is possibly false. So *Y exists* must be a necessary truth. But then Y is not *possible per se* after all. Thus this is not a coherent way of understanding *necessity ab alio*.

Suppose that X is *necessary per se*, that Y is *possible per se*, and that X causes Y to exist. If it is is logically possible that X not cause Y to exist, then that Y is caused to exist by a *necessary per se* being provides a consistent way of understanding the claim that Y is *necessary ab alio*. Whether it will serve all the intended purposes is not something that we will investigate here. If *X causes Y* is a necessary truth, then that proposition, plus the *ex hypothesi* necessary truth *X exists*, entails *Y exists*, so once again Y cannot be *possible per se*.

---

[29]*Ibid.*, p. 304. Cited from *An-Najjah* (1938), pp. 224ff.
[30]*Ibid.*, p. 304.

I think that these complications do not challenge the claim that the understanding of modality sketched above is highly relevant to the notion of modality one finds in Maimonides' tradition. It may well be that there are also differences between the notion of modality sketched above, which is one contemporary account of modality, and the notion of modality expressed in the two recent quotations from Arabic philosophy. The Aristotelian identification of what is always so with what is necessarily so does not allow the possibility that a contingent proposition always be true, whereas the notion sketched above does allow for this possibility. Discussing these matters further would take us well beyond the intended scope of this paper. I shall assume that the notion of modality to which I have expressed allegiance captures enough of the notion of modality in the tradition with which Maimonides is concerned to make the following discussion appropriate.

Assessing the Aristotelian Considerations

The argument offered by the followers of Aristotle concerning possibility is fascinating but fallacious. It assumes that possibility requires an ontological ground, and typically at least conventionalists about the logical modalities would deny that. But suppose, as seems correct, that the conventionalists are wrong. Suppose also that the Aristotelians are right in thinking that the logical modalities (necessity, contingency, and possibility) require ontological grounding. Still, however natural it might be to think that all of the possibilities about something must be grounded in that very thing, that grounding cannot be always in the thing itself.

Assume that *having come from an alligator egg* is an essential property of an alligator. So long as an alligator exists, that is a property it will have. Then the conditional statement *If there is an alligator, then it comes from an alligator egg* is a necessary truth. Being conditional or hypothetical in form, however, its truth is not dependent on there ever being any alligators. Further, it is always logically possible that an alligator exists; no time is such that *An alligator now exists* expresses a contradiction at that time. This is so whether any alligator ever exists or not. So it cannot be true in virtue of there ever, or there always, being alligators. So not all possibilities about alligators can be grounded in alligators. Perhaps none are; but at least not all are.

Apparently, some species have become extinct. If there used to be dodoes, and aren't now, or there now are collies but there didn't used to be, then there are possibilities about dodoes and collies that are not grounded in dodoes and collies. For, as the argument under criticism itself admits, if the production of something is ever impossible, it is always impossible, and similarly whatever is logically possible is always logically possible. These possibilities about dodoes and collies always obtain; dodoes and collies do not always exist.

More generally, that it is always possible that there is a world does not entail that there always is a world; if *There is a world* is always possibly true it does not follow that the world is everlasting.

The third sort of Aristotelian line, then, does not establish its conclusion – a conclusion Maimonides rejects. The first two Aristotelian lines – that time cannot be empty and that some matter must be ungenerated from any other sort – Maimonides accepts. These views are common ground between Aristotle and Maimonides. Of course, the Aristotelian will hold that time and change and matter are uncreated, whereas Maimonides will think that time and change are created things and that the sort of matter not generated from any other sort is also created *ex nihilo*.

A Reservation Concerning Maimonides' View of Time

Maimonides own view of time seems problematic in certain respects. Consider a very simple world, one comprised of a detached (or unattached) heart that everlastingly beats with pristine regularity save for one occasion on which it is completely still for an entire minute. During that minute, we are supposing, absolutely nothing changes, for the heart stands still and there is nothing but the heart. It follows from Aristotle's doctrines, as Maimonides explains them, that since nothing changes during this minute, time has not passed. On those doctrines, apparently nothing can stand entirely still for a minute unless something else changes, for without change there is no time and so without change time does not move. Yet our simple universe seems quite conceivable, whereas if Aristotle's doctrines, as explained by Maimonides, are correct, it is not conceivable.

The obvious real-world analogue to our simple universe that stands still would be everything in our world briefly standing still, an unlikely but apparently conceivable event. One might argue that if this were to happen, no one could discover it (e.g., clocks would stop, but no one's perception would alter so that this stoppage could be noticed). One could further claim that the postulation of undetectable states is meaningless; one might assert that necessarily the real is the in-principle-detectable and if one spelled out "in principle" so that what was being maintained was stronger than the rather innocuous claim that if something exists then it is logically possible to know that it does, one would have embraced a variety of verificationism. Short of such philosophical extravagance, the possibility of time passing in the absence of change remains.

If it is possible that time pass without change occurring, then there is no necessary link between *being temporal* and *being subject to change*. Then there also is no necessary connection between *being temporal* and *being subject to corruption*. Nor it is clear, given these considerations or in any case, that *being temporal* and *existing dependently* are necessarily connected. No doubt one can build a metaphysical system that has as axioms propositions that declare that nothing that is temporal can be free from subjection to corruption and dependence. But one can also build a metaphysical system that does not require assent to those assumptions, and there seems no reason for confidence that such a system is inherently contradictory or is any less credible than its competitors. Such a system might even turn out to be true; this seems a logical possibility (it does not appear contradictory) and an epistemic possibility (it does not seem to be inconsistent with anything that we know to be true). At any rate, it is dubious that Aristotle or Maimonides has demonstrated that these are not possibilities. All of this is encouraging for the fourth alternative, and especially so for its second line.

For that matter, it is not clear that Maimonides has refuted Aristotle insofar as Aristotle's views are incompatible with his own. His strategy regarding Aristotle seems parallel to my own strategy regarding Maimonides. I have argued that there is a fourth alternative regarding the past infinity of the world in addition to the three that he has listed. I have argued somewhat for its consistency and for its having a reply to certain objections, and discussed it enough to give some sense of how it shapes up, both in itself and as a competitor to Maimonides' own view. At any rate, that has been my intent. Maimonides has done much the same concerning his own view that the world and time are both created things. He has made its contours plain, argued for its consistency, and cast it as a competitor to Aristotle's and Plato's view that the world and time are uncreated and beginningless. My strategy toward Maimonides has deliberately mirrored his own toward Aristotle. There is a criticism of Aristotle that is conveniently dealt with in the context of discussing Maimonides' use of philosophical reflection. But even then there is no claim to have demonstrated that Aristotle's views are false or that his own alternative is correct.

One whose concerns are purely philosophical will be unsatisfied with this situation in which (if Maimonides describes it correctly or if we are correct in holding that there is an alternative that Maimonides does not eliminate) one has more solutions than one has problems with no apparent way of deciding between them. Presumably the philosophical ideal is to have a one-to-one correspondence between philosophical problems and undefeated solutions. Maimonides is no enemy of demonstrations; he cheerfully accepts them when he finds them. But his concerns are not purely philosophical, which of course may not taint the genuine philosophical concerns that he does have. Whether it does or not depends on what role he assigns to philosophical thought – what constraints, if any, he places on it.

II. Maimonides on the Role
of Philosophical Reflection on Creation

That there be various alternatives concerning the question of whether or not the world is everlasting between which, so far as he can see, no philosophical decision can be made, will not disturb Maimonides if he can show that the alternatives include the one that is "a basis of the Law." His position is that if that alternative is as acceptable as any other, then it is not irrational to embrace it, particularly if it is entailed by a theological doctrine that one is not irrational in accepting.

One might think that it is presupposition, not entailment, that is relevant here. One might hold that creation is presupposed rather than entailed by the Law, or that "being the basis of the Law" was a matter of being presupposed by the Law rather than being entailed by it. One then should talk of embracing a view concerning the everlastingness or otherwise of the world that is presupposed by a theological doctrine that one is not irrational in accepting. But "A presupposes B" presumably means "If B is false, then A is false" which in turn means "One can validly infer from B's falsehood to A's falsehood." But then not-B entails not-A, and hence A entails B; talk of presupposition, upon analysis, vanishes into talk of entailment.

Maimonides' View on the Everlastingness of the World and the Question of the Existence of God

As we have noted, Maimonides' discussion of the question of whether the world has a finite past has assumed that God exists, something that Maimonides believes can be demonstrated. His philosophical procedure obviously would be deeply faulted if his argument for God's existence required as a premise his view concerning time and the world, but of course it does not. (It is compatible with this that he argue "either the world was created or not, if it was created then God exists, and if not then...", where the blank is filled in by an argument that God exists even if the world was not created.) Thus it is not surprising to find him writing that "the existence of the deity, may He be exalted...is proved by cogent and certain demonstrations, regardless of whether the world has come into being in time after having been non-existent or whether it has not come into being in time after having been nonexistent."[31] He is aware, then, that standard theism, by itself, does not entail his favored alternative, and it is not his assent to the truth of what we called standard theism that brings Maimonides to accept this alternative.

What Maimonides Wished to Establish

When Maimonides comes to describe exactly what he wants to show, it is (perhaps surprisingly) modest: "at present we do not wish to establish as true that the world is created in time. But what we wish to establish is the possibility of its being created in time. Now this contention cannot be proved to be impossible by inferences drawn from the nature of what exists, which do not set at nought. When the possibility of this contention has been established, as we have made clear, we shall go back and we shall make prevail the opinion asserting creation in time."[32] The considerations in favor of Maimonides' alternative, however, are not demonstrations; they have to do with Aristotle's perspective facing worse problems than Maimonides' perspective. "For Alexander [of Aphrodisias] has explained that in every case in which no demonstration is possible, the the two contrary opinions should be posited as hypotheses, and it should be seen what doubts attach to each of them: the one to which fewer doubts attach should be believed."[33]

More carefully, it is not the sheer cardinality of doubts or difficulties that matters. "Know that when one compares the doubts attaching to a certain opinion with those attaching to the contrary opinion and has to decide which of them arouses further doubts, one should not take into the account the number of the doubts but rather consider how great is their incongruity and what is their disagreement with what exists. Sometimes a single doubt is more powerful than a thousand other doubts."[34]

So in the long run Maimonides wants to show that his alternative is logically possible on the one hand, and preferable to Aristotle's when weighed in the only sort of philosophical scales that he thinks are available when demonstrations cannot be given. Both of these efforts are plainly philosophical in nature, and nothing in this methodology

---

[31]*Guide*, 252.
[32]*Guide*, 298.
[33]*Guide*, 320.
[34]*Guide*, 320.

is rendered somehow non-philosophical by the fact that Maimonides' overall purposes in the *Guide* are as described earlier.

Maimonides' View on the Everlastingness of the World and Biblical Exegesis

One issue relevant to whether Maimonides makes philosophy theology's handmaiden in any sense that compromises the objectivity of his philosophical reflections is whether or not his view on the everlastingness of the world derives from exegesis of Biblical texts that Maimonides takes as doctrinally normative, and which he is unprepared to interpret as not requiring the non-everlastingness of the world even if its everlastingness should be demonstrated. Concerning this matter, he writes: "Know that our shunning the affirmation of the eternity of the world is not due to a text figuring in the *Torah* according to which the world has been produced in time. For the texts indicating that the world has been produced in time are not more numerous than those indicating that the deity is a body. Nor are the gates of figurative interpretation shut in our faces or impossible of access to us regarding the subject of the creation of the world in time. For we could interpret them as figurative, as we have done when denying His corporeality."[35] One *could* read creation passages non-literally if one had good enough reason to do so.

The understandable strategy of interpreting a normative text so as to make it consistent with what is demonstrably true may, and sometimes does, lead to interpreting some statements in that text figuratively. Maimonides takes this to be so regarding texts that, taken literally, teach that God has a body. This strategy becomes especially important when two texts, each taken literally, contradict one another, or when one has a demonstration that what a text, interpreted literally, teaches is false. On the other hand, there are limits to what one can do to an allegedly normative text in terms of interpreting it without interpreting its normative status away – without turning the text into a wax nose that one may twist as one wishes, if I may paraphrase Luther in an essay on Maimonides. If one interprets every passage in a normative text figuratively in order to avoid conflict with authorities outside the text, it becomes utterly puzzling what sense it is in which the text retains any normative or authoritative status. Thus figurative interpretations are not to be multiplied beyond necessity, and there is a presumption against a figurative interpretation of an apparently literal passage in a normative text that is overcome only when it is shown that falsehood is otherwise inescapable.

---

[35]*Guide*, 327.

Having said, then, that it would be possible to interpret in a figurative way normative Scriptural texts that, taken literally, teach the non-everlastingness of the world, he also shows a deep lack of enthusiasm about doing so. These texts, he says, differ from texts that, taken literally, teach that God has a body, in crucial ways. One is that it can be demonstrated that God does not have a body whereas it cannot be demonstrated that the world is everlastingly past. Another is that "Our belief that the deity is not a body destroys for us none of the foundations of the Law and does not give the lie to the claims of any prophet."[36] The clear implication is that denial of the creation of the world and of time would destroy some at least of the foundations of the Law and give the lie to some claims of some prophet. But things are more complex than this way of putting the matter suggests.

On the one hand, "the belief in eternity the way Aristotle sees it – that is, the belief according to which the world exists in virtue of necessity, that no nature changes at all, and that the customary course of events cannot be modified with regard to anything – destroys the Law in its principles, necessarily gives the lie to every miracle, and reduces to inanity all the hopes and threats that the Law has held out...."[37] Aristotle's world, at least as interpreted by Maimonides, is a fatalistic world. In it, no miracle can occur, and so no revelation, no action of God in history. Abraham cannot be called from Ur and Moses cannot receive the Law at Sinai. Maimonides knows, of course, that Scriptural references to creation, miracles, and the Law itself, could be interpreted figuratively. He remarks that "this, however, would result in some sort of crazy imaginings."[38]

On the other hand, however, if one, with Plato, accepts belief in an everlasting pastness of the world "according to which the heavens too are subject to generation and corruption, this opinion would not destroy the foundations of the law and would be followed not by the lie being given to miracles, but by their becoming admissible."[39] Miracles generally, and revelation in particular, would be possible. Still, since the Platonic view has not been demonstrated, there is no reason to reinterpret any texts in its light.

---

[36]*Guide*, 328.
[37]*Guide*, 328.
[38]*Guide*, 328. Aristotelian philosophy and the theory of emanation mingle in complex ways in the tradition that influenced Maimonides. See Harry A. Wolfson, *Studies in the History of Philosophy of Religion* (Cambridge: Harvard University Press, 1977), "Hallevi and Maimonides on Design, Chance, and Necessity," pp. 1-59.
[39]*Guide*, 328.

A monotheist who, like Maimonides, accepts a revelation obviously has the task of interpreting that revelation. Maimonides obviously thinks that there are rational constraints on interpretations of Scripture. Neither internal contradictions nor contradiction of what has been demonstrated is permissible. But there are other relevant rational considerations to use in deciding between interpretations.

Maimonides' Doubts About Aristotle's View

Maimonides writes: "Know that with a belief in the creation of the world in time, all the miracles become possible and the Law becomes possible, and all questions that may be asked on this subject vanish."[40] The idea is that there are questions that arise on Aristotle's view that do not arise on Maimonides' view, and that Aristotle cannot answer these questions (though one holding his view should be able to do so).

At first blush, this seems dubious. Maimonides' view does not leave us asking why God waited so long to create, though we have suggested that one who holds that time is not created but that the world is created may be able to answer that question quite nicely. His view does leave us asking why God created at all, and why He created what He did, and why His special revelation came to Israel, and why there is so much evil, to go no further. This Maimonides admits. His claim is that, on his view, there is no reason whatever to think that anyone *should* know the answer to these questions, other than by saying that God's wisdom so ordered things for reasons we do not know. If God's creating the world and time are free actions of His, then while He can answer these questions, we cannot. But one who takes the view that they are His free actions does not thereby take a view on which we should be able to answer them. In that sense, the questions vanish, though they may remain questions that we ask and that we are troubled about. It is not irrational to accept monotheism if one does not know the answers to those questions, because, given the view that an omnicompetent God creates and acts freely, it is not to be supposed that the answers to the questions are in our possession or within our grasp; if anything, it follows that, short of revelation, we are not likely to know the answer to them.

Not so, Maimonides claims, if one accepts Aristotle's views: "If, however, someone says that the world is as it is in virtue of necessity, it would be a necessary obligation to ask all these questions...."[41] The Aristotelian holds that "the world exists in virtue of necessity."[42] If

---

[40]*Guide*, 329.
[41]*Guide*, 329.
[42]*Guide*, 328.

something exists with logical necessity, it need not have any teleological explanation; it is necessarily true that two and two are four, but not because it is good or better than otherwise that this be so. There is no possible *otherwise*. An Aristotelian necessitarianism, however, is teleological, and thus questions of appropriateness do arise in that context. Thus Maimonides asks "What is the cause that has particularized one stretch in such a way that ten stars should be found in it and has particularized another stretch in such a way that no star shall be found in it?...What accordingly can be the cause for the fact that a certain part of the sphere should be more fitted to receive the particular star found in it than another part? All this and everything that is of this sort would be very unlikely or rather would be near to being impossible if it should be believed that all this proceeded obligatorily and of necessity from the Deity, as is the opinion of Aristotle."[43]

One way of coming to see Maimonides' point is by comparing it to a similar criticism of logical fatalism. A logical fatalist holds that whatever is true is necessarily true and whatever is false is contradictory. Thus a logical fatalist is committed to the claim that it only seems logically possible that my pen be empty now unless it is true that it is empty now and it is logically possible that I stand now only if I am standing now. On this view, there are no logically contingent propositions – neither true ones nor false. The fatalist thesis is not the plainly true claim that *It is logically impossible that when I am standing, I am sitting* but the plainly false claim that *When I am standing, it is logically impossible that I am sitting* or *When I am not sitting, it is not only false but also logically impossible that I am sitting*. Concerning the pair of claims *My pen is empty now* and *My pen is not empty now*, the logical fatalist holds not merely that their conjunction is necessarily false, but that one or the other of the pair is by itself contradictory.

One standard criticism of logical fatalism is that if we've not got a firm enough grasp of the modalities to know that propositions like that expressed by *My pen is empty now* or *I am standing now* are logically contingent, we lack sufficient grasp of the modalities even to understand logical fatalism. Another standard criticism, closer to Maimonides' comments on Aristotle, is similar in content: there are plain examples of contingent propositions, some of which we know to be true and some of which we know to be false. Our confident belief that propositions like *Earth has a moon* and *Some people are less than six feet tall* are both contingent and true is entirely reasonable and in

---

[43]*Guide*, 310.

accord with our evidence and our understanding of the modalities. Thus we have good reason to reject any view that conflicts with that belief. Logical fatalism conflicts with that belief. Hence we have good reason to reject it.

Similarly, Maimonides argues that if Aristotle's view is true, it is both necessary that each planet be where it is, and that some parts of the heavens be more populated by heavenly bodies than others; any *necessity* to this entirely escapes us. It seems plainly not necessary. To think otherwise is to reject the appearances. Further, on Aristotle's view, given its *teleological* necessitarianism, it must be somehow better than otherwise that the very portions of space that are densely populated be so and that the very portions of space that are not densely populated not be so. Yet it is hardly evident that this is so, and the appearances are otherwise; it would seem that neither the cardinality nor the positioning of the planets is either logically necessary or teleologically perfect. Of course one can attempt to defend Aristotle here, though it is important to remember that a full-dress defense will have to find reasons why things being as they are is both without real alternative and somehow of maximal value. Maimonides plausibly is dubious about this.

A Difference About Where One Starts

A philosophical watershed between Maimonides and Aristotle lies in their starting point. The Aristotelian argumentation is "based on the nature of what exists, a nature that has attained stability, is perfect, and has achieved actuality."[44] Arguing from this perspective, they conclude that the world is everlastingly past. From the way things are, an inference is made as to how they have always been. Against this, Maimonides protests that "if the philosopher says, as he does: That which exists is my witness and by means of it we discern the necessary, the possible, and the impossible; the adherent of the Law says to him: The dispute between is with regard to this point. For we claim that that which exists was made in virtue of will and was not a necessary consequence. Now if it was made in this fashion, it is admissible that it should be made in a different way."[45]

---

[44]*Guide*, 296.
[45]This difference in perspective is at least very similar to the difference in perspective between those who take scientific, and those who take personal, explanations to be basic. Cf. Richard Swinburne, *The Existence of God* (Oxford: Oxford University Press, 1979), p. 72, where he claims that "the scientifically inexplicable, the odd and the big" are best explained by reference to personal explanations (cf. pp. 125ff and 138ff).

Put in contemporary terms, the Aristotelian takes the fundamental laws of science, insofar as these can be viewed as expressing the basic laws of nature, as primitive or given; there is no such thing as going behind or beyond them in terms of something else that explains them. Or, if they do, it is a God from whose nature they follow and who does not decide what they shall be. (Note that the laws at issue here are those of science, not of logic; Maimonides is no voluntarist about logic.) The Maimonidean does not view laws as primitive or underivative; God has that status, and the laws of nature have Him as author. One could describe this in terms of Aristotle being a philosopher and Maimonides being a theologian, though of course Aristotle's Unmoved Mover is also underivative. With at least equal legitimacy, one could describe this situation as one in which Aristotle and Maimonides have entirely different philosophical starting points.[46] Maimonides endeavors to understand Aristotle's perspective,[47] argues that it has not been demonstrated, and defends the contention that Aristotle's perspective faces greater difficulties than does his own. One can argue about whether or not he has *successfully* carried out these tasks, but they are plainly philosophical tasks, carried out philosophically.

Conclusion

Nothing that we have discovered casts any doubt on Maimonides' philosophizing or shows that he cheats reason to pay faith. But what about the fact that there seems to be a fourth alternative, itself capable of being developed in various ways, that he neglects? We have noted various reasons that may explain why it does not appear among his alternatives. But does its non- appearance damage his case?

He does not *need* to refer to more alternatives than the ones he has referred to. He has his own alternative. He refers to Plato's view which, differing from his own in that for Plato time and the world are beginningless, nevertheless would allow for the Law and the Prophets, and for miracles. For his theological and religious purposes, he needs only *one* alternative that philosophically is at least no worse than Aristotle's and that can make room for the Law and the Prophets, and for miracles. At least on his understanding of it, Aristotle's view can make no such allowance. Since Aristotle's view has not been demonstrated, it is not irrational to refuse to accept it, particularly since it comes off, not better, but worse, than Maimonides' own in the light of what non-demonstrative considerations are relevant. He has,

---

[46]Cf. the list of twenty-five propositions at *Guide*, 235 – propositions actually or allegedly demonstrated by "Aristotle and the Peripatetics."
[47]*Guide*, 211.

then, two alternatives where, strictly speaking, he needs only one. So he has one more alternative than he needs.

The fourth alternative branches into two lines, and one of those lines branches into two; thus there are three versions of the fourth alternative. All of them can allow for the Law and the Prophets, and for miracles. If, in a philosophical heaven, one has a one-problem/one-unrefuted-solution distribution, on philosophical earth a surfeit of alternatives compatible with one's most treasured convictions can be advantageous. From a monotheistic viewpoint, the more internally consistent ways there are of stating a monotheistic metaphysics, the better. Then if one version comes up against a damning objection, there are other versions to turn to. The varieties are sufficiently different so that it is not absurd to suppose that a powerful objection to one of them may not be a powerful objection against another. Perhaps, then, references to the fourth alternative would strengthen Maimonides' philosophical hand. His sympathy to Aristotelianism no doubt would give him pause about the fourth alternative, particularly, as we have noted, in what would appear from that perspective to be its most radical variations. But each of its variations is receptive to the Law and the Prophets, and to miracles, and, as we have seen, that is where Maimonides' ultimate sympathies lie.

34

Maimonides' Fundamental Principles *Redivivus*

Charles M. Raffel
American Jewish Committee

The central focus for a discussion of Maimonides' articles of faith is his *Introduction to Perek Helek*. In this essay, which is an integral part of his *Commentary on the Mishnah*, Maimonides explores misconceptions concerning the Messianic Age, afterlife and resurrection, examines a hierarchy of motivations for observance of the Law, and analyzes three different schools for the interpretation of aggadic texts. Only after this preliminary work does Maimonides offer a formulation of thirteen fundamental principles which serve as the foundation for Jewish belief.

The following are the topics which are covered:

1. existence of God
2. unity of God
3. incorporeality of God
4. eternity of God
5. the prohibition of the worship of beings other than God
6. existence of prophecy
7. superiority of Mosaic prophecy
8. divine origin of the Law
9. eternity of the Law
10. God's knowledge of human deeds
11. reward and punishment
12. days of the Messiah

13.   resurrection of the dead[1]

This kind of listing of the topics, which has dominated popular and scholarly considerations of *Perek Helek*, would seem to violate the substance and style of Maimonides' original presentation. The individual principles are enumerated in the essay/review only after a lengthy prolegomenon and each principle's listing contains an explanation, discussion or clarification of widely varying length, from the simple cross-reference back to the body of the introductory text for the thirteenth principle, to the extended discussions, arguments, examples and digressions which form the lengthy comments on the seventh and eighth principles.

The question which I propose to examine, whether the 'list' of thirteen principles in *Perek Helek* is definitive throughout Maimonides' works, has different shades of meaning and significance within two divergent schools of Maimonidean interpretation. For the interpreter who takes the fundamental principles to have significant metaphysical value, the question is of ultimate philosophic and theological importance: is Maimonides' final formulation of the fundamental principles or beliefs of Judaism as he presents it in *Perek Helek*? On the other hand, for those who see the cognitive status of the principles heavily outweighed by political concerns, a pertinent question still remains: is Maimonides' exoteric formulation of fundamental principles of faith finalized in *Perek Helek* or not?[2] The

---

[1]These shorthand formulations of the topics are adapted from Arthur Hyman's "Maimonides' 'Thirteen Principles,'" in *Jewish Medieval and Renaissance Studies*, edited by Alexander Altmann (Cambridge: Harvard University Press, 1967), pp. 119-144. The topics are listed on p. 128. See Menachem Kellner, *Dogma in Medieval Jewish Thought* (New York: Oxford University Press, 1986) for a comprehensive treatment of Maimonides' formulations, pp. 10-65. A valuable overview is provided in M. Kellner, "Dogma in Medieval Jewish Thought: A Bibliographical Survey," *Studies in Bibliography and Booklore*, Vol. 15 (1984), pp. 5-21. For the relationship of fundamental principles to the whole corpus of Maimonidean thought, see Marvin Fox, "Prolegomenon," to A. Cohen, *The Teachings of Maimonides* (New York: KTAV, 1968), pp. XV-XLIV.

[2]Note, for example, Alexander Altmann's formulation in his entry in the *Encyclopedia Judaica*, Vol. III, Col. 655, "Articles of Faith":

> Maimonides undertook such a presentation to teach the rank and file of the community the true spiritual meaning of the belief in the world to come (*ha-olam ha-ba*) and to disabuse their minds of crude, materialistic notions. Since the ultimate felicity of man depends on the possession of true concepts concerning God, the formulation and brief exposition of true notions in the realm of faith is meant to help the multitude to avoid error and to purify belief.

overall question of the function, purpose and value of fundamental principles in Maimonides' thinking is an issue on which I will suspend judgment initially.

The case has been made that the list of thirteen principles is definitive throughout Maimonides' works. In an extensive study of the thirteen principles, Arthur Hyman writes that Maimonides lists the principles "...with only a slight modification in the *Mishneh Torah,* and in his *Treatise Concerning the Resurrection of the Dead,* a work postdating his *Guide of the Perplexed,* he indicates that he worked out his earlier enumeration of the principles with great care and that he considered this enumeration still definitive."[3]

It is my contention that convincing evidence, from within the *Introduction to Perek Helek* itself, from *Mishneh Torah* and from the *Guide of the Perplexed,* would seem to indicate not only that the list of fundamental principles in *Perek Helek* is not definitive, but that Maimonides himself never conceived of the list in *Helek* to be definitive.

Internal Evidence from *Perek Helek*

It has been demonstrated that the structure of the listing of fundamental principles in *Perek Helek,* represented by three divisions, propositions about God, Torah and Reward and Punishment, is determined by the structure of the three categories in the Mishnah Sanhedrin on which Maimonides is commenting:

The following are those who have no share in the world to come:

A. He who says "there is no resurrection of the dead"
B. And he who says "the Law is not from Heaven"
C. And the *apikoros*[4]

Definition of the believer, in contradistinction to the *apikoros* (C) yields the propositions about God (principles 1-5). Affirmation of Torah from Heaven (B) yields principles 6-9, and the principles concerning reward and punishment (10-13) are expanded counterparts to the affirmation of resurrection (A). Hyman summarizes this point as follows: "It can then be said that the 'thirteen principles' contain Maimonides' account of basic Jewish beliefs *set down according to the structure of the mishnah on which he comments.*"[5]

---

[3]Hyman, "Thirteen Principles," p. 120.
[4]Mishnah, Sanhedrin X:1. See Hyman, p. 122.
[5]Hyman, "Thirteen Principles," p. 138. The italics are Hyman's.

I would like to extend the parallelism between the mishnah and Maimonides' formulation further. This extension would seem to yield a logical conclusion that the structure and contents of the mishnah determine the structure and contents of Maimonides' thirteen principles. The tripartite structure of the mishnah not only determines the tripartite structure of Maimonides' principles, but also the contents of the three major sub-divisions, namely God, Torah and Reward and Punishment. As a result of this revised conclusion, one then wonders whether *Perek Helek* contains Maimonides' independent thinking on fundamental beliefs or Maimonides, as interpreter of the mishnah, offering his interpretation of the Mishnah's view of fundamental beliefs.[6] This conundrum leads to a narrower and verifiable question on which I would like to focus: did Maimonides conceive of another account of basic Jewish beliefs beyond the structure and scope of the mishnah in Sanhedrin? The evidence, within *Perek Helek* itself, would seem to indicate that he did.

Prior to introducing the fundamental principles in *Perek Helek*, Maimonides outlines a plan for a massive work which would put to the test his interpretive scheme for *aggada:*

> I hope to write a book collecting all the sages' teachings on this subject from the Talmud and other works. I shall interpret them systematically, showing which must be understood literally and which metaphorically, and which are dreams to be interpreted by a wakeful mind. There I shall explain the many principles of our faith of which I have discussed a few here....[7]

Conceived as both an encyclopedia of aggadic statements and as a systematic interpretation of *aggada,* this planned work would provide the necessary background for a truly definitive enumeration and analysis of fundamental principles of Jewish belief. This statement would seem to indicate that the enumeration in *Perek Helek,* done prior to the comprehensive work on *aggada,* is, at best, tentative or incomplete, or, to put it simply, an abstract of a work not yet undertaken. The proper method to produce a definitive statement and explanation of fundamental principles involves, according to Maimonides, a comprehensive ordering of aggadic thinking and a

---

[6]Hyman offers the assessment that the structure of the mishnah determined the non-exhaustive nature of the listing in *Helek,* but he refrains from concluding that the list in *Helek* is, therefore, not definitive. pp. 138-9.

[7]*Perek Helek* in *Hakdamot le-Perush ha-Mishnah,* edited by M. D. Rabinowitz (Jerusalem, 1961), pp. 133-4. English translation by Arnold J. Wolf in *A Maimonides Reader,* edited by Isadore Twersky (New York: Behrman House, 1972), p. 417.

systematic analysis of thought (an exclusively aggadic *Mishneh Torah*, if you will).

Maimonides reiterates his plan for a major work on fundamental principles within his discussion of the seventh article of faith in *Helek*, Mosaic prophecy. Realizing the complexity of prophecy's cognitive foundation in general and Mosaic prophecy in particular, and the need in *Perek Helek* to focus on concise formulations of the principles at hand, Maimonides alludes to three different planned works in which these discussions will be dealt with. The three works are: the work on *aggada* and systematic interpretation mentioned above, a Book on Prophecy (on which Maimonides says he is currently working), and a "book I hope some day to write on these fundamental principles."[8]

Without clearly understanding the relationship between the aggadic work and the planned work on fundamental principles (as discussed above), one might have assumed that Maimonides planned a detailed explanation of the fundamental principles listed in *Perek Helek*. It is clear, however, that Maimonides planned a logical sequence of works in which the comprehensive examination of aggadic thinking is the necessary preliminary step for an entirely new and different comprehensive work on fundamental principles. To summarize the internal evidence from *Perek Helek*: Maimonides gives clear indication that the listing and treatment of fundamental principles in *Perek Helek* is not intended as definitive. He outlines an exhaustive program of research that would produce a comprehensive list and discussion. This self-admission by Maimonides enables us to see the treatment of fundamental principles in *Perek Helek* as temporary or transitional, as a preliminary abstract which cannot possibly anticipate research not yet undertaken.

My understanding of the evidence up to this point indicates Maimonides' unequivocal intention to produce a new and comprehensive treatment of fundamental principles, different from the format in *Perek Helek*. We must now consider what Maimonides did, in fact, produce. The evidence from *Mishneh Torah* should not be overlooked.

Evidence from *Mishneh Torah*

If Maimonides did reconsider his own expressed intentions and held the thirteen principles, as formulated in *Perek Helek*, to be definitive for Jewish belief, one might assume that he would preserve the principles intact in his next major work, *Mishneh Torah*. The consensus

---

[8]*Perek Helek* (Rabinowitz, ed.), p. 142.

view, if not the unanimous one, of medieval and modern scholars, is even though reference to the subject matter of *Helek* is scattered throughout *Sefer ha-Mada'* of *Mishneh Torah*, close examination of the texts shows that the list of principles that Maimonides considers to be definitive in *Mishneh Torah* is practically identical with the earlier formulation in *Perek Helek*.[9] My own view, which I feel relates more accurately to the textual evidence at hand, is that the treatment of fundamental principles in *Mishneh Torah* does not equate with the treatment in *Perek Helek*, but represents an evolved view in Maimonides' thinking.

The evidence involves two separate sections in *Yesodei ha-Torah* and two separate sections in *Teshuvah*. The subject matter of the first section, *Yesodei ha-Torah* Ch. 1, parallels the subject matter of the first four principles in *Helek*. But the very first line of *Mishneh Torah* suggests a hierarchical view of fundamental principles which is totally missing from the listing in *Perek Helek*:

> The basic principle of all basic principles and the pillar of all sciences is to realize that there is a First Being who brought every existing thing into being.[10]

Knowledge of and/or belief[11] in the existence of the Prime Being is the basis of all other fundamental principles. Belief in God's existence is coupled with the prohibition against affirming the existence of other gods. This negative corollary is not mentioned in *Helek*. The move to a hierarchical conception of fundamental principles is consistent throughout the first section in *Yesodei ha-Torah*. The subsequent assertion of the principle of divine unity spawns two apparently subsidiary principles, God's incorporeality, and, in a minor role as a premise in the proof of divine incorporeality, God's eternity. The presentation is carefully conceptualized and tightly consolidated around the affirmation of God's existence. Divine unity receives major play, incorporeality has a derivative role, and eternity receives barely a mention.

---

[9]See Isaac Abravanel's harmonizing account in *Rosh Amanah* (Tel Aviv, 1958). See also Menachem M. Kellner's annotated translation, *Principles of Faith* (East Brunswick, New Jersey: Farleigh Dickinson, 1982).

[10]*The Book of Knowledge*, translated by Moses Hyamson (Jerusalem: Boys Town, 1965), p. 34a.

[11]See Simon Rawidowicz's analysis of the influence of the Arabic term *itikad* on Maimonides' conception of belief/knowledge, in his *Studies in Jewish Thought* (Philadelphia: JPS, 1974), pp. 317-323.

This presentation at the very beginning of *Mishneh Torah* seems to be a conscious re-working and refinement (if not implied criticism) of the sequential list in *Helek* of:

1. existence
2. unity
3. incorporeality
4. eternity

The change suggests the shift from one dimension to three. We not only have here a re-working of the same elements in *Helek*, but Maimonides has also made a significant substitution. He has replaced the problematic fifth principle of *Helek*, the prohibition of the worship of beings other than God, with the logically prior prohibition against affirming the existence of other gods. It is clear from the very beginning of *Mishneh Torah* that not only are original elements from *Helek* subject to a hierarchical re-ordering, but substitutions and other adjustments have taken place.

The second section under consideration, *Yesodei ha-Torah* Chs. 7-10, corresponds to the subject matter of the middle division of the listing in *Helek*, principles six through nine:

6. existence of prophecy
7. superiority of Mosaic prophecy
8. divine origin of the Law
9. eternity of the Law

The reformulation in *Mishneh Torah* is a hallmark of Maimonides' famed love of brevity. The main principle is contained in the very first line: "It is one of the basic principles of religion to know that God causes men to prophesy."[12] Belief in the existence of the divine origin of prophecy becomes, in *Mishneh Torah*, the major thrust and organizing principle. The superiority of Mosaic prophecy is extensively discussed in this section, the eternity of the Law is mentioned and the divine origin of the Law is implied. But in this section, Mosaic prophecy, the divine origin and eternity of the Law, are not labelled as independent fundamental principles in the technical language of *Mishneh Torah*.[13] This account on prophecy and the Law parallels the first section's hierarchical scheme of God's existence, unity and incorporeality, and would seem to indicate Maimonides' new method for dealing with fundamental principles in *Mishneh Torah*. One may note tentatively

---

[12]*Yesodei ha-Torah* 7:1.
[13]See Isadore Twersky, *Introduction to the Code of Maimonides* (New Haven: Yale, 1980), pp. 361-2 and particularly n. 12.

that Maimonides' view here is that less is more, the controlling part or major principle may best stand for the whole.

A different kind of evidence occurs in the third chapter of *Teshuvah*. Apparently drawing on sources parallel to the Mishna in Sanhedrin, Maimonides lists twenty-four transgressions which may block one's share in the world-to-come.[14] This listing, unlike the enumeration in *Helek*, mixes both heretical beliefs with actions. A comparison of the elements of heretical belief in *Teshuvah* 3:6 with the listing in *Helek* reveals the following substantive differences: the *Mishneh Torah* account omits reward and punishment and divides the divine origin of the Torah into two separate items, the divine origin of the written Law and the divine origin of the oral Law.

Maimonides' adherence to his source for this listing and his conscious mixing of the realms of belief and action, are designed to fit a particular purpose in *Hilkhot Teshuvah*: to dramatize the severe danger inherent in the multiplicity of beliefs and actions which may take a Jew beyond the pale of normative Judaism. For our own investigation, this list of twenty-four elements indicates possible additions and subtractions to the original formulation in *Perek Helek*.

The final section, *Teshuvah* Chs. 5-9, corresponds in subject matter to the third division of the listing in *Helek*:

10.   God's knowledge of human deeds
11.   reward and punishment
12.   days of the Messiah
13.   resurrection of the dead

Maimonides' reworking of this section in *Mishneh Torah* includes not only organizational and stylistic consolidation, but a rather dramatic shift. Human free will is now the central fundamental principle to which God's knowledge of human affairs is an intimately related problem.[15] Reward and punishment and the Messianic Age are discussed in the related chapters. A discussion of the world-to-come is added in *Mishneh Torah* while mention of bodily resurrection is notably missing from this section. The overarching focus seems to mark a significant transition in Maimonides' thinking on the significance of the root concept of human free will.

---

[14]Hyamson, in his notes to *The Book of Knowledge*, identifies Tosefta, Sanhedrin XIII as a possible source. See p. 84b, notes 2-3. I think this source is potentially revealing as a source for Maimonides' formulation of principles in *Helek* itself.

[15]Teshuvah 5:5.

Traditionally, these corresponding sections in *Mishneh Torah* to the thirteen principles in *Perek Helek* have been examined with a forceful push toward harmonization. The solidity and authority of the original thirteen principles not only remains in tact, but increases as all modifications are described as slight and inconsequential. The motivation for this kind of treatment to preserve Maimonides' original formulation seems to be to standardize Maimonidean, if not Jewish belief. In consideration of the evidence from *Mishneh Torah* discussed above, Arthur Hyman has written: "'The thirteen principles' set down first in the *Introduction to Perek Helek* are retained with barely a modification in the *Mishneh Torah*."[16]

What seems more in line with the evidence from *Mishneh Torah* is not that the thirteen principles have emerged unscathed or that an entirely new, divergent comprehensive treatment has been formulated. *Mishneh Torah* seems to represent a fluid stage in Maimonides' consideration of fundamental beliefs, one in which alternative formulations are being considered, different formats are reviewed and entertained, additional principles are formulated, as either corollaries to existing principles or as independent, new entities, and other principles are subtracted or consolidated. The common denominator behind the three major sections in *Mishneh Torah* (*Yesodei ha-Torah*: 1, *Yesodei ha-Torah*: 7-10 and *Teshuvah*: 5-9) appears to be a shift to a deeper, more consistent understanding of what constitutes a truly fundamental principle of belief. Each section is presented as a hierarchical scheme, controlled by one central fundamental principle. A summary then of the evidence at hand is that *Mishneh Torah*, rather than confirming the thirteen principles as definitive, on closer examination shows Maimonides' thinking on fundamental principles to have undergone major review and revision.

Evidence from *Moreh Nevukhim*

The next piece of the puzzle in determining Maimonides' evolving formulation of fundamental principles is the *Guide of the Perplexed*. In the "Introduction to the First Part" of the *Guide*, Maimonides explains that he abandoned, due to pedagogical reasons, two of the works promised in the *Commentary on the Mishnah*, the "Book of Prophecy" and the work on Aggada, the "Book of Correspondence." The intended formats would have involved adhering to parables and concealment to explain "all difficult passages in the *Midrashim*,"[17] Maimonides

---

[16]Hyman, "Thirteen Principles," p. 133.
[17]*The Guide of the Perplexed*, translated by Shlomo Pines (Chicago: University of Chicago, 1963), p. 9.

writes, and would have amounted to teaching the sophisticated reader that which he already knows and teaching the unsophisticated reader nothing. Rather than focusing and commenting on the *midrashim* themselves, Maimonides' new plan, which is to be followed in the *Guide,* seems to involve structuring his presentation around fundamental principles of belief. He writes:

> In view of these considerations, we have given up composing these two books in the way in which they were begun. We have confined ourselves to mentioning briefly the *foundations of belief* and general truths, while dropping hints that approach a clear exposition....[18]

It is not clear to me whether the scattered references to fundamental principles throughout the three sections of the *Guide* are intended to form a new comprehensive list of fundamental principles. Nevertheless it is clear that Maimonides' thinking on the subject has undergone further change of a significant nature. In the course of the *Guide* the following are identified explicitly as fundamental principles of the Law:

1. God's existence
2. God's oneness
3. God's incorporeality
4. creation of the world
5. prophecy
6. Mosaic prophecy
7. eternity of the Law
8. human free will
9. divine justice
10. divine providence
11. divine knowledge[19]

In light of the original list in *Perek Helek,* discussed implicitly are the eternity of God, the prohibition of the worship of beings other than God, the divine origin of the Law and reward and punishment. But while these elements are mentioned briefly in the *Guide,* they are not identified as fundamental principles. Virtually unmentioned are days of the Messiah and resurrection of the dead.

At least two enormously significant areas of change emerge from a consideration of fundamental principles in the *Guide,* both of which have been well noted in other contexts. First, the newly independent

---

[18]*Guide,* p. 10.
[19]The first four principles are discussed in the *Guide,* I, 35. Principle 5 is identified in II, 32; no. 6 in II, 34 and no. 7 in II, 39. Principles 8-11 are discussed in III, 17-20.

and preeminent status of creation *ex nihilo*, articulated as a fundamental principle, has drawn considerable attention as a problem in the interpretation of the *Guide* as a whole. A suggestive corollary is apparently conclusive manuscript evidence which documents Maimonides' own later efforts to introduce creation *ex nihilo* explicitly back into his original formulation of fundamental principles in *Helek*.[20]

Secondly, the reworking of the tripartite principle of reward and punishment, Messianic Age and resurrection in *Helek* into the principles associated with divine providence in the *Guide* is paradigmatic of Maimonides' ongoing commitment to revamp and refine his formulations of fundamental principles. Again, in order to preserve the definitive stature of *Perek Helek's* listing (or to invest it with greater authority), *Helek's* eleventh principle has been said by some interpreters to contain the outline of a theory of providence. The distance travelled from *Perek Helek* to the *Guide*, in this case, should not be underestimated. *Perek Helek* reads: "The eleventh fundamental principle is that God rewards those who perform the commandments of the Torah and punishes those who transgress its admonitions."[21] This "theological given" is refined by Maimonides in the *Guide* into an explanation of how providence functions. The combined affirmations, as fundamental principles, of human free will and divine justice are joined to an elaborate epistemological model, "providence according to the intellect."[22] I am not saying that Maimonides contradicts the earlier account, but that he transcends it.

This brief overview of the evidence from the *Guide*, which deserves a more detailed examination, as usual raises more questions than it resolves, but, in my own view, points clearly to a further evolution in Maimonides' conception and formulation of fundamental principles.

To summarize our main points:

1) The internal evidence from *Perek Helek* itself indicates that the list of fundamental principles of Jewish belief is not definitive and, furthermore, was never intended to be definitive.

---

[20]See Abravanel, *Rosh Amanah*, Chs. 3 and 16 and see Menachem Kellner, *Dogma in Medieval Jewish Thought*, pp. 240-1, n. 211.
[21]*Helek* (Rabinowitz ed.), pp. 146-7. The translation is in Twersky, *A Maimonides Reader*, p. 422.
[22]*Guide* III, 17-18. For a more detailed explanation see my article "Providence as Consequent Upon the Intellect: Maimonides' Theory of Providence," *AJS Review* XII, 1 (Spring 1987), pp. 25-71.

2) Stated conservatively, the evidence from *Mishneh Torah* and the *Guide* reveals extensive revision, refinement and modifications within Maimonides' thinking on the subject, from the very conception of what constitutes a fundamental principle to the choice of which principles belong ultimately on the list.

Unless one chooses to read the *Guide* in such a manner, what is missing from the Maimonidean corpus is a revised, comprehensive, self-contained enumeration of fundamental principles. One may either surmise that Maimonides never got around to completing this project or that he abandoned it. A careful reading of the first two chapters of the *Treatise on Resurrection*,[23] written after the *Guide*, reveals Maimonides' predicament. A political controversy calling openly into question his own belief in resurrection forces Maimonides himself to invest publicly the earlier accounts of *Mishneh Torah* and *Helek* with renewed authority and completeness. While intellectually committed to the reformulation and revision of fundamental principles, as clearly demonstrated in his *Mishneh Torah* and *Guide*, Maimonides understood that this process of revision was not an enterprise that could be done openly under the hostile glare of an agitated public's scrutiny. The negative public fall-out, revealing indecision, if not chaos in the central core of Jewish doctrine would cancel out any and all possible intellectual gains. The *Treatise on Resurrection*, at least on this score, demonstrates Maimonides' firm conviction that discretion is the better part of intellectual valor, too.

---

[23]Maimonides' *Treatise on Resurrection*, edited by Joshua Finkel (New York: AAJR, 1939).

35

Another *More nevukhim:*

The Italian Background and the Educational Program
of Leon Modena's *More nevukhim*
bikhtivah bilshonenu hakadosh

Howard Adelman
Smith College

Students in Jewish studies, especially those who have had the good fortune to study at Brandeis and with Professor Fox, surely know of Moses Maimonides' philosophical exposition of Judaism, the *More nevukhim,* "The Guide for the Perplexed," and Nahman Krochmal's philosophy of Jewish history, *More nevukhei hazeman,* "The Guide for the Perplexed of our Time." In the course of writing my dissertation at Brandeis with Professor Fox on my committee, I learned about an attempt by a Venetian rabbi in the last decade of the sixteenth century to write yet another *More.* Leon Modena (1571-1648) drafted plans for a *More nevukhim bikhtivah bilshonenu hakadosh,* "The Guide for the Perplexed in Writing in our Holy Language." A study of the attitude towards the Hebrew language in Modena's day which led to his attempt to produce such a manual as part of his educational program is an opportunity for acknowledging Professor Fox's contribution to maintaining Hebrew scholarship at a serious level some four centuries later, a time at which the complaints of Leon Modena and other Venetians about the study of Hebrew in their own community, although not unique,[1] sound very familiar to us:

---

[1] Abraham de Balmes, *Mikneh Avraham* (Venice, 1523), cited in Simhah Assaf *Mekorot letoledot hahinnukh beyisrael* 2 (Jerusalem, 1930-1943), p. 111; Judah

89

- Some Jewish children receive no Jewish education, "because of the sins of their parents."[2]
- Many Jews cannot even read the Hebrew letters.[3]
- One person in each city and two people in a state [Jeremiah 3:14] know basic Hebrew grammar, such as root, form, tense, and conjugation.[4]
- Jews do not know the difference between nouns and verbs, let alone between different vowels and accents.[5]
- Jewish teachers do not consider Hebrew important.[6]
- Jewish students who study the Bible can be compared to magicians who mutter charms without knowing what they mean.[7]
- A student who studies with several teachers might find the differences in Hebrew instruction to be like those between people speaking different languages.[8]
- Students end their Hebrew education at the age of Bar Mitzvah.[9]
- Teaching students Hebrew becomes less and less profitable as the number of students drops and only part-time jobs are available.[10]
- It is not satisfying to teach Hebrew, but positions are held just for the money.[11]

---

del Bene, *Kisaot leveit david* (Venice, 1646), cited in Assaf, *Mekorot* 2, p. 136; *Takkanot beit hatalmud torah beverona*, cited in Assaf, *Mekorot* 2, p. 149.

[2]British Library Or. 5396, 98b, 117a; cf. Meir Benayahu, *Hayehasim shebein yehudei yavan leyehudei italiah* (Tel Aviv, 1980), pp. 207-209, 316-320.

[3]Leon Modena, *Pi aryeh*, (Venice/Padua, 1640), Hebrew Introduction.

[4]Leon Modena *Galut yehudah* (Venice, 1612), Introduction; cf. Abraham de Balmes, *Mikneh Abraham* (Venice, 1523), cited in Assaf, *Mekorot* 2, p. 111.

[5]Leon Modena, "Introduction," Jacob Lombroso *Mikra gedolah* (Venice, 1639), cited in Simon Bernstein, *Divan lerabbi yehudah aryeh mimodena* (Philadelphia, 1932), p. viii and in Peninah Naveh, *Leket ketavim* (Jerusalem, 1968), pp. 287-288.

[6]*Ibid.*

[7]*Ibid.* cf. T. B. Sota 22a.

[8]Modena, *Galut yehudah* (1612), Italian Introduction.

[9]Leon Modena, *Hayyei yehudah, The Autobiography of a Seventeenth-Century Venetian Rabbi: Leon Modena's Life of Judah*, Mark Cohen, tr. (Princeton, 1988), fol. 8b; *Midbar yehudah* (Venice, 1602), fol. 4a; Yakov Boksenboim, *Iggerot rabbi yehudah aryeh mimodena* (Tel Aviv, 1984), no. 9; *idem, Iggerot beit carmi* (Tel Aviv, 1984), no. 1.

[10]Boksenboim, *Iggerot*, no. 24.

[11]Boksenboim, *Iggerot*, nos. 28, 36.

- "Therefore, it is a commandment and an obligation to teach the students that they must void themselves before they come to school and if it happens that one really has to go, he must go alone and no other can go out until he has returned to his place...."[12]

- "...Israel has forgotten its maker [Hosea 8:14] and they build temples, but what good is a splendid synagogue building when the Torah is neglected and their children speak half the language of Rome and half the language of every other people and they do not know how to speak the Jewish language, and the word of the Lord has become as a closed book to them...."[13]

Yet it is also clear from Modena's writings that many Jews in Venice were able to master Hebrew. In Hebrew, they were able to correspond on mundane and academic matters,[14] to keep minutes of their benevolent society meetings,[15] and to maintain a publishing industry which produced for Venice and elsewhere in Italy and the Jewish world at the time hundreds of new Hebrew books each year with at least a thousand copies in each run, including standard editions of Hebrew texts and new Hebrew commentaries "for the mature and knowledgeable,"[16] to enjoy creative Hebrew poetry, to converse with Jews from the Land of Israel, and to demonstrate proficiency in Talmudic texts.

Elementary Jewish Education in Venice

These contrasts in Hebrew knowledge can be explained by the different types of elementary education available for Jewish youth, depending on the background, interests, and assets of their parents.

At one end of the spectrum, were many children of former marranos who had never received any Jewish education,[17] and for them most basic remedial programs were offered. One was sponsored by Joseph

---

[12]Samuel Aboab, *Sefer hazikhronot* (Venice, c. 1631-1651), in Assaf, *Mekorot 2*, p. 141.

[13]Samson Morpurgo, *Shelot uteshuvot shemesh tzedakah* (Venice, 1790), in Assaf, *Mekorot 2*, p. 202.

[14]BL Or. 5395, 5394, Moscow Guensburg 356.7

[15]JTSA 8468, 8593, 8594.

[16]Oxford 2549.1; Adolf Neubauer, "Quelques notes sur la vie de Juda Leon da Modena," *Revue des Etudes Juives* 22 (1891): 82-84.

[17]Leon Modena, *Ziknei yehudah*, Shlomo Simonsohn, ed. (Jerusalem, 1956), no. 80; Ellis Rivkin, *Leon da Modena and the Kol Sakhal* (Cincinnati, 1952), pp. 22-23; Benjamin Ravid, "The First Charter of the Jewish Merchants of Venice," *Association for Jewish Studies Revirew* 1 (1978), pp. 187-222.

Pardo (d. 1619), a prominent Levantine rabbi and merchant,[18] who
hired and supported a teacher to bring the students up to the level at
which they could read and understand the talmudic digest of Alfasi.[19]

Most Jewish youths in Italy received their elementary education in
what was known as *heder*, in large classes which met for most of the
day, often in private homes, and were sponsored by individuals or
benevolent societies.[20] These classes often had many students,
sometimes from twenty to over thirty, and were taught by one teacher,
perhaps with the help of an assistant.[21] This was how Modena tried to
earn much of his living in Venice. Most of his complaints and those of
contemporaries, such as his grandson Isaac min Haleviim, about
teaching concern these large classes in which he spent much of the time
rebuking the students.[22] When other opportunities for income were not
available, he repeatedly returned to teach these classes,[23] even after
he received his ordination at the age of 38. He referred to this
experience as serving his "sentence as the wicked do in Hell,"[24]
especially on account of the discipline problems presented by the
students' behavior.

Schools run by one of the societies of the Venetian Jewish
community required the teachers, in addition to teaching, to be at the
school from early morning before breakfast until late in the evening.
They were required to supervise the students at religious services three
times a day and be available at the school during meal times. Most
societies allowed their teachers only a half hour a day to attend to
personal matters. This kind of confinement, although probably not as
severe for Modena since he still held other positions while he taught,
nevertheless caused much of his frustration as a teacher.[25] In nearby
Verona, the community leaders had to enact a series of regulations for
their school which included financial incentives to keep students in
school till age sixteen, the firing of incompetent teachers, the expulsion
of difficult students, and a truant officer with a whip.[26] As long as it

---

[18]Gershon Cohen, "Letoledot hapulmus 'al stam yenam," *Sinai* 39 (1975), pp. 63, 71, 73.

[19]BL Or. 5396, 98b, 117a; cf. Benayahu, *Hayehasim*, pp. 207-209, 316-320.

[20]Modena, *Hayyei yehudah*, fol. 12a.

[21]Boksenboim, *Iggerot*, no. 105; Modena, *Hayyei*, fol. 12a.

[22]Boksenboim, *Iggerot*, nos. 28, 29, 36, 38, 105. Isaac min Haleviim, *Medabber tahafuhot* Daniel Carpi, ed. (Tel Aviv, 1985), p. 107.

[23]Modena, *Hayyei*, fol. 18a.

[24]Boksenboim, *Iggerot*, no. 105.

[25]Assaf, *Mekorot* 2, pp. 141-165; cf. p. 183.

[26]For regulations typical of the kinds of rules which teachers working for Jewish confraternities in Venice had to follow, in Assaf, *Mekorot* 2, pp. 141-196.

was a small strap and not a full whip, it was allowed by Jewish law to be used on students[27] and was also applied in Venice.[28] There was some opposition to the use of whips on students in Padua,[29] another nearby city under Venetian control.

However, the most effective form of Jewish education was private and semi-private instruction which was enjoyed by the children of the wealthy. Modena himself had received this type of education from the ages of three to thirteen from some of the greatest talmudists in Italy and prominent kabbalists from the Land of Israel, including Azriel Basola, Malachi Gallico, Eliakim ben Isaiah Moses Macerata, Yehiel Tardiolo, Hezekiah Finzi, and Samuel Archivolti.[30] During these years he studied the classical texts of rabbinic Judaism and developed the ability to write Hebrew elegantly. He also received training in music, singing, dancing, preaching, and Latin. For most of his life,[31] like many of the other leading rabbis of Italy, Modena enjoyed giving private lessons to young students, some as young as five years old.[32] One of his former students, the apostate Giulio Morosini, noted that all parents who had the money chose private instruction at home for their children.[33]

The Elementary Curriculum

From Modena's letters and other writings, it is possible to learn what Jewish elementary students in Venice studied. Sunday, Monday, and Tuesday mornings they studied the laws of the Sabbath, Wednesday and Thursday, the Torah portion of the week with the commentary of Rashi, which according to Modena, offered some difficulty because it was printed without vowel points. Friday they turned to the weekly Haftarah selection and commentaries on it, and on weekday afternoons, the prophets, Hebrew letter writing, and Italian

---

[27]Tur, Yoreh De'ah, 245.11.

[28]So depicted on an alphabet wall chart printed in Venice in 1656, see Assaf, *Mekorot* 2, frontispiece.

[29]Daniel Carpi, *Pinkas vaad k. k. padua* 2 (Jerusalem, 1980), no. 765, p. 415. See also Boksenboim, *Iggerot beit carmi*, pp. 314-316.

[30]For further information see Modena, *Hayyei yehudah*, s. v. index.

[31]Boksenboim, *Iggerot*, no. 82; Modena, *Hayyei yehudah*, fol. 28a.

[32]Simhah Calimani, for example, was five years old; see Boksenboim, *Iggerot*, no. 309.

[33]Giulio Morosini, *Via della Fede* (Venice, 1683), pp. 156-166, especially p. 161, cited in Assaf *Mekorot* 2, p. 132.

grammar and composition.[34] The curriculum even called for classes on the Sabbath when they would study the Psalms. This was not unusual; Sabbath study was allowed in rabbinic law,[35] and some Italian Jewish schools at the time even held oral examinations on the Sabbath.[36] The older students worked on what Modena called "compendia of rules of the virtuous life" which included the laws of women and kashrut.[37] In contradistinction to Modena's occasional negative assessment of the progress made by many students, he also described exceptional students who would go on to study Mishnah and Talmud, "the ground work of all, and the best study they can betake themselves to."[38]

These accomplishments in rabbinic texts are particularly impressive because, as a result of Christian policy, only rare copies of the Talmud were available in Italy,[39] and when it was taught the rabbis had to lecture on it in the academies without the students having the benefit of a printed text for study in front of them.[40] Nevertheless, it is clear that Modena owned talmudic tractates which he used for research and which he lent to others.[41] Thus, it is not surprising that under these circumstances a *siyyum*, the completion of the study of a talmudic tractate,[42] was a major event, marked by a

---

[34]Boksenboim, *Iggerot*, nos. 36, 81, 288, 289, 307, 312; Leon Modena, *Riti*, Edmund Chilmeand, tr. (London, 1650), IV, X; Ludwig Blau, *Kitvei harav yehudah aryeh mimodena* (Budapest, 1905), no. 53; Boksenboim, *Iggerot*, no. 323.

[35]Tur, Yoreh De'ah, 245.11.

[36]Assaf, *Mekorot* 2, pp. 129, 156, 174, 175, 192, 195; Carpi, *Pauda*, nos. 528, 765.

[37]Nedarim, Shevuot, Hullin (chapter 8).

[38]Modena, *Riti*, IV, X, 3.

[39]Modena, *Riti*, II, II, 7; Boksenboim, *Iggerot*, no. 56; BL Or. 5396, 89b. Azariah Figo complained that the Venetian Jewish community suffered from a shortage of rabbinic texts, particularly the Gemara, *Zera anashim*, David Frankel, ed. (Husyatin, 1902), no. 23. Judah del Bene noted that permission to possess the Talmud was not granted by the authorities in Italy, *Kisaot leveit david* (Verona, 1646), 92a, cited in I. Barzilay, *Between Reason and Faith* (The Hague, 1967), p. 213; Paul Grendler, *The Roman Inquisition and the Venetian Press* (Princeton, 1977), 91-92, 89, 112, 140; William Popper, *The Censorship of Hebrew Books* (New York, 1899), pp. 34-35; David Kaufmann, "Die Verbrennung der talmudischen Literatur in der Republik venedig," *JQR* o.s. 12 (1901): 533-538. On the availability of some talmudic texts, see Boksenboim, *Iggerot beit carmi*, p. 13.

[40]BL Or. 5396, 89b.

[41]Boksenboim, *Iggerot*, no. 73. BL Or. 5395, 5a, 24b, 13b, 20a; these references were incomprehensibly garbled in Blau, *Kitvei*, no. 191.

[42]Tractates so celebrated included Ketubot, Gittin, and Shevuot.

celebration complete with sermons, songs, musical presentations, and the distribution of fish and candy.[43]

Jewish Higher Education in Venice

The formal training of Jewish children often ended at around thirteen because boys had to work and their parents could no longer afford a teacher. Sometimes it ended sooner for poor children; in Padua the lay leaders refused to give aid to families if the boys had stopped their studies before the age of thirteen.[44] Reflecting this, Modena parodied the mishnaic advice [Avot 5:24] that at five years of age one should begin to study Bible and at ten the study of Mishnah, to read: "At five the age is reached for the Bible and at ten for working in a store."[45] Although Venice had a substantial Jewish community, in 1604 plans were made to establish an advanced talmudic academy in Conegliano, a small town to the north with a Jewish population of about 35 out of around 4,000.[46] There it would be away from the distractions of a big city such as Venice, and the needs of all the students, including room, board, tuition, clothing, and candles without limit, would be provided for. In letters Modena wrote to Jewish communities in Italy, Poland, Bohemia, Germanic lands, and Turkey on behalf of this school he stressed that, removed from mundane matters, the students would be able to pursue their studies.[47] Similarly, in Verona students received subsidies to encourage them to pursue their studies until age sixteen or eighteen.[48]

Some advanced training was also available in Venice itself. Although many Jewish adolescents could not be regular students, there were ways in which they could continue their Jewish education on a part-time basis. Jews attended synagogue services three times each day and part of the obligation of the cantor was to preach, to read the

---

[43]Modena, *Hayyei yehudah*, fol. 18b; Modena, *Divan*, nos. 17, 73, 74, 86, 141; Boksenboim, *Iggerot*, no. 74. Isaac min haleviim, *Medabber*, pp. 48-49.

[44]Carpi, *Padua 2*, no. 555.

[45]Boksenboim, *Iggerot*, no. 124; see also Assaf *Mekorot 2*, pp. 146, 149.

[46]Brian Pullan, *Rich and Poor in Renaissance Venice* (Cambridge, MA, 1971), p. 548 (1609); Federico Luzzatto, "La communita' ebraica di Conegliano Veneto," *Rassegna Mensile di Israel* 22 (1956): 72-80, 115-125, 178-186, 225-238; E. Morpurgo, "Gli ebrei a Conegliano," *Corriere Israelitico* 48 (1910): 205-210; David Kaufmann, "Dr. Israel Conegliano," *Jaresbericht der Landes-Rabbinierschule in Budapest* (1894-1895): 5.

[47]BL Or. 5396, 93b-94a; Boksenboim, *Iggerot*, no. 59; Moise Soave, "Sara Coppio Sullam," *CI* 15 (1876): 197, note 2; Assaf, *Mekorot 4*, pp. 51-52.

[48]Assaf, *Mekorot 2*, pp. 176, 208.

Torah, and to teach Jewish law.[49] In the evenings synagogues and study societies offered regular lecture series on biblical texts.[50]

Additionally, self-study was an important part of the education of many Jewish adolescents. Modena himself, from the age of thirteen to seventeen, while he pursued uncollected accounts for his father, like other young men his age, attended study sessions when he was in Venice and corresponded with friends in Hebrew or Aramaic about academic matters when he was at home in Montagnana.[51] During this period Modena refined his skills as a poet and Hebrew stylist[52] and began to study new fields such as Jewish mysticism.[53] By eighteen, he was able to begin teaching Torah in Montagnana.[54] At nineteen, at the time of his wedding, he qualified for the degree of *haver*. This was an honor that was conferred on young men in recognition of their academic attainments and was the first step towards the rabbinate.[55] Thus, while later in life Modena would complain about the lack of a permanent teacher to guide him through what he considered could have been his most productive years of study,[56] his autodidactic accomplishments enabled him to become one of the most celebrated teachers and scholars of his day.

In a fascinating, recently discovered report of his daily activities, Modena wrote that each day, after leading morning synagogue services, he taught at a *midrash*, an advanced school, also called *talmud torah*, or *hesger*, where he taught law from the *Shulhan arukh*. Next he went to the *yeshivah* for discussion, which he derisively called *pilpul* – casuistry, and also probably decision making, with the other rabbis. Afterwards he taught until lunch at the *heder*, the crowded elementary school where he did not enjoy teaching. After lunch he taught letter writing for an hour to two children of wealthy lay leaders. He then returned for most of the afternoon teaching letter writing to the children in the *heder*. His work day ended with a half-

---

[49]Boksenboim, *Iggerot*, no. 105; JTSA 8594.
[50]Leon Modena regularly reports his involvement with night classes. See also Assaf, *Mekorot* 2, p. 163.
[51]Boksenboim, *Iggerot*, nos. 2, 3, 4, 5, 6, 11, 136; BL Or. 5396, 32b. Cf. Boksenboim, *Iggerot beit carmi*. nos. 123, 130, 160-161.
[52]Modena, *Divan*, nos. 5, 14, 15, 16, 47; Blau, *Kitvei*, no. 25; Boksenboim, *Iggerot*, nos. 1, 10, 137, 221; cf. BL Or. 5396, 15a.
[53]Leon Modena, *Ari nohem*, Nehemiah Libowitz, ed. (Jerusalem, 1929), p. 6.
[54]Boksenboim, *Iggerot*, nos. 297, 298, 299.
[55]Reuven Bonfil, *Harabbanut beitaliah bitkufat harenasans* (Jerusalem, 1979), pp. 21-28, 33-34, 40, 47, 62-63, 111, 216, 237-237.
[56]Modena, *Hayyei yehudah*, fol. 8b; *Midbar yehudah*, fol. 4a; *Boksenboim, Iggerot*, no. 9.

hour sermon at the synagogue. Among these activities he also had to squeeze in time to prepare his lessons and sermons and to answer letters and to write responsa.[57]

Ironically, however, as a tired and overworked teacher himself, Modena had no time or money for the education of his own sons.[58] Thus, at early ages they chose other priorities, and their Hebrew studies were pursued on an irregular basis. At the age of eleven, Modena's middle son Isaac relegated his Jewish education to evenings and Christian holidays while he devoted his days to studying how to be a tailor.[59] Isaac's studies included Torah, the laws of tefillin in preparation for his Bar Mitzvah, and Hebrew writing. Typical of many parents, then as now, by the time Isaac was thirteen in 1607, Modena was not pleased with his progress and characterized a letter from the boy as written "...with the hands of a pig and great difficulty, for his heart turns to evil during the whole day and he seems to count all sins as allowed. And he listens to me like a deaf man; moreover I am tired and over worked by all my occupations...."[60] Modena's oldest son Mordechai, who at fifteen was working at a store in Venice and studying on his own, was criticized by his father for basic errors in spelling, including spelling *holekh*, the word for "going," with a *het* instead of a *khaf* and representing a "t" a *tet* and not a *tav:* "...your letter which I received and read is half a man, half a goat, and as a whole beast. The upper part is a man because it is well and clearly expressed (I did not know who was speaking until I was told). The lower part is a goat since its language is poor like a goat...and the whole is a beast, because the letter from the first to the last line is full of mistakes and misspelled letters."[61] Nevertheless, as a productive student, Mordechai was able to keep the records of the store in which he worked in Hebrew,[62] to become a teacher and preacher,[63] and to write Hebrew poems, one of which was published, testimony to the

---

[57]Boksenboim, *Iggerot*, no. 105, for a complete translation see the historical notes to *Hayyei yehudah*, fol. 15b (pp. 214-215).

[58]For a description of the education of Jewish girls in Italy, see my forthcoming paper on this subject, to appear in a publication of the Harvard University Center for Jewish Studies, edited by Bernard Cooperman.

[59]Boksenboim, *Iggerot*, nos. 47, 92; Jews were not allowed to engage in tailoring according to Pullan, *Rich and Poor*, pp. 551 and 555.

[60]Boksenboim, *Iggerot*, no. 85; Franz Kobler, *Jewish Letters Through the Ages* 2 (New York, 1952), p. 411.

[61]*Ibid.*

[62]Boksenboim, *Iggerot*, no. 82.

[63]Modena, *Hayyei*, fols. 15a-b.

potential of self-study.[64] Similarly, Modena's philandering half brother Abraham Parenzo managed to acquire enough training to be able to correspond in Hebrew and Aramaic and his other half brother Samuel Hezekiah, who was even more derelict, was able to earn his living as a teacher.

Modena's Aids for Self-Study

Modena knew what it meant to be a part-time student and to be torn between the desire to study and the obligation to earn a living. Hence, he devoted much of his early literary effort to meeting the needs of young Jewish students who could not devote all their efforts to full time study. He wrote several Hebrew books which he intended to be practical works, combining topics of popular interest with Hebrew prose and rabbinic scholarship. The books were enriched by his experience as a teacher and reflected his desire to draw students to the study of Hebrew and his own need for additional income. These writings also helped many inexperienced teachers develop an approach to teaching Hebrew which would be appealing to students whose first priority was not always the study of Jewish texts.

Sod yesharim

In 1594/95 Modena's *Sod yesharim* was published. The book was divided into three parts: a collection of 100 *segullot*, which he described as "secrets, marvelous cures, and amazing things," 50 riddles and their solutions, and a curriculum of daily study. In the preface Modena clearly stated his premise:

> To educate the young, I put this curriculum (*seder*) here because the nature of young boys is to pursue the magic formulas (*segullot*) and the riddles which are written in this book. By means of these they will see this wonderful curriculum and will work on it. This way they will find comfort for their souls which desire spiritual matters.[65]

The first section of cures, remedies, and magic translated from Galen, Italian folklore, and popular Italian books,[66] included such

---

[64]Modena, *Galut yehudah.*

[65]This text is reproduced in Leon Nemoy, "A Hitherto Undescribed Edition of Leon da Modena's *Sod yesharim*," p. 48. Cf. Modena, *Hayyei yehudah*, fols. 20a and historical note w.

[66]Modena owned *Magiche illusione*, see Clemente Ancona, "L'inventario dei beni di Leon da Modena," *Bulletino dell istituto di storia della societa' e dello stato veneziano* 10 (1967): 256-267. This magic shows no relation to talmudic or later Jewish magic such as *Sepher harazim* or *Sepher raziel hamalakh.*

formulas as how to remember one's daily lessons.[67] Modena also described sign language for using Hebrew as a secret code with most of the letters being indicated by Hebrew mnemonics such as signaling the letter *'ayin* with the eye, *'ayin*.[68]

In the second section, many of the riddles involved advanced Hebrew and biblical studies, for example:

Q: Your father is my father, your grandmother is my husband, I am your sister, and you are my child..

A: The daughters of Lot are speaking to their children.[69]

Q: Subtract thirty [*sheloshim*] from thirty and you have sixty left?

A: From the word *sheloshim* remove the *lamed*, which has a numerical value of thirty, and the word which remains is the word for sixty, *shishim*.[70]

Q: It is round and not square, fixed in your hand, flip it over and it will walk on all fours.

A: A spear, *romah*, when the letters are reversed it becomes an ass, *hamor*.[71]

Modena also included in Hebrew translation some classical riddles, such as:

Reuben, Simon, and Levy with their three wives, Sarah, Rebecca, and Rachel, are traveling and want to cross a river in a boat which can only hold a man and his wife with no one else to pilot the boat from side to side and each man is too suspicious of his wife to leave her alone with a man. How is it done?[72]

While Modena's answer to this riddle may be interesting, two manuscript reactions to it provide a fascinating opportunity to see the effect Modena's writing had on his readers.

Modena's solution, which does work, is as follows:

Reuben crosses with Sarah his wife and leaves her and comes and takes Simon and they cross. Reuben stays with his wife and Simon returns and takes Rebecca his wife and crosses with her and leaves her and returns and gets Levy and they cross. Simon stays with his wife and Levy returns and takes Rachel his wife and crosses with her.

---

[67] Modena, *Sod yesharim*, formula no. 3.
[68] Modena, *Sod yesharim*, formula no. 29.
[69] Modena, *Sod yesharim*, riddle no. 28
[70] Modena, *Sod yesharim*, riddle no. 15
[71] Modena, *Sod yesharim*, riddle no. 21.
[72] Modena, *Sod yesharim*, riddle no. 49.

In the margins of one of the first editions of *Sod yesharim*, now at the British Library, a contemporary hand penned in an alternative solution:

> It is not correct. Simon cannot cross and leave his wife with Levy so it should be done like this: Sarah and Rebecca will cross, Rebecca will return and cross with Rachel, Rachel will return and stay with Levy, her husband. Then Reuben and Simon will cross and Simon will return with Rebecca. Then Simon and Levy will cross and Sarah will return and Sarah will cross with Rebecca. Rebecca will return and then Rebecca and Rachel will cross.[73]

Another alternative solution, also in a contemporary hand, is found in the margins of a complete manuscript copy of *Sod yesharim* which is now in the Kaufmann collection in Budapest:

> Reuben crosses with Sarah his wife; then Reuben returns and gets off the boat and Rebecca and Rachel get on; then Rachel returns and gets off the boat; and Reuben and Simon get on; then Simon comes with Rebecca his wife; then Rebecca gets off the boat; then Levy gets on the boat with Simon; then Sarah comes and takes Rebecca; then Levy comes and takes Rachel his wife and they cross.[74]

These three different solutions show much about the assumptions which their authors took with them when reading a simple riddle. Modena's solution, which probably was translated from a popular Italian version, chivalrously never permits a woman to have to steer the boat. The unstated but dominant concern of the authors of both the other solutions was not chivalry but halakhah. So when the author of the solution in the British Library said: "It is not correct," he did not mean that this solution would not get the people across the river according to the terms of the riddle, but rather he meant that in doing so it would incur a violation of Jewish law. The unstated concern for the authors of both additional solutions is found in Kiddushin 4:12 (80b) where the Mishnah reads:

> A man must not be alone with two women, but one woman may be alone with two men. R. Simon says, even one man may be alone with two women so as long as his wife is with him, and he may sleep with them in an inn since his wife watches him....

---

[73]Modena, *Sod yesharim*, fol. 14a.

[74]Kaufmann A226, p. 129. In this manuscript the names Abraham, Isaac, and Jacob were used instead of Reuben, Simon, and Levy, as in the other versions of the riddle. Also in the manuscript the verb is usually masculine singular even when referring to a feminine or a plural subject.

Modena's solution is therefore incorrect because it leaves a man alone with two women: Levy is with Rebecca and Rachel, his wife, which would be allowed according to R. Simon, who permitted a man to be alone with two women as long as his wife is one of them, but not according to the first anonymous teaching of the Mishnah, which does not allow a woman to be alone with two men. Similarly, according to Modena's solution, on the other side, Reuben is found with Sarah and Rebecca, his wife. On the surface, Modena's solution appears benign compared with what the author of the British Library solution proposed. There it happens twice that one woman is left with three men. At the beginning this is the position of Rachel and at the end it is Sarah's. The logic according to the later solution is that three men can be trusted to act properly more than two women and that men make better chaperones than women. Indeed, this is the stated thinking in the Gemara to Kiddushin where it is taught that *venashim daatan kalot alehen*, "women are simple minded." Rashi explicitly stated that the reason a man may be with two women is that "because they are simple minded and it is easy for the two of them to be seduced without one being afraid that the other will do the same thing." Rashi then went on to say that a man would be too embarrassed to do such a thing in front of another man. Further, the Gemara allows for three men to accompany one woman if the men are scholars. In fact, the Gemara requires that on the road there must be three man traveling with a woman so that if one man must leave to relieve himself there will still be two men accompanying the woman. However, while following halakhah, the solution in the Kaufmann manuscript allows for one woman to pilot the boat alone, for one woman to be alone with three men, and for two women to be alone on the shore together. All the solutions allow a woman to be left alone by the side of the river, showing that they all thought it would be better to leave a woman alone by the side of a river at the mercy of who or what might come along than with another known man.[75] Interestingly, Modena's

---

[75]The similar work of Jacob Heilpronn, *Shoshanat ya'akov* (Venice, 1623), must be studied further. It is interesting to note that manuscript versions of Modena's riddles were also circulated among the Jews of Yemen. One researcher of Yemenite Jewish folklore reported many of Modena's riddles exactly as they appear in *Sod yesharim* as oral traditions, "from the mouth of the people" created by Jews from the East whose Hebrew was influenced by Arabic; Yehudah Ratzhaby, "Ahudah na," *Yeda'-'am* 2 (1954): 36-42; cf. Dan Pagis, *'Al sod hatum* (Jerusalem, 1986), pp. v, 17-19, 49-50, 60, 72.

contemporaries still discussed these issues and rabbinic texts in several responsa.[76]

In the third section of *Sod yesharim* Modena offered a curriculum for self-study. In this curriculum Modena apportioned on a weekly basis the study of Torah, Prophets, Writings, and Mishnah so that by the end of a year each of these works would be completely covered. Modena assured his readers, citing a rabbinic dictum, "a three-fold cord would be created which could not be easily broken." He introduced the curriculum with an overview of Jewish education. He wrote that the rabbis of old had advised that each student's day be divided into three parts: Bible, Mishnah, and Gemara.[77] Undoubtedly reflecting his own extensive experiences studying with teachers from Safed, he noted that recently in the Land of Israel a method of study had been devised for the benefit of students which would lessen the burden of studying Gemara, *lehakel me'alehem 'iyyun begemara*. Here Modena's curriculum with its emphasis on Mishnah instead of Gemara reflects the growing influence of the Jewish mystics of Safed for whom, in addition to the attempt at regular use of Hebrew in conversation with each other,[78] the Mishnah was central to their course of studies and their contemplative exercises. Joseph Caro's (1488-1570) *maggid*, his mentor-angel, whom he identified with the Mishnah as well as the Shekhinah, God's presence, revealed itself to him usually during or after a session of Mishnah study. Many other kabbalists of Safed, such as Abraham Galante, Moses Galante, Abraham Berukhim, Solomon Shlomiel, Isaac Luria (1534-1572), Joseph Ashkenazi, Hayyim Vital (1543-1620), and Moses Cordovero (1543-1570), also pursued the regular study of Mishnah on a daily and weekly basis, orally, to musical tunes, in groups, and especially on the Sabbath. Caro tended to emphasis the study of large quantities of Mishnah while Vital stressed the

---

[76]Joseph Colon, *Sheelot uteshuvot* (Jerusalem, 1973), no. 160; Maharam Padova, *Sheelot uteshuvot* (Cracow, 1882; Jerusalem, 1980), no. 26; Judah Minz, *Sheelot uteshuvot (ibid)*, no. 6; Yacov Boksenboim, ed. *Sheelot uteshuvot matanot baadam* (Tel Aviv, 1983), no. 161.

[77]T. B. Kiddushin 30a: *Le'olam yeshalesh adam shenotav shelish bemikra shelish bemishnah shelish betalmud.*

[78]Modena, *Midbar yehudah*, fols. 79a-80a; Schecter, "Safed," p. 294; Lawrence Fine, *Safed Sprituality* (New York, 1984), p. 38: "A person ought to converse in Hebrew with the associates at all times." This is one of the few rules of behavior not regularly repeated in several of the collections. Ancona 7, fol. 6a: *Lo yedaber 'im hahaverim beshabatot veyom tov verosh hodesh ele lashon hakodesh 'im yod'im.* "Do not speak with the Associates on Shabbat, holidays, and new moons except in Hebrew with those who know it." Clearly a different tone than the first admonition on the same subject.

repetition of short sections. Some considered memorization of the Mishnah to be essential, others engaged in serious textual criticism of it. The study of Mishnah was seen as having spiritual as well as redemptive qualities.[79] Although most of the kabbalists of Safed were also adept at the study of Gemara and some spiritual regimens included the study of Gemara (Moses Cordovero suggested covering it three times every twelve months!), voices among them were heard suggesting that those who could not understand the study of halakhah concentrate on the study of Torah, legal judgments, rabbinic homilies, and Kabbalah. Gemara was omitted from the lists of texts covered in some of the kabbalistic regimens of Safed.[80] From Modena's own remarks it is apparent that his curriculum was intended for remedial purposes for students with difficulties in the basics of Bible and Mishnah and who were not yet ready for Gemara study. Although later Modena would be known for his critique of Kabbalah,[81] it is important to see here, as elsewhere, its influence upon him and his curriculum.[82] Modena would demonstrate his own need for such a curriculum when he gave it to his son Mordechai to help him structure a self-study program.[83]

---

[79]David Tamar, "'Al hahevrot shel tzfat," *Mehkarim betoledot hayehudim beeretz yisrael uveitaliah* (Jerusalem, 1970), pp. 96-97; Lawrence Fine, "Recitation of Mishnah as a Vehicle for Mystical Inspiration: A Contemplative Technique taught by Hayyim Vital," *Revue des Etudes Juives* 141 (1982): 183-199; idem. *Safed Spirituality*, pp. 22, 43, 51, 55, 68; R. J. Zwi Werblowsky, *Joseph Karo: Lawyer and Mystic* (London, 1962), p. 272; Samuel Aboab, *Sefer zikhronot*, in Assaf, *Mekorot* 2, p. 140.

[80]Lawrence Fine, "The Study of Torah as a Rite of Theurgical Contemplation," *Approaches to Judaism in Medieval Times* 3 (Atlanta: Scholars Press, 1988), 38-39; *idem.*, *Safed Spirituality*, pp. 43, 68, 51, 55.

[81]Howard Adelman, "Rabbi Leon Modena and the Christian Kabbalists," *Renaissance Rereadings: Intertext and Context* (Urbana, 1988), Maryanne Cline Horowitz, Anne J. Cruz, and Wendy A. Furman, eds., pp. 271-287.

[82]In an article on spiritual regimens, Zeev Gries suggested that books like Modena's were even influenced stylistically by the short imperative sentences of the kabbalistic regimen vita literature, Zeev Gries, "'Itzuv sifrut hehanhagah ha'ivrit bemifneh hameah hashesh-'esreh uvemeah hashevah-'esreh umashma'uto hahistorit," *Tarbitz* 56 (1987): 574.

[83]Boksenboim, *Iggerot*, no. 85. The translator did not understand this reference, Kobler, *Letters* 2, pp. 411-412.

Tzemah tzaddik

In 1600 Modena published *Tzemah tzadik,* a Hebrew version of the most popular Italian book of the period, *Fior di virtù.*[84] *Tzemah tzadik* was devoted to discussions of virtues and their corresponding vices, such as happiness and sadness, peace and anger, kindness and cruelty, generosity and stinginess, and each chapter was supported by copious quotations from ancient authors. Sometimes, Modena substituted quotations from Christian sources with passages from Jewish texts. Other times, he retained the quotation but removed the Christian attribution. For example, the anonymous definition of *gemilut hasadim* in Modena's translation was identical to the definition of mercy attributed to Augustine in the original: "To have compassion in one's heart for other people's misfortune."[85]

Modena's most important addition was his introduction, which stated that the highest virtue for Jews was to fulfill the commandments of the Torah. The contrast between this and the first six chapters which stated, in Hebrew translation, that the highest virtues were love of God, faith, and hope, raises a question as to how much Modena's alterations affected the substance of *Fior di Virtù.* Most of the quotations in it were attributed to classical pagan literature. Moreover, the Christian texts cited were used to illustrate mainly general ethical values.[86] Thus, for Modena the aesthetic qualities, the great popularity, and the neutral outlook made *Fior di Virtu'* an ideal medium for attracting Jewish readers to a Hebrew text and Jewish citations.

More nevukhim bikhtivah bilshonenu hakadosh

In 1605 while living in Ferrara Modena turned in earnest to a project which for over ten years he had felt would be of benefit to students because, in his view, it had not been done before. He undertook what he would call "Guide for the Perplexed in Writing in our Holy

---

[84]*Fior di virtù* appeared in 66 editions while Boccaccio's *Decameron* and Dante's *Divine Comedy* only appeared in 15 editions each. It also was translated into almost every European language.

[85]Modena, *Tzemah tzadik,* chapter 12; Nicholas Fersin, *The Florentine Fior di Virtu' of 1491* (Washington, D. C., 1953), p. 32; cf. *Fior di Virtu'* (Napoli, 1870).

[86]Lessing Rosenwald, "Introduction," *The Florentine Fior,* p. v; Carlo Frati, "Ricerche sul 'Fiore di Virtù,'" *Sudj di Filologia Romanza* 6 (1893): 247-447; Maria Corti, "Le fonti del *Fiore di Virtu'* e la teoria della 'nobiltà' nel duecento," *Giornale Storico della Letterature italiana* 136 (1959): parte 2, 1-82.

Language."[87] In preparation, he wrote to his colleagues asking for five or six short samples of their best letters on different subjects as well as for some of their poems, making it clear however that their names would not appear on the letters and that he did not have "beans to give as payment."[88] He explained that he wanted to use these as examples "to teach the children of Israel the way of writing in our language which has almost been erased from the earth, the creation of a letter, its arrangement, and its rhetoric."[89] In addition, he hoped to include examples of writing such as contracts, minutes, memoranda, commentary, responsa, endorsements, exegesis ("with and without errors"), treatises, prayers, ethics, proverbs, and jokes, as well as simple, serious, bombastic, and free-style writing.

Some of the rules Modena drafted in preparation for the books provide insight into his Hebrew literary style, for example,

- Do not cite a complete biblical verse.
- Above all it is necessary to know grammar, through experience or expertise, in matters of the verbs, the pronominal suffixes, and the tenses.
- Be careful of Song of Songs, of making holy profane, and of using praises of God for flesh and blood.
- Consider to whom you are writing, whether it is a Talmud scholar, a philosopher, a Bible expert, or an ignoramus.
- Do not use words ambiguously.
- Do not use the same word two different ways in the same letter.
- He also planned to write against the convention that a biblical verse with bad connotations should not be used in a good context.[90]

On an eight day trip to Venice in July 1606, Modena, who was now two-thirds finished with this project, heard that his former teacher, Samuel Archivolti, whom he had asked to contribute letters for this

---

[87]He also called it *More hanevukhim likhtov yosher divrei emet*, Boksenboim, *Iggerot*, no. 75.
[88]Boksenboim, *Iggerot*, no. 89.
[89]Boksenboim, *Iggerot*, no. 76.
[90]Among those he hoped to include were the late Joseph Arli (whose letters he possessed), Samuel Archivolti, Barukh Simhah Calimani of Correggio (who had written an article on letter writing which had never been published), the late Judah Moscato, two members of the Sanguini family of Modena, Jacob Segre, a rabbi of Casala Monferrato, and Moses Cohen Porto, BL Or. 5396, fols. 135b, 136b, 137b, 138a, 141a, 143a, 145b; Boksenboim, *Iggerot*, nos. 76, 78, 79, 80, 81, 87, 88, 89; pp. 343-345.

book, was preparing a work for teaching Hebrew composition and was using similar materials and methods as Modena. Modena became panic stricken because he thought Archivolti's work would surpass his own. Also Modena was afraid that he would be embarrassed for abandoning his own work without having completed it. He communicated his fears to Archivolti, expressing his hope that what he had heard was not true, and advising Archivolti that he had kept a copy of his letter to Archivolti from the fall of 1605 in which he had described this project. There is no evidence of Archivolti's response to Modena's letter nor did he ever publish a sequel to *Arugat habosem*. During the next year Modena continued to work on his *Moreh*, following up on requests he had made for sample letters over a year earlier. Like anyone trying to impose deadlines on scholars he had to cajole his busy writers: "If the sages of the present refuse their wheat, corn, and wine, then I (an ignoramus) will provide grain to all the people from my saddlebag."[91] He would finish the book and record its completion in his autobiography and in two letters, but it was never published, and, except for some rough drafts, it is no longer extant.[92]

Galut yehudah

Another result of Modena's interest in Hebrew composition was that between 1604 and 1607 he began to write in Italian a short summary of the rules of Hebrew grammar to serve as an introduction to his vocabulary list of biblical and rabbinic terms, *Galut yehudah*. In his Italian preface, in addition to dismissing the old method of translating into a Judeo-Italian jargon as clumsy and graceless, he stated his views on the role of teaching grammar as part of Jewish education:

> I have considered many times the way that we usually teach the interpretation of our scripture to our children; it is perforce exclusively practical, by means of reading and explaining word by word in the language of the country we are living in, without first teaching the rules of grammar – as the others do – because there are those who think that this would be a waste of time....[93]

---

[91]Boksenboim, *Iggerot*, nos. 79, 80.

[92]Boksenboim, *Iggerot*, nos. 88 and 161. For other examples of guides to Hebrew letter writing, see David Ruderman, "An Examplary Sermon from the Classroom of a Jewish Teacher in Renaissance Italy," *Italia* 1 (1978): 12.

[93]Leon Modena, *Galut yehudah* (Venice, 1612), "L'autore," cf. Nave, *Leket ketavim*, pp. 285-286; Modena, *Hayyei yehudah*, fols. 15b, 20a, 26b, 37b, and historical notes.

Lev ha-aryeh

At the same time as *Galut yehudah,* Modena published *Lev ha-aryeh,* a Hebrew course in memory improvement with particular emphasis on the Hebrew language. He was especially proud that his use of non-Jewish ideas in the serive of Hebrew was the first of its kind. *Lev ha-aryeh* was a preface to a list of the 613 commandments according to Maimonides. The book was filled with references to the study of Hebrew, Jewish life, rabbinic literature, and devices for remembering the Hebrew letters. Thus it was intended to provide lesson ideas for elementary Hebrew teachers as well as to amuse advanced students who might need some motivation to read and an understand the Hebrew.[94]

Conclusion

In 1618, when he was forty-seven years old, at the beginning of his autobiography, despite all his complaining about teaching, Modena still took great comfort in the rabbinic maxim, "Students are called sons."[95] In 1624 he claimed that schools had been established for him to teach at in several synagogues in Venice as well as in other communities in Italy.[96] Yet, in 1639, he wrote with great bitterness:

> I have grown old, and as is the law of the masters of Torah in Italy, particularly in Venice, their houses are empty and there is nobody to look after them.[97]

Nevertheless, old and abandoned, Modena still could encourage a young man to become a teacher of children.

> And now to teach children God's instruction, my son, do not hate and do not despise His work because ultimately it is a divine task....In any case, one who teaches another person so that he achieves knowledge will himself acquire greater understanding, as the sages said, '[I learned] from my pupils more than from all others.'[98]

---

[94]Cf. Modena, *Hayyei yehudah,* fols. 15b, 20a, 37b, and historical notes.

[95]Sifre, Deut. par. 34, ed. L. Finkelstein, (New York, 1969), p. 61; see Assaf, *Mekorot* 2 p. 209, note 4.

[96]Leon Modena, *Beit lehem yehudah* (Venice, 1625), Introduction.

[97]Boksenboim, *Iggerot,* no. 131.

[98]Avot 2:14. Boksenboim, *Iggerot,* no. 134.

Part Twelve
JUDAISM IN THE MIDDLE AGES
PHILOSOPHERS: JUDAH HALEVI

36

Judah Halevi and Karaism[1]

Daniel J. Lasker
Ben-Gurion University of the Negev

According to a letter written by Judah Halevi, discovered in the Cairo Geniza, the first edition of Halevi's *Book of Kuzari* was composed as a response to a Karaite from Christian Spain. Halevi seems to have been none too pleased with this literary effort, since, in the letter, he dissociated himself from the tract which he had written.[2] Nonetheless, in the final edition of the *Kuzari*, the only

---

[1]The preparation of this paper was made possible by grants from the Memorial Foundation for Jewish Culture and from the Research Committee of the Humanities and Social Sciences Faculty of Ben-Gurion University. My friend and colleague, Dr. Howard T. Kreisel, offered me his usual insightful comments.
[2]Shlomo Dov Goitein, "Autographs of Yehuda Hallevi," *Tarbiẓ*, 25 (1955-56): 393-412 (Hebrew); *Idem*, "The Biography of Rabbi Judah Ha-Levi in Light of the Cairo Geniza Documents," *Proceedings of the American Academy for Jewish Research*, 28 (1959): 41-56; David H. Baneth, "Some Remarks on the Autographs of Yehudah Hallevi and the Genesis of the *Kuzari*," *Tarbiẓ* 26 (1956-57): 297-303 (Hebrew). Both Goitein and Baneth assume that Halevi's Karaite correspondent was a philosopher, explaining thereby why Halevi wrote what they consider to have been the first edition of the *Kuzari*, i.e., a tract which criticizes both Karaism and philosophy. Halevi's letter, however, has no such indication, and what Halevi's exact motives were in writing the non-extant first edition of the *Kuzari* remains unknown. In addition, the extent of that edition and the reason for Halevi's later disapproval of it are matters of dispute among scholars; see, in addition to the articles mentioned above, Yohanan Silman, *Thinker and Seer*, Ramat Gan, 1985 (Hebrew); and Shlomo Pines, "Shi'ite Terms and Conceptions in Judah Halevi's *Kuzari*," *Jerusalem Studies in Arabic and Islam*, 2 (1980): 210-217; and see below.

edition known today, a polemic against Karaism was included,[3] and Halevi stated specifically at the beginning of the book that the *Kuzari* was intended to provide answers against the claims of the philosophers, the other religions (i.e, Christianity and Islam), and the Jewish heretics (i.e., the Karaites).[4]

In light of Halevi's anti-Karaite aims, it is somewhat ironic that for many centuries Karaites relied upon Judah Halevi's *Kuzari* as the main source for their own reconstruction of Karaite history.[5] In his

---

[3]While there is no reason to assume that the anti-Karaite chapters of the extant *Kuzari* are not the original ones, it is impossible to establish the exact relationship between the first edition and those chapters, which are found in Judah Ha-Levi, *Kitāb al-Radd wa-'l-Dalīl fī'l-Dīn al-Dhalīl (Al-Kitāb al-Khazarī),* ed. by David H. Baneth, prepared for publication by Haggai Ben-Shammai, Jerusalem, 1977, III:22-63, pp. 112-137. The remaining sections of *Kuzari* III, namely the attack on asceticism (chaps. 1-22, pp. 90-112) and the account of Rabbinic tradition and literature (chaps. 64-74, pp. 137-146), might also be seen as anti-Karaite; see Eliezer Schweid, *Ta'am Va-Haqashah,* Ramat Gan, 1970, pp. 48-54.

Hartwig Hirschfeld's English translation, *The Kuzari,* 2d ed., New York, 1964, was consulted for this paper, but all direct translations from the Arabic will be my own. The Hebrew translations of Judah ibn Tibbon, *Sefer Ha-Kuzari,* ed. Hirschfeld, Leipzig, 1887 (reprinted, Jerusalem, 1970), and Yehuda Even Shmuel, *Sefer Ha-Kozari,* Tel Aviv, 1972, were consulted as well.

[4]*Al-Khazarī,* p. 3. Halevi referred to the Karaites as *al-khawārij* (dissenters, rebels). Despite Halevi's explicit statement that the Karaites, unlike the Sadducees, are not *minim* (III:65, p. 139), Ibn Tibbon; Even Shmuel; and Nehemia Allony, "The *Kusari* – An Anti-Arabiyyeh Polemic," *Eshel Beer-Sheva,* 2 (1980), p. 142, translated *al-khawārij* as *ha-minim* (Allony added *ha-Qara'im* in parentheses). Judah ben Isaac Cardinal translated it as *ha-Qara'im;* see Allony, "Two Book-Titles from Jewish-Arabic Literature," *Kirjath Sepher,* 38 (1962-63): 115, n. 32 p. 115, n. 22. The contradiction between Ibn Tibbon's translation of *minim* and Halevi's statement in III:65 is the subject of comment by Judah Moscato, *Qol Yehudah,* ad I:1, and Israel of Zamosc, *Oẓar Neḥmad,* ad I:1, neither of whom had the original Arabic in front of him.

Halevi's terminology, however, does not seem to be consistent. In the letter from the Geniza mentioned above (see n. 2), Halevi did refer to the Karaite recipient of his work as being "one of the exponents of heresy *(al-minut)*"; (Goitein's comments in "Autographs," p. 411, were made before the Arabic original of *Al-Khazarī* was available). In III:49, pp. 128-131, Halevi stated a number of times that the Karaite reliance on personal effort *(idjtihād)* and logical analogy *(qiyās;* on these terms, see below) leads to *minut.* On the other hand, in III:65, p. 138, Zadoq and Boethus, founders of Sadduceenism, are said to be the root of the heretics *(khawārij).*

Halevi's three-fold division of the opponents of Rabbinic Judaism may be reflected in a similar classification in Maimonides' Hilkhot Teshuvah, 3:8 (deniers of the Torah).

[5]For a history of Karaite historiography, see Samuel Poznanski's introduction to his edition of Mordecai Sultansky's *Zekher Ẓaddiqim,* Warsaw, 1920, pp. 5-69.

discussion of Rabbinic tradition in *Kuzari* III:65, Halevi asserted that the Karaite schism began in the Second Temple Period and that the Karaites were not Sadducees. At a time when most of his contemporaries were convinced that Karaism was started by the eighth century C.E. disgruntled exilarchic candidate Anan ben David, and that its religious doctrines consisted of revived Sadduceeism,[6] Halevi gave an entirely different interpretation of Karaite origins and religion. Basing himself on the Talmudic account of King Yannai's persecutions (Qiddushin 66a), he stated that, in the generation of Judah Ben Tabbai and Simeon ben Shettah, one of the sages questioned the propriety of Yannai's being both King and High Priest. In response, Yannai's friends advised him to kill or exile the sages. When Yannai hesitated because he was afraid that there would be no one to teach the Torah, his friends replied: "We have the Written Torah and anyone can learn from it; as for the Oral Torah, just ignore it." Yannai took their advice and exiled the sages. Simeon ben Shettah went to Egypt, where he kept the Oral Torah alive, but returned to the Land of Israel when it became apparent that the Written Torah could not be observed by logical analogy *(qiyās)* alone. He was, however, too late to prevent a schism; Karaism, according to Halevi, had already been born.[7] As an additional feature of his account, Halevi distinguished between the Karaites who rejected the Oral Torah and the Sadducees who were the *minim* referred to in the prayers.[8] Anan was not mentioned in this context at all.[9]

When the fifteenth-century Elijah Bashyatchi addressed the question of Karaite origins, it was to Judah Halevi that he turned. Claiming that works written by Karaites did not provide enough information about the origins of Karaism,[10] Bashyatchi used Halevi's account to show the antiquity of his religion. This Karaite's version of the story is slightly different than Halevi's, as might be expected. Bashyatchi wrote that when King Yannai killed the scholars, all of

---

[6]See, for instance, Halevi's younger contemporary, Abraham ibn Daud, *The Book of Tradition (Sefer Ha-Qabbalah),* ed. Gerson D. Cohen, Philadelphia, 1967, pp. 48-50, 91-92.

[7]*Al-Khazarī,* p. 138. Halevi elaborated upon the version of the story in the Talmud; cf. also T. Berakhot, 48a; Josephus, *Antiquities,* 13. 10. 5-7.

[8]*Al-Khazarī,* p. 139; see above, n. 3. According to the Ibn Tibbon translation, one of the differences between Karaites and Sadducees is the formers' belief in world to come; see below, n. 11.

[9]Anan is mentioned only in III:38, p. 121.

[10]See Zvi Ankori, "Elijah Bashyachi: An Inquiry into his Traditions Concerning the Beginnings of Karaism in Byzantium," *Tarbiz,* 25 (1956/57): 183-186 (Hebrew), for a discussion of the significance of this fact.

whom believed in the one Written Torah, only Simeon ben Shettah survived. He escaped to Egypt, made up the idea of an Oral Torah, and eventually returned to the Land of Israel. Simeon was able to impose his new religion upon a majority of the people because he had the backing of his sister the queen and because all the other scholars had been killed. "If only all the scholars had remained alive and we were all one people," Bashyatchi opined wistfully, "or if only Simeon ben Shettah had been killed with the rest of the sages we would be all one people." Furthermore, according to Bashyatchi, most Rabbanites had distorted history, making Karaism into a medieval sectarian heresy. Halevi, however, told the truth because he was afraid to lie to the King of the Khazars.[11]

Bashyatchi's reconstruction of Karaite history on the basis of Halevi's account in the *Kuzari*, with appropriate later embellishments, such as the assertion that Judah ben Tabbai was loyal to the one Written Torah, became the standard Karaite explanation of the schism between the two Jewish groups.[12] The recent discovery of the Dead Sea Scrolls has strengthened the Karaite claim of a Second Temple origin of the schism, but for years Judah Halevi's *Kuzari* had been their main evidence of Karaite antiquity.[13]

* * *

[11]Elijah Bashyatchi, *Adderet Eliyyahu*, Odessa, 1860 (reprinted, Israel, 1966), introduction (unpaginated). According to Bashyatchi, Halevi distinguished between the Sadducees who denied the afterlife, and the Karaites who accepted it. This statement does not appear in the original Arabic but is present in Ibn Tibbon's translation; see Hirschfeld, *Sefer Ha-Kuzari*, p. xxxix, n. 115. The difference between Karaite and Sadducean eschatology is often cited by Karaite authors as proof that Karaism is not related to Sadduceeism; see my "The Destiny of Man in Karaite Philosophy," *Daat*, 12 (winter, 1984): 5-13 (Hebrew).

[12]See, for instance, Caleb Afendopolo, *Sefer Asarah Ma'morot*, quoted in Mordecai ben Nisan, *Sefer Dod Mordecai*, Israel, 1966, pp. 44-51; Simhah Isaac Luzki, *Sefer Oraḥ Ẓaddiqim*, in *ibid.*, pp. 85-86.

[13]See Poznanski (above, n. 5). It should always be remembered that from the Karaite perspective the issue is *not* when did Karaism break away from Rabbanism, but when did Rabbanism break away from true (i.e., Karaite) Judaism. For the Karaites, their religion was founded at Sinai.

For modern Karaite reconstructions of Karaite history, see, e.g., Simon Szyszman, *Le Karaïsme*, Lausanne, 1980, pp. 20-48; Joseph Algamil, *Toledot Ha-Yahadut Ha-Qara'it*, vol. 1, Ramle, 1979, pp. 38-63; Hayyim Halevi, *Qiẓẓur Ha-'Adderet*, Ramle, 1982, 113-122 (this is a mimeographed booklet for use by Karaite pupils).

The relation between the Dead Sea Scrolls and Karaism is a matter of debate among scholars; see, e.g., Naphtali Wieder, *The Judean Scrolls and Karaism*, London, 1962; Andre Paul, *Écrits de Qumran et sectes juives aux premiers siècles de l'Islam*, Paris, 1969.

Undoubtedly, the Karaite reliance upon Halevi's reconstruction of history was based on its compatibility with their own belief that the Karaite-Rabbanite schism dates back to the Second Temple. It is possible, however, that the Karaites were predisposed to cite the *Kuzari* because they detected in Judah Halevi a certain sympathy for Karaism.[14] On the face of it, Halevi was a committed anti-Karaite polemicist, one in a long line of Rabbanite writers beginning with Saadia Gaon. Nevertheless, there are a number of indications in the *Kuzari* that Halevi found Karaism attractive. For instance, the whole first section of the *Kuzari* is based solely upon the Bible, with no references to Rabbinic works. The *haver* stated in I:115: "My talk with you from the beginning has been concerned with what is explicit in the text of the words of the prophets."[15] In other words, the King, who converted to Judaism at the beginning of the second part of the *Kuzari*, could, theoretically, just as easily have become a Karaite.

In IV:3, Halevi discussed different opinions of the divine glory *(kavod)*. One view held that the *kavod* is a thin body which can assume different shapes according to the divine will. The other view maintained that the glory is the sum of the angels and the divine beings. The first of these opinions is that of Saadia, while the second one is that of the Karaites.[16] For Halevi, apparently either interpretation of the *kavod* was acceptable.[17]

---

[14]Ankori, "Elijah Bashyachi," p. 185, states that Byzantine Karaism was drawn especially to the works of Abraham ibn Ezra, Judah Halevi, and Maimonides. It is of interest that while some Karaites argued that Ibn Ezra and Maimonides, both strong opponents of Karaism, were secretly supporters of this sect, no such claim was made for Halevi despite what will be argued here, namely that Halevi did indeed sympathize with Karaism. Of course, Ibn Ezra, as a Biblical commentator, and Maimonides, as a halakhic authority, were much more important authors for the Karaites than Judah Halevi; see Ankori, *ibid.*, pp. 60-63, 194-199.

[15]*Al-Khazari*, p. 40.

[16]See Alexander Altmann, "Saadya's Theory of Revelation: its Origin and Background," in *Studies in Religious Philosophy and Mysticism*, London, 1969 (originally published in *Saadya Studies*, ed. by Erwin I. J. Rosenthal, Manchester, 1943), pp. 154-55; see also my "The Philosophy of Judah Hadassi the Karaite," in *Shlomo Pines Jubilee Volume* Part I, (*Jerusalem Studies in Jewish Thought*, 7, 1988): 487-489 (Hebrew).

[17]*Al-Khazari*, IV:3, pp. 158-59. Harry A. Wolfson, "Hallevi and Maimonides on Prophecy," in *Studies in the History of Philosophy and Religion*, II, Cambridge, Mass. and London, 1977 (originally published in *Jewish Quarterly Review*, 32 [1943]: 345-370; 33 [1942]: 49-82), pp. 90-95, maintains that Halevi accepted both views, while Israel of Zamosc, *Ozar Nehmad*, ad IV:3, says that the first view (of Saadia) is Halevi's choice. In any event, Halevi did not specifically reject the Karaite view (which Wolfson sees as Philonic in origin).

Halevi sided with the Karaites in another disagreement with Saadia, in this case concerning the rationality of the revelational commandments. Saadia maintained that those commandments which are not enjoined by reason are at least not rejected by it.[18] The Karaites, however, considered certain actions to be rejected by reason, and were it not for the divine command to observe them, one would be obligated to refrain from them. Circumcision and the slaughter of animals were two prime examples of this type of commandment.[19] In III:7, Halevi stated that the divine actions are rejected by reason (*'aql*) and gave circumcision as an example of a commandment which is far from logical analogy *(qiyās)*.[20] A similar opinion is offered in III:53 (in the polemic against Karaism) about the sacrifices.[21] Halevi and the Karaites agreed, then, that God could command actions which seemed to be at variance with reason.

Halevi's desire to move to the Land of Israel may also have been affected by Karaism. In the late ninth century, Daniel al-Qūmisī, one of the three important early Karaite leaders, propounded a theory of hastening the messiah by a Jewish return to the Land of Israel. He even set out a practical plan – each diaspora Jewish community would send five families to the Land of Israel and support them so that they could remain in the Holy Land, and he himself immigrated to the Land of Israel.[22] The *"avele zion"* (mourners of Zion) movement was apparently a predominantly Karaite enterprise, and in the tenth and eleventh centuries (until the Crusades), there was a vibrant Karaite community

---

[18]*Emunot ve-De'ot*, III:1-2; see Alexander (Shimon Zevi) Altmann, "Saadya's Classification of the Law," in Y. L. Maimon (Fishman), ed., *Rav Saadya Gaon*, Jerusalem, 1943, pp. 658-673 (Hebrew); Haggai Ben-Shammai, "The Classification of the Commandments and the Concept of Wisdom in Rav Saadia's Thought," *Tarbiz*, 41 (1971-72): 170-182 (Hebrew).

[19]See, e.g., Ya'qūb al-Qirqisānī, *Kitāb Al-Anwār Wal-Marāqib (The Book of Lights and Watchtowers)*, ed. Leon Nemoy, New York, 1939-1943, II:14, p. 289 (the context is the necessity for revelation since reason ['aql] alone is not sufficient for knowing the correct actions). For a later source, see Aaron ben Elijah, *Ez Ḥayyim*, ed. by Franz Delitzsch, Leipzig, 1841, p. 179.

[20]*Al-Khazarī*, p. 96.

[21]*Ibid.*, pp. 132-135.

[22]Jacob Mann, "A Tract by an Early Karaite Settler in Jerusalem," *Jewish Quarterly Review*, n.s. 12 (1921-22): 257-298; Leon Nemoy, *Karaite Anthology*, New Haven, 1952, pp. 34-39; (*Idem*, "A Pseudo-Qūmisīan Sermon," *Proceedings of the American Academy for Jewish Research*, 43[1976]: 49-105, casts doubt upon the Qumisian provenance of this tract); Haggai Ben-Shammai, "A Fragment of Daniel El-Qūmisī's Commentary on Daniel as a Source for the History of Eretz-Israel," *Shalem*, 3 (1981), pp. 295-307 (Hebrew); Samuel Poznanski, "Reishit Ha-Hityashvut Ha-Qara'it Birushalayim," *Jerusalem* (ed. A. M. Luncz), 10 (1913): 83-116.

in Jerusalem.[23] Therefore, while Halevi's planned journey to the Land of Israel may have been somewhat unusual for a Rabbanite Jew of his time, he certainly had Karaite precedents.[24]

Despite Halevi's possible sympathy to Karaites and Karaism, he still found it necessary to reject their interpretation of Jewish law.[25] His spirited attack on Karaism, however, was possibly more a function of a perceived Karaite threat than a deep-seated antagonism. Karaites arrived in Spain at least by the end of the tenth century.[26] Abu'l-Taras, a student of Yeshua ben Judah (the eleventh century Karaite thinker, student of Yūsuf al-Baṣīr) returned to Spain in the middle of the eleventh century, and by the twelfth century, there must have been a sizable Karaite community there.[27] This can be seen from the following references to Karaites in the works of twelfth century Jewish writers. Halevi's contemporary Joseph ibn Zaddiq quoted long passages from al-Baṣīr's *Kitāb al-Muḥtawī* in his *Sefer Ha-'Olam*

---

[23]Moshe Gil, *Palestine During the First Muslim Period* (634-1099), I, Tel Aviv, 1983, pp. 627-660 (Hebrew); Jacob Mann, *Texts and Studies in Jewish History and Literature*, II, Philadelphia, 1935, pp. 3-127; Haggai Ben-Shammai, "The Karaites," in Joshua Prawer, ed., *The History of Jerusalem. The Early Islamic Period (638-1099)*, Jerusalem, 1987, pp. 163-178 (Hebrew).

[24]There were small communities of Spanish Jewish Rabbanites in the Land of Israel before the time of Judah Halevi, some of whom even converted to Karaism; see Simhah Assaf, "Sources for Jewish History in Spain," *Zion*, 6 (1940-41): 33-45 (Hebrew); Ben-Zion Dinaburg (Dinur), "'Aliyyato shel Rabbi Yehudah Halevi Le-Erez Yisrael," in Simhah Assaf et al, eds., *Minḥah Le-David*, Jerusalem, 1934-35, pp. 157-182; Gil, *Palestine*, p. 646.

[25]Halevi also objected to the Karaite use of Kalam; see *Al-Khazarī*, V:2, p. 191. This difficult passage is discussed by Harry A. Wolfson, *The Philosophy of the Kalam*, Cambridge, Mass., and London, 1976, pp. 86-88. In addition, Halevi criticized the Karaite notion, supported by the citation of I Chron. 28:9, that one must first prove the existence of God before accepting the obligation of the commandments (V:21, p. 227). This view, with the same Biblical prooftext, can be found, e.g., in Judah Hadassi, *Eshkol Ha-Kofer*, Eupatoria, 1836 (reprinted, Westmead, England, 1971), p. 18b; see Georges Vajda, *Al-Kitāb al-Muḥtawī de Yūsuf al-Baṣīr*, ed. by David R. Blumenthal, Leiden, 1985, p. 30, n. 116. Halevi referred to the Karaites also in his discussion of Kalam in V:15, p. 213.

The above three references to Karaite thought (as contrasted with Karaite Halakhah) occur in Part V of the *Kuzari*, which, according to a number of scholars, was written later than the first (anti-Karaite?) edition of the book; see above, n. 2. It would seem, then, that Karaism remained an interest of Halevi throughout the writing of the *Kuzari*.

[26]They are mentioned by the Spanish Muslim historian Ibn Hazm in the middle of the eleventh century; see, Ibn Daud, *The Book of Tradition*, p. xlvi.

[27]*Ibid.*, pp. xlvi-xlvii; but cf. Ankori, "Elijah Bashyachi," pp. 193-194.

Ha-Qatan.[28] Abraham ibn Daud's *Sefer Ha-Qabbalah* was written as an anti-Karaite polemic.[29] Abraham ibn Ezra's commentaries are full of references to Karaites, especially Yefet ben Eli.[30] Judah ben Barzilai al-Barzeloni in his *Perush Sefer Yezirah* also made reference to Karaite views.[31] In addition, according to Maimonides' *Commentary on the Mishnah*, Rabbanites in Spain used to put Karaites to death for heresy.[32] When we add to this information the fact that Halevi originally wrote the *Kuzari* as an answer to a Karaite, we are left with the strong impression that Rabbanite Jews in twelfth-century Spain perceived Karaism as a real threat. It is against this background that we must view Halevi's anti-Karaite polemic.

* * *

Halevi's initial argument against Karaism can be summarized as follows: they try too hard. At first glance, this is Karaism's strongest asset, as the King mentioned at the very beginning of the discussion of Karaism in III:22.[33] The Arabic term rendered here as "trying hard" is *mudjtahadīn*, that is, they use *idjtihād*. *Idjtihād*, namely, personal effort or diligent striving, is an important principle in Islamic law, and it refers to the process by which individuals derive new laws from four sources: holy text *(Qurān)*, tradition *(sunna)*, logical analysis *(qiyās)*, and community practice *(idjmā')*.[34] The early Karaites employed much

---

[28] *Sefer Ha'Olam Ha-Qatan*, ed. S. Horowitz, Breslau, 1903, pp. 44, 47 (in the reprinted edition, no place, no date, pp. 46, 49); see also Harry A. Wolfson, *Repercussions of the Kalam in Jewish Philosophy*, Cambridge, Mass., 1976, pp. 52-72; 121-123.

[29] See Gerson D. Cohen's long Introduction to his edition of *The Book of Tradition*.

[30] P. R. Weiss, "Ibn Ezra, the Karaites and the Halakhah," *Melilah*, 1 (1944): 35-53; 2 (1946): 121-134; 3-4 (1950): 188-203. Despite Ibn Ezra's explicit anti-Karaite stance, later Karaites tried to claim him as a supporter who had been taught by Yefet ben Eli (the tenth-century Karaite Bible commentator); see above, n. 14.

[31] *Perush Sefer Yezirah*, ed. S. J. Halberstam, Berlin, 1885, p. 13. For further references, see Ibn Daud, *The Book of Tradition*, p. xlviii, n. 18.

[32] On Hullin 1:2; for Maimonides' attitude towards Karaites and Karaism see my "The Karaite Influence on Maimonides," to appear in *Sefunot*, 20 (Hebrew), and Gerald J. Blidstein, "*Ha-Gishah la-Qara'im be-Mishnat ha-Rambam*," *Tehumim*, 8 (1986-87), pp. 501-510.

A review of our present knowledge of Spanish Karaism is found in Judah Rosenthal, "Karaites and Karaism in Western Europe," in *Mehqarim U-Meqorot* 1, Jerusalem, 1967, pp. 238-244 (Hebrew); see, also, Martin Schreiner, *Stüdien über Jeschu'a ben Jehuda*, Berlin, 1900, pp. 86-90.

[33] *Al-Khazarī*, p. 112.

[34] The theory of four principles of Islamic law was fully developed by Shafi'i, born in 767, the putative year of Anan's revolt. Elements of this theory, however,

the same legal methodology as did the Muslims, but without the use of tradition *(sunna)*.[35] Only later, when *idjtihād* had led to a certain amount of anarchy in both religions, was its use discontinued both by Muslims and Karaites. At this time the Karaites adopted the concept of tradition *(sevel/sevel ha-yerushah/ha'ataqah)*, but they claimed that it was non-Sinaitic and also that it did not contradict the Written Torah (in contrast to the Rabbanite Oral Law).[36] When Halevi wrote against Karaism in the twelfth century, *idjtihād* was no longer a Karaite legal characteristic. Nevertheless, the memory of *idjtihād* lingered on sufficiently to be considered a prime element of Karaite law and a major characteristic of the Karaite religion.[37]

According to Halevi, the fact that Karaites try harder (i.e., they use *idjtihād*) is a sign of their ultimate weakness. The King of the Khazars, himself, is described twice in the opening passage of the *Kuzari* as striving diligently *(yadjtahedu; idjtahada)* to fulfill the Khazarian religion, which, it may be recalled, was an insufficient form

---

were already in use before Shafiʻi; see Joseph Schacht, *The Origins of Muslim Jurisprudence* (Oxford: Clarendon Press, 1953).

[35]The relation between the Karaite and Islamic *usūl al-fiqh* was apparently noted first by Samuel Poznanski, "Anan et ses écrits," *Revue des Études Juives*, 44 (1902): 182, n. 3; see Ankori, *Karaites in Byzantium*, New York-Jerusalem, 1959, p. 223, n. 38. Karaites presumably did not want to use the word *Qurān* with its Islamic connotations, so they employed the term *naṣṣ* (text) instead; for Yaʻqūb al-Qirqisānī's use of *naṣṣ*, see, e.g., *Al-Anwār*, II:11, p. 101. In Hebrew, the terms were *ketav*, *mashmaʻ*, and *shemaʻ*. For further discussion, see my "Islamic influences on Karaite Origins," to appear in *Studies in Islamic and Judaic Traditions*, II, ed. by William M. Brinner and Stephen D. Ricks.

References to *idjtihād* (in Hebrew *ḥippus*) as a Karaite technique, can be found in Ankori, *Karaites*, pp. 54, n. 72; 209-210; 249; Moshe Zucker, "Fragments from Rav Saadya Gaon's Commentary to the Pentateuch from Mss.," *Sura*, 2 (1955-56): 325 (Hebrew).

[36]Karaites eschewed the term *sunna* for tradition because of its Rabbanite connotations and closeness to the term Mishnah. On *sunna's* being the equivalent of Mishnah, see John Wansbrough, *Quranic Studies*, Oxford, 1977, p. 57; and Judith R. Wegner, "Islamic and Talmudic Jurisprudence, The Four Toots of Islamic Law and Their Talmudic Counterparts," *The American Journal of Legal History*, 26 (1982): 34-39. Saadia used the term *sunna* for tradition; see George Vajda, "Études sur Qirqisâni," *Revue des Études Juives*, 107 (1946-47): 93, n. 47. On the Karaite Hebrew terms, *sevel/sevel ha-yerushah/ha'ataqah*, which all mean "tradition," see Naphtali Wieder, "Three Terms for Tradition," *Jewish Quarterly Review*, 49 (1958-59): 108-121; Ankori, *Karaites*, pp. 223-230. Transmission or tradition apparently replaced consensus as a principle of the law; see Judah Hadassi, *Eshkol Ha-Kofer*, p. 64d.

[37]The development of Karaite legal theory in the period preceding Judah Halevi is discussed by Ankori, *Karaites*, pp. 204-251.

of worship.[38] In I:97 the worshippers of the Golden Calf and those who built high-places *(bamot)* are also described as *mudjtahadīn*.[39] In I:98, *idjtihād* is said to be practiced by the astrologer, the magician, the fire worshipper, the sun worshipper, and dualists.[40] In III:23, dualists, believers in the eternity of the world, worshippers of spirits,[41] hermits, and those who sacrifice their children are described as striving *(mudjtahadūn)* to become close to God.[42] In III:37, even those who worship the stars *(melekhet ha-shamayim)* are characterized as using *idjtihād*, unlike the worshippers of God who follow the commandments.[43] Halevi stated further that the person who has the true religion is like someone who lives in a city and can, therefore, walk without fear of being attacked, whereas the pursuer of personal effort *(idjtihād)* is like the person walking in the desert who is constantly afraid of attack. That person must prepare for any eventuality. Karaites are *mudjtahadūn* because they do not have reliable tradition and need a fortress for their defense. Rabbanites can afford to be lazy, lying on their comfortable couches in the fortified city of the Oral Torah.[44] The Karaites should not be so proud of their *idjtihād*, Halevi argued, because even the non-Jewish nations use this method more than the Karaites do.[45]

While Halevi argued that the Karaite strong point, *idjtihād*, was really a sign of weakness, he also claimed that a possible Rabbanite weak point, namely Rabbinic disagreement, was more apparent than real. The Karaites had argued that there should be no internal

---

[38]*Al-Khazarī* I:1, p. 3.

[39]*Ibid.*, pp. 31-32; the term *qiyās* is also used in the context of the Golden Calf.

[40]*Ibid.*, p. 32.

[41]See Shlomo Pines, "Shi'ite Terms," pp. 196-207.

[42]*Al-Khazarī*, p. 112.

[43]*Ibid.*, p. 120.

[44]*Ibid.*; according to David Kaufman, "R. Yehudah Ha-Levi," in Y. L. Maimon (Fishman), ed., *Rabbi Yehudah Ha-Levi*, Jerusalem, 1940-41 (Hebrew), p. 18, n. 112, Halevi's imagery was borrowed from the Muslim Abu Hamid Al-Ghazali.

Surprisingly, Halevi referred to the *idjtihād* also of the Massoretes, the Rabbinic sages, and the students of the Rabbis; see *Al-Khazarī*, III:31-32, pp. 116-117; III:48, p. 127; III:51, p. 131; III:73, pp. 144, 146. Some of the usages of this term may be ironical since they occur within the context of the anti-Karaite polemic.

[45]*Ibid.*, III:50, p. 131; cf. also IV:23, p. 173, where the Christians and Muslims are portrayed as striving diligently concerning God's unity. Halevi's use of the term *idjtihād* may have been influenced by the works of Abu Bakr Muhammad al-Razi (850-923) as well as by Karaite sources; see Shlomo Pines, "Shi'ite Terms," p. 204.

Rabbinic arguments because the Oral Torah was said to be from Sinai.[46] It is Karaite *idjtihād*, Halevi wrote, not the rabbinic Oral Torah, which leads to anarchy and uncertainty among the worshippers, because, as a matter of fact, the Karaites have more internal dissension than the Rabbanites. Halevi no doubt had in mind Anan's famous dictum (if, in fact, Anan said it), namely, "Search scriptures diligently, and do not rely upon my opinion."[47] This attitude led to the situation described by Ya'qub al-Qirqisani in the tenth century when no two Karaites agreed on anything, a condition which was getting worse every day.[48]

While the allusion to Karaite anarchy was already anachronistic by Halevi's time, he obviously believed that the principle which led to the former situation was still applicable: in the absence of reliable tradition, and a central, legally constituted authority, such as the Sanhedrin, it would follow that ten different Karaites would have ten different opinions, none of whom would be convinced that even his own opinion was correct. If the Karaites finally agree on something, Halevi continued, they say it is because they received the tradition from Anan or Benjamin (al-Nahawendi, the leader after Anan) or Shaul (Anan's son). Why, then, do they not accept Rabbinic traditions from the sages who were so many?[49] Halevi contended, then, on two levels: if the Karaites wished to argue that internal Rabbanite disagreements belie the truth of Rabbinic Judaism, the answer would be that, historically, internal Karaite disagreements have been even greater; if the Karaites

---

[46]Karaites raised the question of divergence in opinions and practice among the Rabbanites in their anti-Rabbanite polemics; see, e.g., Qirqisānī, *Al-Anwār*, I:10, pp. 48-51; Leon Nemoy, "Al-Qirqisānī's Account of the Jewish Sects and Christianity," *Hebrew Union College Annual*, 7 (1930): 377-382. Qirqisani held that internal Karaite disputes, unlike the Rabbanite ones, were reasonable given the Karaite claim that their interpretations of Biblical law are not Sinaitic; see *Al-Anwār* I:19, pp. 63-64; "Sects," p. 396.

[47]"Ḥapisu be-'Oraita shapir, ve'al tish'anu al da'ati." This dictum was recorded by the tenth-century Yefet ben Eli in his commentary to Zachariah; see Poznanski, "Anan," p. 184. One of the reasons for doubting its authenticity is the fact that the first half of the statement is in Aramaic, the second half in Hebrew: see Wieder, *Judean Scrolls*, pp. 88-89. Cf. the discussion of Salo W. Baron, *A Social and Religious History of the Jews*, 2nd ed., vol. 5, New York and Philadelphia, 1957, pp. 389-390, n. 4; Paul, *Écrits de Qumran*, pp. 31-33; Ankori, *Karaites*, 209-212. Ya'qub Al-Qirqisani (fl. 937). while not mentioning the motto, did attribute the principle of *ḥippus* (i.e. *idjtihād*; the Aramaic of the credo reads *ḥapisu*) to Anan; see his *Kitāb Al-Anwār* II:9, p. 79; trans., Vajda, "études," p. 67.

[48]Qirqisānī, *Al-Anwār*, I:9, p. 63; Nemoy, "Sects," p. 396.

[49]These arguments are made in *Al-Khazarī* III:38, pp. 120-121; 41, pp. 124-125; 49, pp. 128-129. For the changes in Karaite law by Halevi's time, see above, n. 37.

now claimed uniformity, Halevi would respond that this uniformity came about only because they accepted traditions from Anan or Benjamin who were mere individuals who could not provide certainty.

* * *

There is one other aspect of Halevi's criticism of Karaism. Karaites prided themselves on the use of logical analogy (*qiyās/heqesh*) for the derivation of laws. Prima facie, this is an attractive feature of their religion. Nevertheless, Halevi argued that in religion, tradition, and not logical analogy, is absolutely necessary. The Karaites themselves would admit that the Torah cannot even be read correctly without reliance on received guidance concerning vocalization. If *qiyās*, rather than tradition, were used in order to read the Torah, numerous errors would be made.[50] In similar fashion, when it comes to the commandments, unrestrained logical analogy will undoubtedly mislead worshippers rather than help them achieve religious perfection.[51]

Halevi's response to Karaism on this issue has wider implications than just which branch of Judaism understands the Torah correctly. After all, the unreliability of logical analogy, both for beliefs and for practices, is one of the central motifs of the *Kuzari*.[52] From Halevi's viewpoint, the Karaites were not the only group to be deceived by the employment of *qiyās* uncontrolled by tradition. The use of logical analogy was a prime technique of the philosophers, who advocated asceticism and solitude in order to cultivate it.[53] Yet, it was this very

---

[50]*Al-Khazarī* III:25-33, pp. 115-117. If it is true that some, or all, of the Massoretes were Karaites, then this argument is even stronger: if the Karaites as Massoretes used tradition, then certainly Karaite halakhists should do so.

[51]In *Ibid.*, III:38, pp. 120-121, Halevi argued that Karaite reliance on *qiyās* leads to the anarchy referred to above. In III:49, pp. 129-130, general reliance upon *qiyās* as a source of truth is called into question, while in III:50, p. 131, logical analogy (*taqāyus*) and personal effort (*idjtihād*) are said not to be sufficient for achieving certainty.

[52]In *Ibid.*, I:13, p. 10, Halevi referred to political religions based upon logical analogy, and, indeed, Christians and Muslims are portrayed as using *qiyās* (III:21, p. 111). Astrologers and believers in charms are said to use *qiyās* in I:79, p. 20 and I:97, p. 31, as are the modern astronomers in III:20, p. 52. Certain Jewish practices or beliefs are said either to be in conflict with *qiyās*: circumcision (III:7, p. 96), resurrection (III:17, p. 106), certain *midrashim* (III:68, p. 142; 72, p. 143), and prophecy and miracles (IV:3, pp. 156-157); or to be unlearnable by logical analogy: priestly gifts, tithes, and sacrifices (III:19, p. 108), sanctuary (III:23, p. 113), and the laws of animals whose deaths are caused by physical defects or injury (*terefot* – IV:31, p. 187). *Qiyās* is also said to reject the Biblical description of water above the firmament (IV:25, p. 181).

[53]*Ibid.*, III:1, p. 90. Halevi wrote that in the case of special individuals, for example Socrates, such asceticism is justified.

same technique of *qiyās* which misled the philosophers into adopting major erroneous conclusions. First of all, they believed that the world is eternal, since they used logical analogy instead of depending upon reliable tradition.[54] In addition, philosophers believed that all religions are equally valid[55] and that God does not act in the world.[56] Most importantly, since the philosophers had at their disposal only *qiyās*, their conception of God was inadequate: they realized the existence of God only on the level of Elohim, not on the level of the Tetragrammaton.[57]

The parallelism between Karaism and philosophy can be seen in other ways. Just as the Karaite use of *qiyās* led to halakhic anarchy, the philosophers' use of it led to philosophical anarchy.[58] In addition, the philosophers, like the Karaites, were described by Halevi as employing *idjtihād* in addition to *qiyās*.[59] It is obvious, then, that, for Halevi, Karaism was the Jewish religious equivalent of Aristotelian

---

[54]*Ibid.*, I:65-67, pp. 17-18; see also IV:13, p. 164; V:14, p. 212.

[55]*Ibid.*, II:49, p. 69.

[56]*Ibid.*, II:54, p. 72.

[57]*Ibid.*, IV:15-17, pp. 167-169. The Tetragrammaton is the God of Abraham, who left *qiyās* behind him when he reached this level of revelational knowledge (IV:27, p. 184).

Halevi apparently had an ambiguous attitude toward *qiyās*. Usually, he condemned it as leading to wrong conclusions. He also stated that if one had the correct information through experience, revelationary or otherwise, *qiyās* could be manipulated to explain the perceived phenomena; see *ibid.*, I:5, p. 8; 65, pp. 17-18; IV:3, pp. 156-157. Occasionally, Halevi himself referred to *qiyās* positively and even proved his contentions through recourse to that method; see I:110, p. 38 (immortality of the soul); II:68, pp. 79-80 (superiority of the Hebrew language); and III:21, p. 110 (trust in God). In IV:25, p. 181, *qiyās* is said to reject the philosophical view of emanation.

[58]*Ibid.*, V:14, p. 212. Many of the same terms used here were employed by Halevi in his discussion of Karaite anarchy in III:38, pp. 120-121. In that section, Halevi argued that if there were any Karaite uniformity, it was because of acceptance of a tradition from Anan, Benjamin, or Saul; concerning philosophy, uniformity was attained by accepting traditions from Pythagoras, Empedocles, Aristotle, Plato, or others.

[59]*Ibid.*, I:4, p. 6; II:49, p. 69.

philosophy. Both are to be rejected in favor of Rabbanite Judaism, which arrived at the truth concerning beliefs and practices through revelatory experiences and reliable tradition.[60]

* * *

In addition to Halevi's basic arguments against Karaism, namely, 1) *idjtihād* is a sign of weakness; 2) Karaite internal disagreements and uncertainty show that they do not have the true religion; and 3) logical analogy *(qiyās)* in the pursuit of religious duties is misleading; he added a number of short comments on particular commandments. Here, Halevi was firmly in the mainstream of Rabbanite anti-Karaite polemics. These topics include the calendar, the correct method of slaughtering animals, prohibited fats (such as the famous fat-tail), the measurements of prohibited and prescribed activities, kosher birds, the Sabbath-limit, prohibited work on the Sabbath (such as riding on the animals of non-Jews and conducting business), civil law, laws of inheritance, circumcision, ritual fringes, the tabernacle *(sukkah)*, prayer,[61] the correct date for Shavuot,[62] purity and impurity,[63] and the *'eruv*.[64] Halevi asserted, regarding all these issues, that the

---

[60]The parallelism between the criticism of Karaism and the criticism of philosophy shows that even if the first edition of the *Kuzari* were a small anti-Karaite tract (just Part III, for instance, and not Parts I-IV, as Goitein, Baneth, and Pines maintain), Halevi underwent no change of position when he incorporated that edition into the final work, which is characterized by an anti-philosophical stance. The criticism of Karaism presupposes a critical attitude towards Aristotelianism. Cf., however, Y. Silman, *Thinker*, p. 85, who argues that the first edition of the *Kuzari* was written as an anti-Karaite polemic while the young Halevi was still under the influence of Aristotelian philosophy. See also Silman's earlier article, "The Distinctiveness of Book III of the *Kuzari*," *Eshel Beer Sheva*, 1 (1976): 94-119 (Hebrew).

As partial support of his thesis, Silman writes *(Thinker, p. 124)* that in III:65 (presumably an earlier part), Halevi stated specifically that the Karaites are not *minim*, but in 1:1 (presumably part of his mature thought), Halevi referred to them as such. The Arabic original does not support this conclusion; see above, n. 4.

The relationship between Halevi's anti-Karaite polemic and the general tenor of the *Kuzari* was noted by Baneth, "Remarks," pp. 298-299, and Goitein, "Biography," pp. 46-47. Neither, however, elaborated upon this point.

[61]The above items are all discussed in *Al-Khazarī*, III:35, pp. 117-120. The calendar is discussed also in III:38, p. 121; civil law in III:46-47, p. 126; *sukkah* in III:63, p. 137.

[62]*Ibid.*, III:41, p. 125.

[63]*Ibid.*, III:49, pp. 127-128.

[64]*Ibid.*, III:49-53, pp. 130-132.

Karaites have no way of determining what the law should be in the absence of reliable traditions.[65]

* * *

Judah Halevi was no Karaite. He was also no Aristotelian philosopher. He criticized both, using their own terminology and assumptions, as being in contradiction with the truth of Judaism (Rabbanite Judaism, of course). Nevertheless, both held a certain attraction for Halevi.[66] The philosopher and the Karaite tried to achieve through individual effort and the use of logical analogy what the Rabbanite Jew had achieved through revelation and reliable tradition. As a result, they were both bound for failure, since logic and personal effort are not the true means of achieving the divine influence. Yet, philosophy and Karaism still fascinated Judah Halevi. He was able to take from each, without, however, succumbing to either one, in order better to explain and justify Rabbanite Judaism. The *Kuzari* was written, among other reasons, to explain the failure of both philosophy and Karaism despite their obvious attractions.

---

[65]In *ibid.*, III:43, p. 126; 47, p. 127; the *ḥaver* told the King not to pay too much attention to the details of particular laws once the general principle of the need for reliable tradition is established. Could this mean that Halevi recognized that certain Karaite legal interpretations (judged solely on the basis of *qiyās* and *idjtihād?*) were superior to Rabbanite ones?

[66]In *Al-Khazarī* V:14, pp. 211-213, Halevi stated that the philosophers were to be praised for their achievements made through the use of *qiyās*. Without revelation, philosophers could not arrive at real truth; through *qiyās*, they at least made a valid attempt at such knowledge. The philosophers' achievements in the fields of logic and mathematics were also said to be a result of their use of logical analogy. Karaites, on the other hand, do strive diligently in their attempt to fulfill God's will; they just do not understand how to reach their goal.

37

The Superiority of Oral Over Written Communication:

Judah Ha-Levi's *Kuzari* and Modern Jewish Thought

Raphael Jospe
The Open University of Israel

The influence of Judah Ha-Levi's theory of Jewish particularity on such modern Jewish thinkers as Moses Mendelssohn, Ahad Ha-'Am, and Mordecai Kaplan was the subject of a study I published some years ago.[1] In this study I propose to assess the influence of Ha-Levi's *Kuzari* on modern Jewish thought, especially that of Moses Mendelssohn, on the question of the superiority of oral over written communication, a question that arises in Ha-Levi's discussion of the superiority of the Hebrew language.

Ha-Levi on the Origin of Human Language

In the *Kuzari* 1:53-56, Ha-Levi states explicitly that human languages are not natural and eternal; they are, rather, merely conventional:

> The Rabbi said: Do you consider languages to be eternal and without beginning?

> The Kuzari said: No, they were generated, and are conventional....

---

[1]See my study, "Jewish Particularity from Ha-Levi to Kaplan: Implications for Defining Jewish Philosophy" in *Go and Study: Essays and Studies in Honor of Alfred Jospe*, ed. Raphael Jospe and Samuel Fishman (New York, 1980), pp. 307-325; reissued in *Forum* (No. 46/47, Winter, 1982), pp. 77-90.

The Rabbi said: Have you ever seen anyone invent a language or heard of such a person?

The Kuzari said: I have neither seen nor heard of this. Undoubtedly [languages] arose at some generation, prior to which there was no human language about which any nation could agree.[2]

It is noteworthy that the usual order of the *Kuzari* is reversed here: it is not the King but the Rabbi who asks the questions here, and it is not the Rabbi but the King who responds. As the conversation progresses, when the King and Rabbi are discussing the universal division of time into weeks and the universal application of the decimal system of numbers, the *Kuzari* is forced to reach the conclusion that such universal assent could only have occurred "if all humans are the children of Adam or Noah or some other individual" (*Kuzari* 1:58).

Nevertheless, despite the conventional nature of human language, there is one language which is unique. Unlike human languages, which arise at a given time by common agreement, the Hebrew language is neither conventional nor temporal; it is the divine language of creation, and was the language of Adam and Eve:

> The Kuzari: Is Hebrew superior to the other languages? As we can see, they are more perfect and comprehensive than it.

> The Rabbi: What happened to it is what happened to those who bear it, becoming poorer and weaker as they became fewer. In itself, it is the noblest of languages. According to reason and tradition it is the language in which God spoke to Adam and Eve and which they spoke to each other....(*Kuzari* 2:67-68)[3]

---

[2]English translations of Ha-Levi's *Kuzari*, Mendelssohn's '*Or La-Netivah* and *Be'ur*, and Ahad Ha-'Am's "Torah Sheba-Lev" are mine. See the discussion of Ha-Levi on conventional languages in Yochanan Silman, *Bein Pilosof Le-Navi'* (Ramat Gan, 1985), pp. 86-87. Rambam (*Guide of the Perplexed* 2:30) agrees with Ha-Levi that "languages are conventional, not natural." However, in *Pirqei Moshe Bi-Refu'ah*, Ch. 25 (which may also be found in Yosef Kafih's edition of '*Iggerot Ha-Rambam* [Jerusalem, 1972], Appendix B, p. 149), Rambam agrees with Galen and Al-Farabi that such natural conditions as clime affect language. In contradistinction to Ha-Levi and Mendelssohn, Rambam does not argue for the superiority of Hebrew. Those languages produced in the median clime – Greek, Arabic, Hebrew, Syriac, and Persian – all share in the benefits of that ideal clime, and Rambam understands Hebrew and Arabic to be closely related, and also close to Syriac.

[3]The king refers to the purported superiority of other languages over Hebrew, but Judah ibn Tibbon's Hebrew translation reverses the argument specifically in favor of the superiority of Hebrew over Arabic.

In another context, when discussing different types of causes and free will, and different types of speech (*Kuzari* 5:20), the Rabbi explains that "in conventional languages, both natural power and free will function." "Natural speech" had already been defined as "motions and hints which conform to the thoughts the speaker wishes to express; their origin is in the soul. This requires no prior agreement." "Voluntary speech," on the other hand, is "what the prophet says when he is not prophesying, or what any rational, thinking person says, who connects his phrases and chooses words which conform to his intention," in contradistinction to "accidental speech, which is the speech of madmen at the time of their madness, which has no order of subjects and aims at no known end." Such meaningless accidental speech cannot be attributed to God.

The Superiority of Hebrew as the Original Language

Hebrew qualifies as the "natural language" par excellence, in terms of conforming to the thoughts of the speaker without prior agreement, because it is the language of God and the angels, the original human language, the language of creation:

> Some languages and scripts are superior to others. In some cases, the name conforms to the qualities of the objects named, while other names are remote from them. The divine language which God created and taught to Adam and placed on his tongue and in his heart is undoubtedly the most perfect of languages, for its terms conform best to the things they indicate, as Scripture says (Genesis 2:19), 'Whatever Adam called a living creature, that was its name.' In other words, this name was appropriate for it and conformed to it and characterized it. This is the superiority of the holy tongue, and [this is why] the angels employ it more than any other tongue. This is also the basis for their saying that the shapes of the letters of the Hebrew script are not accidental or unintentional; each of them conforms to what is intended by them. (*Kuzari* 4:25)

The Superiority of Oral Communication

Thus far, we have cited Ha-Levi's views on the superiority of the Hebrew language and script. The Rabbi, however, adds another dimension to this superiority, first in general terms, and then, again, in terms of Hebrew.

> The purpose of language is that what is in the soul of the speaker be attained by the soul of the listener. This purpose can only be completely fulfilled orally [Arabic: *mushafahatan*; Hebrew: *panim el panim*] (*Kuzari* 2:72)

As we shall see, this, too, is one of the points in which Hebrew excels. Why, however, is oral communication superior to written communication, according to Ha-Levi? As the Rabbi continues:

> For oral [communication] is superior to written [communication], as they said: 'From the mouth of the authors, and not from books' (*mi-pi soferim ve-lo mi-pi sefarim*). For in oral [communication] one is assisted by pauses, when a person stops speaking, or by continuing, in accordance with the subject; or by raising or lowering one's voice; or by various gestures to express amazement, a question, a narrative, desire, fear, or submission, without which simple speech will be inadequate. Sometimes the speaker may be assisted by motions of his eyes, eyebrows, or his whole head and his hands, to express anger, pleasure, requests or pride in the appropriate measure. (*Kuzari* 2:72)[4]

It is precisely here that biblical Hebrew is superior to other languages. The written biblical text was given an oral dimension by means of the masoretic cantillation notes (*ta 'amei ha-miqra'*).

> The remnant of our divinely created and formed language, contains subtle and profound elements in place of those oral gestures, namely the notes by which the Bible is read. They indicate pause and continuity, and separate question from answer, beginning from continuation, etc. (*Kuzari* 2:72)

"From the Mouth of Authors, and Not from Books"

What did Ha-Levi mean by citing what seems to have been a popular aphorism, "From the mouth of authors, and not from books?" The aphorism, cited in Hebrew in the Arabic text of the *Kuzari*, may have been widely known in Ha-Levi's time, but it is unknown to us from any other source. Yehuda Even-Shemu'el suggests that "it is based, apparently, on the talmudic interpretation 'from their mouths [i.e. from the oral testimony of the witnesses in a case], and not in writing.'"[5] The Talmud (Gittin 71a) makes this stipulation regarding testimony, regarding only direct oral testimony as acceptable, and disqualifying written testimony. (Cf. Rashi and Tosafot *loc. cit.*). Elsewhere (Makkot 6b) the Talmud stipulates that the Sanhedrin might only hear the testimony directly from the witness himself, and not from a translator. In both cases, the Talmud's ruling is based on the biblical verse, "From the mouth of two witness or from the mouth of three witnesses" (Deuteronomy 19:15), which Rashi accordingly interprets as meaning that "they may not write their testimony in a letter and send it to the court; nor may a translator stand between the witness and the judges."

---

[4]Cf. the discussion in Silman, *Bein Pilosof Le-Navi'*, pp. 212-213, 248, 281.
[5]Yehuda Even-Shmu'el, trans., *Sefer Ha-Kuzari* (Tel Aviv, 1972), p. 87 note 3.

This is also what Rambam (Maimonides) understands the verse to mean: "The Torah law is that one does not accept testimony in either civil law or criminal law except from the mouth of the witnesses, as it says, 'From the mouth of two witnesses,' [meaning] from their mouth, and not from their writing."[6]

It is, therefore, difficult to accept Even-Shemu'el's suggestion that the aphorism "From the mouth of authors, and not from books" refers to this halakhic issue. In the first case, contextually, we note that Ha-Levi is dealing here with a linguistic matter, namely the superiority of oral to written communication, as well as the superiority of the Hebrew language. Ha-Levi is not dealing here with a halakhic or juridicial question. In addition, there is a critical difference of terminology and nuance. The word-play in our aphorism is based on the preference for authors (*soferim*) over their books (*sefarim*), a play entirely missing in the talmudic passages in which neither term is used.

However, in another passage (*Kuzari* 4:25), Ha-Levi has a word-play based on the root *s-f-r*, in his commentary on the statement in *Sefer Yezirah* 1:1 that God "created the world by three *sefarim, sefer, sefar, and sippur.*" Without treating the corpus of early philosophical commentaries on this passage, and also without examining in detail Ha-Levi's innovative interpretation of the passage, as I do in my article "Early Philosophical Commentaries on the *Sefer Yezirah*,"[7] I wish merely to note that, as far as I know, Judah Ha-Levi, who generally is regarded as the archetypal anti-Aristotelian Jewish philosopher, was the first philosophical commentator on the *Sefer Yezirah* to understand the unity of "*sefer, sefar, and sippur*" in terms of the Aristotelian unity of subject, act, and object of intellection (Arabic: *'aql, 'aqil, ma'qul*; Hebrew: *sekhel, maskil, muskal*):

> Among them is the *Sefer Yezirah* by Abraham our ancestor. It is profound and requires lengthy interpretation. It teaches about (God's) unity and mastery by things which are changing and multiple in one respect, but which are, in another respect, unified and coordinated. Their coordination is in respect of the one who orders them. Among these things are *sefar, sippur,* and *sefer*. The term *sefar* refers to the measure and apportionment of created bodies, for the measure required for the proper arrangement of a body can only be effected on

---

[6]Rambam, *Mishneh Torah*, Shofetim, Laws of Testimony, Ch. 3, #4. This is the law in both criminal and civil cases. However, Rambam continues, whereas in criminal cases only oral testimony is thus acceptable, in civil cases one may ultimately accept written testimony, for otherwise people would not be able to get loans.
[7]Cf. my study, "Early Philosophical Commentaries on the *Sefer Yezirah*" (*forthcoming*).

the basis of number. Area, volume, weight, uniformity of movements, and musical harmony all are based on number, on *sefar*. So you see that a house cannot be produced by a builder unless it is preceded by its representation in his soul. *Sippur* means speech, i.e., divine speech...as it says, 'Let there be light' (Genesis 1:2). The action was simultaneous with the speech. This (action) is *sefer*, namely the writing, for the writing of God means his creatures, and the speech of God is his writing, and the number of God is his speech. Thus, in terms of God, *sefar* and *sippur* and *sefer* are one thing, whereas in terms of man they are three. For man measures with his mind (*dhihn*), speaks with his mouth, and writes with his hand....Human measure and speech and writing are signs (*'alamat*) indicating something, and are not the thing itself, whereas (God's) measure and speech are the thing itself, which is also the writing....If we had the ability, by saying the word 'man,' or by drawing a human body, to make his form exist, then we would have the power of divine speech and divine writing, and we would be creators, **although we are endowed with some of this ability in our intellectual representation**....What resembles these is speech and writing, which are preceded by measure. I mean by this the thought of the pure soul which resembles the angels. Thus the three *sefarim, sefar, sippur,* and *sefer* are joined together as one thing, thereby generating that measured thing as it was measured by the one possessing that pure soul, as he spoke it and as he wrote it. In this way, the author of the book says, God created his world by three *sefarim, sefar, sippur,* and *sefer*, which, in terms of God, are all one.[8]

Now Ha-Levi's thorough familiarity with the Aristotelian doctrine cannot be questioned. In fact, his *Kuzari* 5:12 presents a concise summary of Ibn Sina's psychology, including the identity in the actual human intellect of the subject, act, and object of thought. The analogy of the creative unity of the three *sefarim* to the human mind is explicit: "we are endowed with some of this ability in our intellectual representation." In this respect, Ha-Levi, for all his alleged "anti-rationalism," anticipates "rationalist" Rambam's explicit equation of the unity of subject, act, and object of thought in both man and God (in the *Guide of the Perplexed* 1:68). Ha-Levi's general opposition to "the

---

[8]The *Sefer Yezirah* commentaries of Sa'adiah Ga'on, Dunash ibn Tamim, Shabbetai Donnolo, and Judah ben Barzillai al-Bargeloni do not draw this analogy of *sefer, sefar,* and *sippur* to human intellection, nor do we find it in the passages relating to *Sefer Yezirah* in Solomon ibn Gabirol's *Meqor Hayyim* and poetry. On the other hand, the concept of three (from a human perspective) which are one (in God) is reminiscent of the three essential attributes of God (life, power, knowledge), which, according to Sa'adiah (*'Emunot Ve-De'ot* 2:4), are understood by us as one, as implied in the concept of creator, but they can only be expressed verbally in the plural, since "there is not word in our language which indcludes these three subjects, and therefore we have to express them as three words." Ha-Levi rejects this view of the divine attributes.

God of Aristotle" notwithstanding, we have here a thoroughly Aristotelian re-interpretation of God's creative unity in intellectual terms.

And yet, the discussion of the three *sefarim* does not necessarily resolve our problem of the meaning of the aphorism, "From the mouth of the authors, and not from books," because none of the three *sefarim*, however etymologically close to our root, is punctuated as *sofer*, and because the unity of the three *sefarim* presumably precludes one (*sofer*) being preferred over the other (*sefer*).

The commentary to the *Kuzari* "Qol Yehuda" by Judah Moscato suggests a third solution to our problem. According to Moscato (*loc. cit.*), the meaning of the aphorism "From the mouth of the authors, and not from books" is:[9]

> In accordance with the saying 'Let your eyes behold your teachers' (Isaiah 30:20). This is what Samuel ibn Tibbon said in the introduction to his commentary on Ecclesiastes: A wise teacher may engage in many ruses, transfigurations and reversals to enable intelligent students to understand his meaning, although he does not explain it or make it explicit, whereas this is impossible to do when writing a book....All this is difficult to do in a book, and in some cases is impossible, such as a facial expression or vocal characteristic.[10]

Moscato's commentary, and especially his citation from Samuel ibn Tibbon's commentary to Ecclesiastes, seem to suggest another meaning of *sofer* (translated above as "author"), which in rabbinic literature also means a school-teacher (school = *beit sofer*[11] and not the modern Hebrew *beit sefer*[12]). It is precisely the personal, face to face contact between teacher and pupil which is essential for meaningful communication, which is why such frontal teaching is superior to learning from the written word alone.

As for the Bible, according to such a view, the masoretic cantillation notes (*ta'amei ha-miqra'*) convert the dry, written

---

[9]Judah Moscato, "Qol Yehuda," in *Sefer Ha-Kuzari* (Warsaw, 1790), p. 161. Cf. "Judah ben Joseph Moscato" in *Encyclopedia Judaica* 12:357.

[10]Samuel ibn Tibbon's Commentary to Ecclesiastes has not be published, but may be found in manuscript Parma - De Rossi 272.

[11]My thanks to my friend Professor Yehuda Liebes for calling this to my attention.

[12]For example, see the term *sofer* as teacher in Talmud, Bava Batra 21a, and Tosefta Megillah 4 (3) 38 (Lieberman ed. p. 228). In Midrash Lamentations Rabbah 2:4, p. 42, "Rabban Gamli'el said, There were 500 schools (*batei soferim*) in Beitar...." Cf. Marcus Jastrow, *Dictionary of the Targumim, the Talmud, etc.*, p. 968, and Avraham Even-Shoshan, *Millon Hadash* (Jerusalem, 1972), p. 1777.

scripture, which cannot be understood alone, into a living text (*miqra'*, that which is read, rather than that which is written), namely into a word heard by the reader.

The Superiority of Biblical Poetry

Biblical Hebrew poetry is similarly superior to the poetry of other languages. Foreign poetry requires a metric structure; Hebrew poetry is not constrained by such artificial devices. In response to the Kuzari's observation that Hebrew poetry seems inferior to the poetry of other nations, "for the others are superior to it in metered poetry conforming to melodies" (*Kuzari* 2:69), the Rabbi says that the beauty of Hebrew poetic expression does not require meter. Therefore, biblical poetic verses of differing lengths are capable of being sung to the same melody regardless of the number of syllables in the verse. For example, Psalm 136:1, *hodu l'adonai ki tov* (7 syllables) can be sung to the same tune as Psalm 136:3, *le-'oseh nifla'ot gedolot levado* (12 syllables).[13]

Meter can beautify poetry, but the poetry of the Bible aimed at a "superior and more beneficial quality" than such beauty (*Kuzari* 2:70). Meter, accordingly, has merely an esthetic value. The problem is that this formal esthetic advantage comes at the expense of effective communication of the poetic content, the meaning, which is what is truly important. Meter constitutes an artificial and divisive structure which often fails to conform to the meaning of the words. The biblical masoretic cantillation notes, on the other hand, conform to the meaning of the words, punctuate the words, and thereby make it possible to understand their meaning. Therefore, according to the Rabbi:

> A person who has this intention must reject metered poetry, for metered poetry can only be recited in one way. It generally connects where there should be a pause, and pauses where there should be a connection. One can only avoid this with great effort. (*Kuzari* 2:72)

The Kuzari adds:

> It is proper that the excellence of sound give way before that of meaning. Meter is pleasing to the ear, whereas this [masoretic biblical] vocalization (*dabt*) [clarifies] the meaning (*Kuzari* 2:73).

That Ha-Levi, himself a great and prolific author of metered Hebrew poetry, should regard poetic meter so negatively, is, to say the

---

[13]It is ironic that Ha-Levi picks as an example of independence from metric structure a psalm manifesting such structured literary form as Psalm 136, which Judge Jacob Bazak has shown to have triangular geometric structure. For Bazak's theory in general, cf. his book *Zurot U-Tekhanim Be-Mizmorei Tehillim* (Structures and Contents in the Psalms) (Tel Aviv, 1987).

least, paradoxical. In the words of my late revered teacher, Alexander Altmann, Ha-Levi's attitude is "a bit strange."[14]

However, perhaps Ha-Levi's attitude is not entirely strange. There is a fundamental difference between secular poetry, which need be merely pleasing aesthetically, and sacred poetry. Biblical poetry (from a perspective such as Ha-Levi's) was not merely meant to please, however aesthetically pleasing it may be; its purpose was to instruct.

Artificial devices such as meter, as we have seen, do not facilitate understanding of the meaning. To the contrary, meter may even constitute a formal impediment to comprehension of the content of the poem. Metered poetry which obscures its meaning thus resembles, in some respects, "accidental speech" which lacks meaning and is the speech of a madman, unlike meaningful "natural speech" which accurately conveys meaning, "prophetic speech" which is divinely inspired, and "voluntary speech" which a person freely chooses to express his intention. (Cf. *Kuzari* 5:20). The poet is free to choose whatever formal expression he wishes, but when his meter artificially connects what should meaningfully be separated or separates what should meaningfully be connected, his poetry can no longer be categorized as meaningful voluntary speech, and has become, instead, meaningless accidental speech. In fact, Ha-Levi categorizes poetry together with the accidental, meaningless speech of madmen and infants, as well as the dubiously meaningful speech of an orator or preacher (*khatib*).[15]

> All these classes may be attributed to God only indirectly....Otherwise, the words of an infant and the words of madmen and the speech of orators and the poems of a poet would be divine speech.

In the best of cases, then, poetic meter may be aesthetically pleasing, but when the form of the poem, i.e., its meter, obscures its

---

[14]Alexander Altmann, *Moses Mendelssohn: A Biographical Study* (Alabama, 1973), p. 410: "Mendelssohn here paraphrased Jehuda Ha-Levi's statement in the *Kuzari* (II, 70-74), which rejected the notion that melodies required the use of meter, and which saw the superiority of ancient Hebrew poems in their power to enhance the understanding, rather than to flatter the ear...Jehuda Ha-Levi had deplored the imitation of the metrical systems of Arabic poetry by Hebrew writers as alien to the Hebrew tongue and causing only disharmonies – a view that seems a bit strange when uttered, in this case, by a great Hebrew poet who had used this method himself."

[15]*Kuzari* 5:20. Similarly, according to Rambam (*Guide of the Perplexed* 3:25-26), one may not attribute to God any futile (*'abath*) or frivolous (*la'ib*) actions, just as, according to Ha-Levi, one may not attribute to God accidental speech, which serves no purpose or only a silly purpose.

content and prevents comprehending its meaning, the poetic meter degrades voluntary speech and renders it accidental and meaningless speech, which cannot be attributed to God.[16]

The Need for Visible Symbols

Despite Ha-Levi's clear claim that oral communication, with its greater vibrancy and immediacy, is superior to written communication, Ha-Levi also says that what a person sees and experiences personally makes a greater impression than what he is told by others. Similarly, seeing the sensible object facilitates understanding abstract ideas. This is why the prophets employed anthropomorphisms, rather than referring in abstract terms to God's unity, power, and wisdom.

> We see that the human soul is more afraid in the presence of fearsome things that it senses than it is afraid when told of such things, just as it desires more a beautiful form which is present than it does if told about it. Do not believe someone who considers himself so intelligent that he claims his thought is so well arranged that he can grasp all metaphysical ideas by his intellect alone, without relying on any sensible object, or without apprehending something visible, such as words, writing, or any visible or imagined form. (*Kuzari* 4:5)

The need for visible symbols to facilitate comprehension does not contradict Ha-Levi's preference for oral over written communication, because the issue is not the superiority of something audible to something visible. Oral communication is not superior because it is audible, rather than visible, but rather because it is immediate, alive, and facilitated by aids (gestures, tone of voice, etc.) which by their very nature are present in a face to face encounter, but not in a written text. Similarly, sensible symbols (which are usually visible, but can just as well be audible) assist in our comprehension of otherwise abstract ideas. Just as the biblical cantillation notes lend an oral quality to the written text, thus punctuating it and giving it concrete meaning which we can more easily understand, so do sensible symbols give an immediate and living quality to abstract ideas, thus aiding our understanding of them. The notes give specific, punctuated form to an otherwise unpunctuated and unvocalized text, much as the symbols give concrete form to otherwise formless abstractions.

Moses Mendelssohn

Moses Mendelssohn's Hebrew introduction to the Torah, the *'Or La-Netivah* ("The Light for the Path"; cf. Psalm 119:105, "Your word is a

---

[16]Cf. Judah Moscato, "Qol Yehuda" on *Kuzari* 2:72, pp. 160-161, and the citation from Samuel ibn Tibbon's Introduction to his Commentary to Ecclesiastes.

lamp for my feet, and a light for my path"), and also his Hebrew commentary (*Be'ur*) to the Song of Moses (Exodus 15), as well as his German philosophical work *Jerusalem*, clearly manifest the influence of Ha-Levi's *Kuzari* on the points we have discussed: Hebrew as the original language of creation and of Adam and Eve; the superiority of the Hebrew language; the superiority of biblical poetry; the superiority of oral communication; the need for concrete symbols; the role of the biblical cantillation notes. It is only in his German *Jerusalem*, intended for a non-Jewish audience, that Mendelssohn went farther than Ha-Levi on the question of the superiority of oral communication and the need for visible symbols, although he failed to take the next logical step, or, perhaps, to realize the radical consequences of the additional step he did take. That next step was taken, later on, by Ahad Ha-'Am, although in a completely different context and direction.

Let us first examine Mendelssohn's theory of the Hebrew language and biblical poetry, as it was influenced by the *Kuzari*, in his Hebrew biblical studies, the *'Or La-Netivah* and *Be'ur*. Since Mendelssohn often discusses at great length intricate issues that are discussed more briefly in Ha-Levi's *Kuzari*, we will limit our citations to illustrative selections.

In the *'Or La-Netivah*, Mendelssohn follows Ha-Levi in arguing that Hebrew was the original language of creation:

> The Holy Tongue in which the books of the Bible which we have today were written is the language in which God spoke with Adam, Cain, Noah, and the Patriarchs, and in which he revealed the Decalogue on Mount Sinai and the two tablets were written, in which he spoke with Moses and the prophets. This gives (Hebrew) a sufficient advantage, response, and glory over the other languages to be called the 'Holy Tongue.'[17]

---

[17]Moses Mendelssohn, *'Or La-Netivah*, in Vol. 1 (Genesis) of *Sefer Netivot Ha-Shalom* (Pentateuch with Mendelssohn's German translation and Hebrew commentary, *Be'ur*), (Prague, 1836), p. 2. In addition to Alexander Altmann's discussion of this work in his *Moses Mendelssohn: A Biographical Study*, see Edward Richard Levenson, "Moses Mendelssohn's Understanding of Logico-Grammatical and Literary Construction in the Pentateuch: A Study of His German Translation and Hebrew Commentary (The *Bi'ur*)" (Ph.D. Dissertation, Brandeis University, 1972, and University Microfilms, Ann Arbor). Also see Perez Sendlar, *Ha-Be'ur La-Torah Shel Moshe Mendelssohn Ve-Si'ato* (Jerusalem, 1940). Levenson's valuable study deals extensively with Mendelssohn's attitude toward and interpretative use of the masoretic system of biblical cantillation notes.

Mendelssohn then cites various rabbinic *aggadot* (legends), which purportedly prove, on the basis of biblical Hebrew names and word plays that Hebrew, and not Greek or Aramaic, was the original human language and the language of creation.

The Importance of the Biblical Cantillation Notes

The biblical cantillation notes are for Mendelssohn, as they were for Ha-Levi, one of the unique features of the Hebrew language, in light of which it is superior to other languages. The notes have, of course, a purely linguistic function, that of punctuating the text, without which the text would be unintelligible. But then Mendelssohn adds a new point, which, as far as I know, is not made in the *Kuzari*. According to Mendelssohn, the notes were revealed to Moses together with the words; Moses actually heard the words punctuated by the notes. The notes, heard by Moses at Sinai, were then transmitted orally from generation to generation.

> No intelligent person can doubt that when God speaks to humans, he makes his voice heard with whatever is necessary for its pronunciation...with the musical pauses in the appropriate places. Without all this the statement would not be comprehensible to the listener as it should be....All this is well-known to linguists. The rules of the notes and their melodies were based on some of these things, and it is in virtue of (the notes) that the Holy Tongue was distinguished from the other languages known to us. Because of their profound precision, the connection and separation of the words agree with the connection and separation of the ideas, so that the ways of the language thereby conform to the ways in which the soul thinks. External speech is thus arranged in agreement with internal speech.[18]

---

[18]*'Or La-Netivah*, p. 3a bottom-3b top. On the question of Mendelssohn's careful attention to connections and pauses, cf. Levenson, Thesis, pp. 8-9: "A better translation of *hemshekh ha-ma'amar* than 'the continuity of the account' might be 'the connectedness of the account.' Careful study of the translation and commentary, in fact, yields the insight that Mendelssohn manifests an acute sensitivity in the rendering of various kinds of 'connections': between both phrases and clauses within individual sentences, between whole sentences, and between larger units such as *pisqa'ot*, chapters, portions, and even whole books. He uses the term itself or its equivalent only in explaining the connection of Biblical sentences and groups of sentences, but its meaning actually embraces the connections of the larger units, as well as the intra-sentence connections....For intra-sentence connections, the accents, or *te'amim*, emerge as major guides; they serve a unique hermeneutical function in the *Bi'ur* as indicators of the separations and connections between phrases and clauses....The accents were an important concern of Mendelssohn in his translation throughout the Pentateuch." Similarly, Levenson writes that "the

However, as Ha-Levi had already said, the notes do not merely punctuate the text by connecting and separating the words. Rather, they add an oral dimension to the written word:

Know that the cantillation notes do not merely guide in the connection and separation of words. If the words were said with all the precise continuations and pauses, but without changing or varying the level of the voice or pitch or intonation, in accordance with the subject, they would be like dry bones lacking any living spirit, and one would scarcely be able to understand the speaker's intention....Every single idea has its own level of the voice and intonation, according to how it functions in the soul, for example, a question or astonishment....Although all these matters do not have written signs and marks, in any event one who wishes to give meaning to his words must change and vary the sounds he pronounces, in accordance with the subject understood by them, and according to the relation between the feelings of the soul and the levels of the voice and their intonation. Hence, there is no doubt that Moses heard all the words of the Torah divinely revealed together with the vowels and the notes related to them, in all their precision and purity, without any of them being lacking.[19]

The Torah, therefore, was not transmitted from generation to generation in written form alone. In a manner reminiscent of Ha-Levi's aphorism, "From the mouth of authors, and not from books," Mendelssohn said:

The child learning from his father or the pupil listening to his teacher would hear one of these statements with whatever was appropriate for its pronunciation, just as he had also received it from his father or teacher. He would similarly teach it to his children and pupils, for the commandment 'teach them diligently to your children' (Deuteronomy 6:7) [means] that these words should be ever ready in his mouth. They did not merely hand over the sacred scriptures to their children or

---

accents, in fact, serve no mean role as aids in Mendelssohn's analysis of the structure and meaning of the Pentateuch, as reflected in the *Bi'ur* and in the German translation as well" (Thesis, p. 14). Regarding the revelation of the notes to Moses, Levenson says: "Mendelssohn discusses the accents at greater length, expressing the view that they were revealed with all their combinations by God to Moses at Sinai, and were thenceforth transmitted orally from generation to generation by the leaders and scholars of the Jewish people, until they were finally set to writing at some later date" (Thesis, pp. 19-20). The notes thus support Mendelssohn's thesis that the perfect literary structure of the Torah, involving a close inter-relatedness of its parts, is evidence of its textual integrity, against the views of Bible critics. Cf. Levenson, Thesis, p. 66, that Mendelssohn's "concentration on the 'continuity of the text,' 'connections,' and 'the order of the accounts' exemplifies this literary purpose."
[19]*'Or La-Netivah* p. 3b.

pupils, and let them read the written text alone, in which case they would have been like the words of a closed book. Rather, they would read it in front of them and repeat it with them, out loud and by chanting. They would thereby transmit to them the Torah's cantillation notes, and would sweeten its words like honey, so that the words might enter into their hearts.[20]

A similar view of the need for living, face to face, oral instruction is found in Chapter 2 of Mendelssohn's *Jerusalem*. In this passage, to which we shall return later, Mendelssohn argues not only that the written text alone is not fully intelligible, as Ha-Levi had maintained, but that books tend to isolate people from each other. Thus isolated, people are deprived of the opportunity

> to develop social contacts, to emulate others, and to seek oral communication and living instruction. For this reason, there were but a few written laws; and even those were not completely intelligible without oral instruction and tradition. Nevertheless, it was forbidden to add explanations and comments in writing. In was the unwritten laws, the oral tradition, the living instruction from person to person and from mouth to mouth that were to explain, enlarge, limit, or define more clearly what, by wise intent and in wise moderation, had been left undefined in the written law. In everything a youth saw being done, in all acts, public no less than private, at every gate and doorpost, wherever he turned his eyes or ears, he found an incentive to probe, to think, and to follow in the footsteps of an older and wiser man whose smallest acts and practices he could observe with filial attention to every detail. He felt stimulated to emulate his teacher with a child's eagerness to learn, to discover the meaning and intent of these practices, and to obtain the instruction for which his master considered him ready and prepared. In this way, study and life, wisdom and action, intellectual activity and social intercourse were intimately interwoven. At least this was the way it was meant to be, according to the original arrangement and intent of the lawgiver.[21]

Returning to his discussion of the Hebrew language in the *'Or La-Netivah*, Mendelssohn cites the discussion, in *Kuzari* 3:30, of the question of the original alphabet in which the Torah was first

---

[20] *'Or La-Netivah* p. 3b.

[21] Mendelssohn, *Jerusalem, oder ueber religioese Macht und Judentum* (Berlin, 1919), pp. 102-103. Unless otherwise indicated, citations from *Jerusalem* are taken from the translation by Alfred Jospe, *Jerusalem and Other Jewish Writings* (New York, 1969). This passage may be found on pp. 90-91. Cf. the translation by Allan Arkush, with Introduction and Commentary by Alexander Altmann, *Jerusalem or On Religious Power and Judaism* (Hanover, New Hampshire, 1983), pp. 118-119.

written.[22] Mendelssohn then concludes his discussion of the Hebrew language, as did Ha-Levi, with a survey of Hebrew grammar.[23]

Biblical Poetry

In the introduction to the Song of the Sea (Exodus, Chapter 15), in the *Be'ur*, Mendelssohn follows and amplifies Ha-Levi's theory of biblical poetry, and explicitly cites the *Kuzari*.[24] Like Ha-Levi (in the *Kuzari* 2:70), Mendelssohn appreciated biblical poetry's freedom from the constraints of meter, such as typifies Greek and Latin poetry, as well as its freedom from the constraints of rhyme. As for rhyme, Mendelssohn wrote:

> The similarity of the final syllables of the verses to which we today are accustomed in Hebrew [poetry], has no advantage or superiority, except for its being pleasing to the ear. Even this is only the case with plain reading, and not with singing. To the contrary, the wise person who sings will dislike that precision [of rhyme]....[25]

Therefore, Mendelssohn says,

> the ancients abandoned this weak superiority, and instead chose a greater superiority, which is the order of the subjects, preserved in an appropriate manner, and intending toward the desired end, so that the words might not merely enter into the ears of the listener, but also into his heart. They would then remain engraved in his heart, and would give birth to happiness or sadness, faint-heartedness or confidence, fear or hope, love or hate, whatever is appropriate to the intention, and would establish in him fine qualities and excellent characteristics....[26]

Mendelssohn then makes explicit what is implicit in Ha-Levi's theory. Secular poetry, with its meter and rhyme, aims at "the superiority of sound, which is nothing but the delight of a sense, [something] pleasing to the ear," whereas sacred poetry aims at "the superiority of the subjects and the thoughts which correct the rational soul." Sacred poetry thus does not merely please; it instructs and corrects the person, and aims at "controlling the faculties of the soul and ruling its qualities, and changing its characteristics as it wishes."[27]

---

[22] *'Or La-Netivah* p. 6a, middle.

[23] *'Or La-Netivah* pp. 14b-21a.

[24] Cf. *Be'ur*, Vol. 2, p. 82b, "Note," Introduction to the Song of the Sea (Exodus, Chapter 15).

[25] *Be'ur*, Introduction to the Song of the Sea, p. 82a.

[26] *Ibid*, p. 82b.

[27] *Ibid*.

Biblical poetry thus serves a moral, and not merely esthetic, purpose. The cantillation notes serve this end by dividing the verses into phrases (what Mendelssohn terms *ma'amarim qezarim*, short statements) of two to four words.

> They did this for two reasons. First, the shorter the phrases are, the more pauses and rests there are. Increasing the number of rests serves a great purpose, to arouse one's intention (*kavanah*) and strengthen it in the heart....It also benefits the memory....The second reason is the benefit of melody....The aim of all this is to preserve one's intention.[28]

Mendelssohn concludes by commenting that he dealt at length with the theory of biblical poetry in order to demonstrate to the youth, who are influenced by trends in foreign poetry,

> that the ways of sacred poetry are as high over these of secular poetry as the heaven is above the earth, not merely in respect of the superiority of the poet, who is the agent, and the precious and glorious phraseology, which is the matter of the poem, but also in respect of its purpose, which is to direct one to eternal bliss and true felicity, by means of lofty and sublime subjects. For it is also in respect of its form, which is the arrangement, composition and order of the phrases, that sacred poetry is also of great advantage of enormous superiority, in terms of majesty and beauty, over the [secular] poems which they regard as so praiseworthy.[29]

In short, in these two Hebrew works on the Bible (*'Or La-Netivah* and the *Be'ur* to Exodus), written in a traditional manner and aimed at Jewish readers, Mendelssohn cites the *Kuzari* and further develops Judah Ha-Levi's theories of the superiority of the Hebrew language, biblical poetry and the system of biblical cantillation, positions appropriate for internal Jewish discussion but scarcely appropriate for the Gentiles.

Mendelssohn's *Jerusalem:* The Superiority of Judaism

Mendelssohn's *Jerusalem*, however, written in German and aimed at non-Jewish readers, also manifests Ha-Levi's influence, but takes the argument of the superiority of oral communication in a different direction. Here, in the *Jerusalem*, the superiority of oral communication proves not the superiority of the Hebrew language and biblical poetry, but the superiority of the Jewish religion as such, in terms of its proximity to the universal and rational religion of nature. Mendelssohn

---

[28]*Ibid.*
[29]*Ibid*, p. 86a.

thus employs Ha-Levi's arguments, but transforms them on new levels and in new directions.

Ha-Levi's arguments regarding the superiority of the Hebrew language, biblical poetry, and oral communication were linguistic and pedagogic; they deal with the most effective way of communicating meaning and facilitating understanding. Mendelssohn starts with such linguistic and pedagogic arguments, but proceeds from the level of communicating meaning to the level of apprehending metaphysical and religious truth. It is not merely the Hebrew language and biblical poetry which are superior, because they effectively communicate the author's intention. It is now Jewish religion which is superior, because it conveys its adherents to the highest truth, with the least interference with or dilution of that truth by plastic symbols and the fixed, immutable and inflexible written word.

Ha-Levi (in the *Kuzari* 5:20) had recognized that visible symbols may be needed to represent abstract truths. As we shall see, Mendelssohn takes this further, and introduces two new elements into the discussion, both of which prove the superiority of Jewish religion, in general terms and specifically over Christianity.

First, since plastic symbols inevitably lead to idolatry, Judaism employs the commandments, rather than images, as concrete means of inculcating abstract truths, and is accordingly the closest religion to the universal religion of nature.

Second, we witness today a breakdown in immediate oral communication because of the spread of the written word. Much of Jewish teaching (the Oral Torah) was originally transmitted only orally to preserve its flexibility and immediacy, again demonstrating Judaism's superior ability to communicate truth.

These two elements, in turn, manifest another shift of emphasis, from the individual to the group (the nation or community). Mendelssohn, like Ha-Levi, deals with the problem of communicating meaning and intention by oral instruction, which is primarily a problem of the individual. The individual's comprehension of another individuals' intended meaning is facilitated by visible images and oral communication. But Mendelssohn again takes the next step, on the level of the group. Visible symbols may be effective concrete means of inculcating abstract truth; but, on the group level, such visible symbols historically and inevitably led to idolatry, and Judaism therefore had to evolve a different, safer method for inculcating abstract truths to the people.

The safer method that Judaism evolved was a system of ceremonial laws which lead the thinking Jew to consider the truths they embody. These laws were originally, by and large, transmitted orally, and were not committed to writing for centuries, until changed historic circumstances required that radical change.

The shift is thus clear: Mendelssohn takes Ha-Levi's arguments, but adds to them new dimensions and directions. Religious and metaphysical considerations are now added to pedagogic and linguistic ones, and the discussion of oral communication and visible symbols similarly provides a transition from the level of the individual seeking to understand meaning, to the level of the group seeking to attain ultimate religious truth.

Let us now examine how Mendelssohn develops his arguments and makes these shifts of level and direction.

Oral Instruction

Oral communication is not only more flexible and adaptable than the written word, but the ritual or ceremonial laws of Judaism, which are necessary to inculcate abstract truth, are themselves a kind of "living script," facilitating oral instruction (*muendlich Unterricht*), and encouraging the immediate and personal encounter of teacher and pupil that Ha-Levi (at least according to Moscato's interpretation) also had in mind with his aphorism, "From the mouth of authors, and not from books." According to Mendelssohn, originally the doctrines and laws of Judaism were, for the most part, preserved as "oral Torah," and thus

> were not connected to words or written characters which always remain the same, for all men and all times, amid all the revolutions of language, morals, manners, and conditions, words and characters which invariably present the same rigid forms, into which we cannot force our concepts without disfiguring them. They were entrusted to living, spiritual instruction, which can keep pace with all changes of time and circumstances, and can be varied and fashioned according to a pupil's needs, ability, and power of comprehension. One found the occasion for this paternal instruction in the written book of the law and in the ceremonial acts which the adherent of Judaism had to observe incessantly. It was, at first, expressly forbidden to write more about the law than God had caused Moses to record for the nation. 'What has been transmitted orally,' say the rabbis, 'you are not permitted to put in writing.' It was with much reluctance that the heads of the synagogue resolved in later periods to give the permission – which had become necessary – to write about the laws. They called this permission a destruction of the law and said, with the Psalmist, 'There is time when, for the sake of the Eternal, the law must be destroyed.' According to the original constitution, however, it was not supposed to be like that. The ceremonial law itself is a kind of living script, rousing the mind and heart, full of meaning, never ceasing to inspire contemplation and to provide the occasion and opportunity for oral instruction. What a student himself did and saw

being done from morning till night pointed to religious doctrines and convictions and spurred him on to follow his teacher, to watch him, to observe all his actions, and to obtain the instruction which he was capable of acquiring by means of his talents, and of which he had rendered himself worthy by his conduct.[30]

Visible Symbols

Thus far we are still on the pedagogic level of communicating meaning; oral instruction is superior to learning from books alone. However, we already discern Mendelssohn's shift to the level of religious truth, when he introduces the element of the ceremonial law, which was meant to be transmitted orally. For Ha-Levi, as we have seen, a person cannot attain the abstract truth "by his intellect alone, without relying on any sensible object, or without apprehending something visible, such as words, writing, or any visible or imagined form" (*Kuzari* 4:5). Mendelssohn also regards visible symbols as important.

> If at any time we wish to reawaken abstract concepts in our soul and to recall them to our mind through signs or symbols, these symbols will, of necessity, have to present themselves to us of their own accord....Here visible symbols are more helpful. Being permanent, they need not be re-created over and over again in order to be effective. Concrete objects probably served as the first visible symbols which mankind used to denote abstract concepts. Since every natural object has its own distinctive character which distinguishes it from all other objects, the impression it makes upon our senses will direct our attention chiefly upon the particular features which distinguish it, and stimulate the appropriate conceptualization and designation.[31]

Such graphic representations evolved into hieroglyphics, although it would take a subsequent "leap...[of] extraordinary human ingenuity" to progress from hieroglyphics to the written alphabet.

The problem is that visible, graphic representation, however beneficial it may be in inculcating abstract truths and in serving as

---

[30]Mendelssohn, *Jerusalem* (German, p. 84; Jospe ed. p. 74; Arkush ed. pp 102-103). This citation is from the Arkush and Altmann edition. The reference is to Psalm 119:126, "It is time to act for the Lord, for they have violated (*heferu*) your Torah." The rabbinic interpretation of this in Talmud Berakhot 54a to which Mendelssohn alludes involves a play on the word "violated": Rabbi Nathan says: "Violate (*haferu*) the Torah, because it is a time to act for the Lord." In other words, there are times when circumstances require that one act for the Lord even by transgressing a prohibition of the Torah. In this case, changed historic circumstances after the destruction of the Temple necessitated committing the Oral Torah to writing, despite the earlier prohibition.

[31]*Jerusalem*, German p. 90, Jospe ed. p, 79, Arkush and Altmann ed. p. 107.

aides-memoire, results in the two problems that Ha-Levi did not anticipate: the idolatrous corruption of the visible symbols, and the subsequent inflexibility of the written word which eventually supplants graphic symbols.

The first problem, that of idolatry, arose when people began to perceive the graphic symbols they employed to express abstract ideas as sacred in themselves, as embodying and being identified with what they were supposed to represent:

> Thus, misunderstanding or misuse transformed what should have been an instrument for the improvement of man's condition into a means for its decay and destruction....The masses had little or no understanding of the concepts and ideas which were to be associated with visible symbols. They tended to regard them not as symbols but as the things themselves....Objects had a reality of their own, in addition to their function and meaning as symbols.[32]

The Ceremonial Commandments instead of Symbols

Therefore, in order to provide the Jewish people with concrete and tangible means to preserve and inculcate abstract truth, and at the same time to avoid employing visible symbols which inevitably degenerate into idolatrous objects of veneration, God gave the Jews the ceremonial commandments of the Torah.

We have seen how difficult it is to preserve abstract religious concepts by the use of permanent symbols. Images and hieroglyphics lead to superstition and idolatry, while alphabetic script makes man too speculative – it displays and interprets the symbolic meaning of things and their relationship far too superficially, spares us the effort of penetrating and searching the material, and creates too wide a gap between doctrine and life (Lehre und Leben). To correct these defects, the lawgiver (Gesetzgeber)[i.e., Moses] gave the ceremonial laws (Zeremonialgesetz) to this nation. Man's daily dealings and conduct were to be linked to religious and moral insights. The law, to be sure, did not impel man to contemplation; it merely prescribed his acts, what he was to do or not to do. The great maxim of this constitution seems to have been: Men must be driven to action but merely stimulated to contemplation. Therefore each of these prescribed acts, each rite, each ceremony, had its special meaning and profound significance. It was closely linked to the affirmation of religious truth and moral law through speculation, and it provided an incentive for a man in search of truth to reflect about these sacred matters or to seek instruction from men of wisdom. The truths necessary for the happiness of the entire nation as well as its individual members were to be absolutely independent of all imagery. This was the fundamental purpose and aim of the law. Eternal verities were to be associated

---

[32]Jerusalem, German p. 93, Jospe ed. p. 82, Arkush and Altmann ed. pp. 110-111.

solely with deeds and practices, and these were to take the place of the symbols without which truth cannot be preserved. Man's actions are transitory; there is nothing permanent or enduring about them which, like hieroglyphic script, could lead to idolatry through misuse or misunderstanding. Moreover, deeds and practices have an advantage over written symbols: they do not isolate man, do not transform him into a solitary creature, poring over books and articles. On the contrary, they stimulate him to develop social contacts, to emulate others, and to seek oral communication and living instruction (*zum muendlichen, lebendigen Unterricht*).[33]

Oral instruction is accordingly superior to the written word for both the individual and the nation. The continuation of the passage (cited above; cf. note 21) argues that such living, oral instruction encourages the student to explore and emulate the living example of his teacher.

What then follows in the *Jerusalem*, an account of the ancient Israelites' worship of the Golden Calf (cf. Exodus, Chapter 32) appears at first glance to be a non-sequitur. But the connection is clear and real. It was in the prolonged absence of Moses (traditionally called "Moshe Rabbenu," "Moses *our teacher*") that the people, lacking the opportunity for such immediate, living, oral instruction, resorted to idolatrous imagery. In Mendelssohn's interpretation of the story (which, as Alexander Altmann has noted, is based on Judah Ha-Levi's interpretation in *Kuzari* 1:92-97),[34] the people "at first...probably did not intend to worship it as a deity....They spoke merely of a divine being that was to be their leader and take the place of Moses." Aaron, while providing them the Golden Calf as a surrogate leader, attempted to ensure their loyalty to God by proclaiming "Tomorrow will be a festival for the Lord," but on the morrow the "dancing and carousing mob" proclaimed "This is your God, O Israel, who brought you out of Egypt."

The Superiority of Judaism

Idolatrous corruption is thus the inevitable consequence of the use of plastic symbols to represent abstract religious and metaphysical truth. In sharp contrast with those who thought that his views on religious toleration were more in accord with a liberal Christianity than with traditional Judaism, Mendelssohn thus asserts the superiority of Judaism on two correlative levels, content and form. In terms of content, the basic teachings of Judaism, those truths necessary for human

---

[33]*Jerusalem*, German pp. 102-103, Jospe ed. p. 90, Arkush and Altmann ed. pp. 118-119.

[34]Cf. Altmann, *Commentary* in *Jerusalem*, p. 227.

fulfillment, are none other than the basic rational truths of the universal religion of nature. In the words of Alexander Altmann,[35]

Clearly, many readers of the Preface [to Mendelssohn's German edition of Menasseh ben Israel's *Vindiciae Judaeorum*] inferred from its tone and temper that Mendelssohn's stress on forbearance, love, and tolerance as the essence of religion indicated what they considered a growing closeness to Christian principles. They disregarded his explicit references to the Jewish tradition...for the purpose of showing its tolerant ethos, and they failed to perceive that in his view the 'true divine religion' (the religion of reason, or natural religion) formed the sole credal element of Judaism.

But it is also in terms of its religious forms that Judaism is superior, in its avoidance of plastic symbols in favor of the ceremonial laws as the means for inculcating the truth. Those laws were originally primarily transmitted orally, because of the superiority of living, oral instruction, which retains the quality of immediacy as well as the flexible capacity for adapting to changed circumstances of life.

Judaism, Mendelssohn concludes, thus consists of "religious doctrines and tenets, or eternal truths about God, His rule and Providence, without which man cannot be enlightened or happy," which are known purely rationally. In addition, Judaism teaches corollary "historical truths" which "disclose the fundamental purposes of the people's national existence," and which form the foundation for the law.[36] These historical truths are accepted on faith. Finally, Judaism as "revealed law" consists of "laws, precepts, commandments, rules of conduct: they were to be peculiar to this people, and their observance was to bring happiness to the entire nation as well as to its individual members."

As he then explains the function of these laws:

These laws were revealed, that is, they were made known by God through the spoken and written word. However, only their most essential part was embodied in letters; and even these written laws remain largely incomprehensible without the unwritten commentaries, elucidations, and specific definitions transmitted by oral and vivid instruction. They are unintelligible, or had to become

---

[35]Cf. Altmann, *Introduction* to *Jerusalem*, pp. 6-7.
[36]*Jerusalem*, German pp. 111-113, Jospe ed. pp. 97-98, Arkush and Altmann ed. pp. 126-127. According to Mendelssohn's interpretation of the Decalogue (*Be'ur* to Exodus, Chapter 20), the statement "I am the Lord your God who brought you out of the land of Egypt" (Exodus 20:2) is not a commandment, since only actions, and not convictions, can be commanded. It is, rather, a historical truth, which serves as a preamble to the other commandments, and on which they are founded.

unintelligible in the course of time, since no words or letters can retain their meaning unchanged from one generation to the next. The ultimate purpose of the written and unwritten laws prescribing actions as well as rules of life is [the attainment of] public and private salvation. But to a certain degree, they must also be regarded as a type of script and have significance and meaning as ceremonial laws. They guide the seeking mind to divine truths – partly eternal, partly historical – on which the religion of this people was based. The ceremonial law was to be the link between thought and action, between theory and practice. The ceremonial law was meant to stimulate personal relations and social contact between school and teacher, between student and instructor, and it was supposed to encourage competition and emulation.[37]

The Oral Torah

The superiority of oral communication, with its greater flexibility and immediacy, is thus one of the strengths of Judaism which, at least originally, was transmitted primarily as oral Torah. As we have seen, Mendelssohn says that

> written words are fixed forever, immutable. They represent rigid and unchangeable forms into which our concepts cannot be forced without being mutilated. [In Judaism, however,] our doctrines became part of a living tradition which was transmitted through oral instruction. Thus it could keep pace with all changes of time and circumstances; it could be altered and molded according to the needs and intellectual capacities of each student.[38]

It was only because of radically changed circumstances that the Oral Torah was committed to writing:

> It was only much later that the heads of the Synagogue decided, albeit with considerable reluctance, to grant permission – which by then had become necessary – to record some legal traditions in writing.[39]

This brings us, however, to a critical point in Mendelssohn's theory. Ha-Levi's theory of the superiority of oral communication is limited to the plane of individual communication and oral instruction. The arguments concerning the necessity for and superiority of the Oral Torah in the *Kuzari* are directed against Karaism, which threatened to undermine the authority of rabbinic teaching and law by its rejection of the talmudic traditions and by its acceptance of the Bible alone as

---

[37]*Jerusalem*, German pp. 113-114, Jospe ed. p. 99, Arkush and Altmann ed. pp. 127-128.
[38]*Jerusalem*, German p. 84, Jospe ed. pp. 73-74, Arkush and Altmann ed. p. 102.
[39]*Jerusalem*, German p. 84, Jospe ed. p. 74, Arkush and Altmann ed. p. 102.

the source of legitimate authority.[40] In other words, Ha-Levi cites the Oral Torah in the context of an internal Jewish debate which split much of the Jewish community in the Middle Ages. The Oral Torah was not, for Ha-Levi, evidence of the superiority of Judaism as such, but of the superiority and truth of the rabbinic traditions within Judaism.

For Mendelssohn, however, the Oral Torah is a crucial element in proving the superiority of Judaism itself. Since, as he explicitly acknowledges, it became necessary to commit the Oral Torah to writing, the obvious question is, what was the effect of that radical change on subsequent Jewish developments? After all, the change was not a recent one. To the contrary, the change took place at about the same time that Christianity was splitting away from Judaism.

Mendelssohn, however, fails to address this question. After stating (in the passage cited above) that it became necessary to commit the Oral Torah to writing, and stating that "this development was not in harmony with the original intent," he again shifts the discussion to the general question of written versus oral instruction, and laments the depersonalization of written communication:

> The ready availability of books and other printed materials, whose number has enormously increased since the invention of the printing press, has changed man radically. It has revolutionized human thought and knowledge. This development has, of course, been beneficial and contributed to the improvement of mankind....But like every good thing that happens to man on earth, it also has some evil side effects....We teach and instruct each other through writings; we get to know nature and man only from writings....Everything is reduced to the dead letter; the spirit of living dialogue no longer exists anywhere....As a result, a man has lost almost all value in the eyes of his fellowmen....This was not the case in ancient times....Man was more urgently in need of man; theory was more intimately connected with practice, contemplation more closely associated with action.[41]

This is such an important point for Mendelssohn that he then promises "to show the influence of these factors upon religion and morals more clearly."[42] However, in fact, Mendelssohn never does so explicitly in regard to Judaism. That is to say, Mendelssohn discusses at length and in general terms the problems inherent in representing

---

[40]Cf. *Kuzari* 3:33-74, and also Abraham ibn Ezra's commentary to Exodus 21:24 and Leviticus 24:17-21. For a concise survey of the issues, see Daniel J. Lasker, "Rabbanism and Karaism: The Contest for Supremacy" in *Great Schisms in Jewish History*, ed. Raphael Jospe and Stanley Wagner (New York, 1981), pp. 47-72.

[41]*Jerusalem*, German p. 85, Jospe ed. pp. 74-75, Arkush and Altmann ed. p. 103.

[42]*Jerusalem*, German p. 86, Jospe ed. p. 76, Arkush and Altmann ed. p. 104.

abstract truth by plastic symbols. But, except for his brief discussion (based on Ha-Levi's interpretation) of the Golden Calf, he does not examine the "influence of these factors upon religion and morals" in specifically Jewish terms.

If it is true that Judaism is superior, in large measure, due to the oral quality of its teaching and the concomitant flexibility inherent in the Oral Torah, then surely one needs to question the effects on the Oral Torah and its alleged flexibility once it came to be written down. For a millenium and a half the "oral" Torah of Judaism had, in fact, been transmitted in written form, and Mendelssohn promises to assess the "influence of these factors (i.e. writing) on religion and morals," but he does not do so with regard to Judaism since the time of the editing of the Mishnah! Mendelssohn's silence on this point is deafening.

Mendelssohn's innovation is thus incomplete. On the one hand, he extended logically Ha-Levi's theory of the superiority of oral communication from the level of the individual to the level of the group, and from the question of oral instruction to Oral Torah. On the other hand, he fails to apply his own theory of the superiority of oral communication to Judaism as it has, by his own acknowledgement, existed for most, if not all, of the centuries of its encounter with Christianity. Mendelssohn does not answer in Jewish terms the question he poses in general terms of religion and morals. What is more, he does not even ask the question in Jewish terms.

Ahad Ha-'Am

Our question was asked by, among others, Ahad Ha-'Am (Asher Ginzberg), more than a century after Mendelssohn. Ahad Ha-'Am is not ordinarily categorized, like Mendelssohn, as a religious thinker; his Hebrew essays are usually included in anthologies of Zionist thought and Hebrew literature. And yet, Ahad Ha-'Am did write on religious questions, such as his opposition to the Reform movement in his essay "'Al Shetei Ha-Se'ipim" ("Between the Two Branches"),[43] and his

---

[43]"'Al Shetei Ha-Se'ipim" was published in 1910, in response to the publication in 1909 of Claude G. Montefiore's commentary on the Synoptic Gospels. The title, which can be translated as "Between the Two Branches" or "Between the Two Opinions," means something like the English expression "straddling the fence," and is a reference to Elijah's challenge to the people on Mount Carmel, "How long will you skip between two opinions?"(I Kings 18:21). The essay was translated into English by Leon Simon under the title "Judaism and the Gospels" (in *Ten Essays on Zionism and Judaism*, 1922) and subsequently partially re-issued by him under the title "Jewish and Christian Ethics" (in *Ahad Ha-Am: Essays, Letters, Memoirs*, 1946). The passages from Ahad Ha-'A m

earlier critique of rigid Orthodoxy in "Torah Sheba-Lev" ("The Law of the Heart").[44]

"The Law of the Heart" was written in 1894, in reaction to the arrest and jailing of Eliezer Ben-Yehuda by the Turkish authorities in Israel (then Palestine), after he was accused of sedition by the extreme Orthodox leadership of the "Old Yishuv" (i.e., the Jewish community which existed for centuries before the modern Zionist settlement in the Land of Israel).[45] As Joseph Goldstein has shown, Ahad Ha-'Am's earlier essays had related to Jewish religion in a relatively positive light, reflecting Ahad Ha-'Am's view of Jewish religion as a transcending and unifying factor in national life, "raising the heart of the nation" above the various divisions into which it was split.[46]

---

cited here are my translation. It should be noted here that Ahad Ha-'Am refers in a number of his writings to Judah Ha-Levi, for whom he had great respect as both a Hebrew poet and Jewish philosopher. For example, cf. his references to Ha-Levi in "'Emet Me-'Erez Yisra'el," in *Kol Kitvei Ahad Ha-'Am* (Tel Aviv, 1965), p. 30; "Li-She'elat Ha-Lashon," *ibid*, p. 94; "Shinui Ha-'Arakhin," *ibid* pp. 157-159, where he reacts to earlier criticism of his theory that the Jews have become a "people of the book" instead of a "literary people"; "Moshe," *ibid* p. 346; "Shilton Ha-Sekhel," *ibid*, p. 365.

[44]"Torah Sheba-Lev" ("The Law of the Heart"), written in 1894, was partially translated by Leon Simon under the title of "The People of the Book" (in *Ahad Ha-'Am*, etc., 1922, and included under the title "The Law of the Heart" in *The Zionist Idea*, ed. Arthur Hertzberg [Philadelphia, 1959], pp. 251-255). In his essay "Shinui Ha-'Arakhin" ("A Transvaluation of Values," 1898), Ahad Ha-'Am defends his "Torah Sheba-Lev" and criticizes a group of young Nietzschean authors, such as M. J. Berdichevsky, who followed Nietzschean idealization of brute physical force. The Jewish people, Ahad Ha-'Am argues, has lost its status as a "literary people," and degenerated into the "people of the book," not because it lacked physical might, but because, lacking the natural setting of a national homeland, it needed a moral and spiritual renewal. The true "superman" is not characterized by brute force but by moral and spiritual superiority. The national renewal would thus not be based on physical strength, as the Nietzscheans mistakenly thought, but on the combination of national and moral goals. Ahad Ha-'Am then cites Ha-Levi as an example of a person combining such national and moral goals. Cf. "Shinui 'Ha-'Arakhin" in *Kol Kitvei Ahad Ha-'Am*, pp. 157-159. The essay was translated under the title "A Transvaluation of Values" in Leon Simon's *Selected Essays by Ahad Ha-'Am* (1948), and under the title "Judaism and Nietzsche" (in *Ahad Ha-Am*, etc., 1946).

[45]Joseph Goldstein, "Yahaso shel Ahad Ha-'Am La-Dat Be-Aspaqlariyah Historit," in *Temurot Ba-Historiah Ha-Yehudit Ha-Hadashah*, (Presented to Shemu'el Ettinger) (Jerusalem, 1988), pp. 159-168.

[46]Ahad Ha-'Am, "Milu'im Le-Derekh Ha-Hayyim," cited by Goldstein, p. 165.

Such a morally despicable act as the rabbis' informing on Ben-Yehuda and turning him over to the hostile authorities apparently led to a change in Ahad Ha-'Am's attitude to Jewish religion or to a crystallization of what may have been latent in his earlier attitude. What kind of religion is it which can produce such moral obtuseness and outright immorality?

"The People of the Book" and not "a Literary People"

According to Ahad Ha-'Am, such an act cannot be the behavior of a "literary people" (*'am sifruti*), possessing a living culture and living values. It could only occur in "the people of the book" (*'am ha-sefer*), a people enslaved for hundreds of years by and to the written word.

> Our tragedy is that we are not a literary people but the people of the book. The difference between these is very great. Literature, like the people, is a living force, acquiring or shedding a form. Generations come and go, but the people lives on in all of them. Books come and books go, and literature lives on in all of them. Therefore, one can only call "a literary people" a [nation] whose life and whose literary life, i.e., generations and books, progress and develop together, the literature according to the needs of the generation, and the generation according to the spirit of the literature....However 'the people of the book' is the slave of the book, a people whose soul has flown away from its heart and completely entered the written word.[47]

Unlike Y. L. Gordon, Ahad Ha-'Am did not accuse the rabbis themselves of moral insensitivity. The problem is much more serious and profound than that, and the issue is not a particular individual rabbi or group of rabbis. The true problem is that the rabbis, like the entire nation, are enslaved to the written word. They do not in fact have any choice; they can do nothing else, because they have no living Torah. This is the true national-religious tragedy.[48] The written and sealed book constitutes a barrier between the heart and real life.

Mendelssohn, it will be recalled, had complained that

> as a result, a man has lost almost all value in the eyes of his fellowmen....We no longer need the man of experience; we only need his writings. In one word: we are literati, men of letters [in the literal sense of the word]. Our whole being depends on the printed word, and we can no longer comprehend how mortal man can educate and perfect himself without books.[49]

---

[47]Ahad Ha-'Am, "Torah Sheba-Lev," in *'Al Parashat Derakhim* (Tel Aviv, 1964), Vol. 1, pp. 82-83.

[48]"Torah Sheba-Lev," p. 84.

[49]Mendelssohn, *Jerusalem*, German p. 85, Jospe ed. p. 75, Arkush and Altmann ed. p. 103.

Mendelssohn, however, is describing a general human predicament, and as we have noted, he does not in fact relate specifically to the Jewish component of the problem, by asking what impact being written down had on the (originally) Oral Torah. This is precisely the next step, missing in Mendelssohn, that Ahad Ha-'Am takes.

According to Ahad Ha-'Am, when the Oral Torah became written down, the Jewish people ceased to be "a literary people," creating a living literature, and came instead to be "the people of the book," a people incapable of reacting freely and immediately to the needs of the hour, a people enslaved to what had been written down long before by a different generation, in different times and circumstances.

> Everything exists only by the written word. Any natural or moral vision capable of arousing some motion in the heart must invoke written approbation permitting it to do this thing. Even then, the arousal is no longer simple and natural, but must accord with a particular, artificial program, fixed and limited from the outset. Therefore both of them, the people and its book, stand in their position, and their form does not change much over the generations, since both of them lack the forces which could impel them: the people [lacks] a direct, immediate relationship between the heart and whatever is outside it; and the book [lacks] the heart's rebellion, based on that relationship, against those things which are not in accordance with its needs.[50]

This petrification of the national heart and spirit is a direct result of the increasing reliance on the written word, once the Oral Torah became written down, and the Jewish people ceased to create literature, and became ever more enslaved to the book. But this was not the case, Ahad Ha-'Am believed, in the period of the Bible (exemplified best by the prophets) and the Second Temple.

> All this changed later on. The Oral Torah, which should properly be called the 'Torah of the heart,' became petrified in the written word, and the heart of the people became completely filled by one clear and strong recognition: the recognition of its own absolute insignificance and eternal enslavement to the written word.[51]

Conclusion

Judah Ha-Levi's theory of the superiority of oral communication in the *Kuzari* focuses on the excellence of the Hebrew language and biblical poetry, an excellence manifested in the biblical cantillation notes which effectively transform the written words into spoken words. Scripture thus becomes audible, and is endowed with the superior

---

[50]Ahad Ha-'Am, "Torah Sheba-Lev," pp. 82-83.
[51]Ahad Ha-'Am, "Torah Sheba-Lev," p. 83.

qualities of oral communication. These theories are replicated and amplified in Moses Mendelssohn's *'Or La-Netivah* and *Be'ur.* However, Mendelssohn's *Jerusalem* expands the theory in two directions. First, the use of concrete, plastic images to represent abstract truth inevitably leads to idolatry. Second, there is a tendency, especially and increasingly pronounced in modern times, to rely on the written word alone, at the expense of true, immediate, and flexible oral communication.

According to Mendelssohn, Judaism, to avoid the first danger (idolatrous images) relies on the system of ceremonial commandments, rather than images, to inculcate the truth. Similarly, to avoid, insofar as possible, the second danger (the inflexibility of the written word), and in order to ensure maximum flexibility for its necessary legislation, it communicated most of its laws in the form of the Oral Torah.

Mendelssohn fails, however, to fulfill his promise to assess the impact on religion and morals of these dangerous developments in specifically Jewish terms; his discussion is limited to their effects in general terms, and avoids any reference to the consequences of the Oral Torah's having been finalized in written form after the destruction of the Second Temple.

Mendelssohn thus takes Ha-Levi's theory of the superiority of oral communication one step further, applying it not only to individual instruction, but to the nation's Oral Torah, and extending it from Ha-Levi's argument for the superiority of the Hebrew language and biblical poetry to an argument for the superiority of Judaism itself. But Mendelssohn failed to take the next logical step, and to examine the implications of his own theory of the superiority of oral law for the Oral Torah, once it came to be written down.

Did Mendelssohn, who was fundamentally a traditionally religious Jew, believing in the Torah and observing its precepts, remain silent on this critical point in his theory because he simply did not see its logical implications? Did he, perhaps, believe that this was not a Jewish problem at all, because the Talmud remained, despite its being written down, fundamentally a flexible oral system of law? Or did Mendelssohn, on the other hand, possibly believe that this was, in actuality, a Jewish problem, but that the *Jerusalem,* a book written for a non-Jewish audience in defense of his Jewish commitment, was not the appropriate forum for airing internal Jewish problems? Or, perhaps, did Mendelssohn, who encountered difficulties with the established rabbinic leadership of his day on account of various innovative theories he propounded, in fact anticipate further problems and therefore remain silent? If so, we would need to read between the lines, as Leo

Strauss recommended for understanding the medieval Jewish philosophers.

Ahad Ha-'Am took the next step that Mendelssohn failed to take. His position is clear and unambiguous: when the Oral Torah became written down, it became petrified and ceased to be a living Torah. The nation, which had been "a literary people," producing living and dynamic literature in immediate response to its experiences in life, now became "the people of the book," a people enslaved to the fixed, dead written word, and incapable of responding to life's challenges. Without extending further the scope of this study, we may also find an echo of Ha-Levi's theory of the superiority of oral communication in the theories of Franz Rosenzweig (whose indebtedness to and interest in Judah Ha-Levi's *Kuzari* and poetry are well known), in his essay "Die Bauleute" (1923), where he argues against Martin Buber's anti-nomianism. The written law (*Gesetz*), which has the objective quality of the past, must be transformed into a commandment (*Gebot*) experienced in the present, and subjectively addressing each individual Jew. From a historical perspective, therefore, the Jewish people had to commit the Oral Torah to fixed, written form in the Talmud after the destruction of the Temple. From a religious perspective, however, the individual Jew today must restore the written law to its prior, original status of oral commandment.

Ha-Levi's theory of the superiority of oral communication, which simply aimed at proving the the superiority of the Hebrew language and biblical poetry, was thus expanded by Mendelssohn into a theory of the superiority of Judaism. But what Mendelssohn failed to address, the impact on Jewish religion of the Oral Torah's being written down, became central to Ahad Ha-'Am's attack on the inflexibility and impotence of the *halakhah* and Jewish spiritual life. Rosenzweig, on the other hand, saw the need to restore an immediate oral quality to the objective written law.

Part Thirteen
HASIDISM: MESSIANISM IN MODERN TIMES

38

Hasidism as the Image of Demonism: the Satiric Writings of Judah Leib Mises

Yehuda Friedlander
Bar Ilan University

"The demon Jonathan told me that they have a shadow, but they do not have a shadow of a shadow" (BT Yev. 122a).[1]

The book *Kin'at ha-Emet* and its appendix *Likutei Perahim* (Vienna: 1828), Judah Leib Mises' scholastic satire, consists of a fictitious study marked by a mixture of routine and innovation, both in terms of its type and structure, and in terms of its contents and the manner in which they are fashioned. Regarding type and structure, this is a "conversation in Heaven" between Maimonides and Rabbi Solomon ben Moses of Chelm (1717?-1781), the author of *Sefer Mirkevet ha-Mishneh* (Frankfurt-am-Main: 1751).[2] The genre of conversations in the "World of Truth," which come to the knowledge of the audience of readers on earth by all manner of ways, was developed in the new Hebrew literature at the end of the eighteenth and the beginning of the nineteenth centuries, and not only by satirists. To mention only a few

---

[1]See: Rashi, Yev. *op. cit.*, c. v. *"Limdani Yonatan Shida:"* "He was a demon or erudite regarding them." The version in BT Git. 66a: "Jonathan my son [beni] taught me." See *Alfasi*, Yev. 56a: "He concludes that a demon has a shadow, but does not have a shadow of a shadow."

[2]Novellae on *Mishneh Torah* by Maimonides. The first section of the book was first published in Frankfurt-am-Main in 1751, while sections II and III were printed for the first time in Salonika in the year 1782, posthumously. See also: Avraham Brik, "R. Shelomo Helme, Ba'al Mirkevet ha-Mishneh" (R. Solomon of Chelm, the author of Mirkevet ha-Mishneh), *Sinai* 61 (1967), pp. 168-184.

159

examples: the theoretical dialogue *Sihah be-Olam ha-Neshamot beyn ha-Rav R. David Kimhi u-veyn ha-Hakham R. Yoel Brill* (A Conversation in the World of Souls between Rabbi David Kimhi and the Sage, Rabbi Joel Brill), by Solomon Levisohn (Prague: 1811);[3] the satire *Kol Mehatzetzim* (The Sound of Archers), by Tobias Gutman Feder (written in 1813);[4] and the satire *Sihah be-Eretz ha-Hayim* (A Conversation in the World of Life) by Aaron Wolfsohn of Halle (*Ha-Me'assef*, Berlin: 1794-1797).[5] Conversations by the dead had therefore become a quite prevalent genre during this period, and it should come as no surprise that Judah Leib Mises also made use of it in his writings. This genre developed in the polemical and satirical literature under the inspiration and influence of, *inter allia*, the work of the second-century Greek writer Lucian, through the translation of his writings into German by Christoph Martin Wieland (1733-1813).[6] The fact that these conversations take place in the "World of Truth" imparts to them credibility, and needless to say, a great deal of authority, in the eyes of the reader who lives with the awareness of the difference between this world as a vestibule, as the world of degradation, and the World to Come as the banquet hall, in which the righteous enjoy the brilliance of the Divine Presence.

Tobias Feder, in his satire, and Solomon Levisohn, in his linguistic studies, made no mention of how the conversations came from the world of souls to their hands, while Aaron Wolfsohn of Halle writes as a publisher that *Sihah be-Eretz ha-Hayim* was written by a friend "while lying on his deathbed, suffering from the illness from which he died."[7] In contrast, Mises writes in "A Word to the Reader" that "Towards evening, when I went to meditate in the field, I met a man with a scroll in his hand. He stood before me, and said, 'Take this scroll...and now, if my words will find favor in your eyes, please do this for the sake of the truth, and publish them.' So spoke the man to me, and he placed the scroll in my hands, and he departed. Since I was

---

[3]Rabbi David Kimhi (Radak, 1160-1235); Joel Brill (1760-1802).

[4]See: Yehuda Friedlander, *Be-Misterei ha-Satirah - Perakim ba-Satirah ha-Ivrit ha-Hadashah ba-Me'ah ha-Yud-Tet* (Hebrew Satire in Europe in the Nineteenth Century) (Ramat Gan: Bar Ilan University Press, 1984), pp. 11-75.

[5]See: Yehuda Friedlander, *Perakim ba-Satirah ha-Ivrit be-Shilhei ha-Ma'ah ha-Yud-Het be-Germaniya* (Studies in Hebrew Satire in Germany) (Tel Aviv: Papyrus, 1980), pp. 121-200.

[6]This issue was discussed extensively in Shmuel Werses's study, "Hedei ha-Satirah shel Lucianus be-Sifrut ha-Haskalah ha-Ivrit" (Echoes of Lucian's Satire in the Hebrew Enlightenment Literature), *Criticism and Interpretation* 11-12 (1978), pp. 84-119. See: *ibid.*, pp. 88-97.

[7]Friedlander, *Perakim*, p. 145.

startled by this vision, I could not speak and ask him what was his name."[8]

Mises, like Aaron Wolfsohn, is therefore a presumed publisher; unlike the earlier works, however, the setting in which he is given the work for publication is of a mystic nature. The book is given to him towards evening, when the persona of the narrator is alone, and an unidentified character of a "man" stands before him and quickly vanishes. The persona of the narrator receives a sort of "revelation," for it is possible that this "man" is none other than an angel, one of those angels "who speak with the prophets and appear to them in the prophetic vision. Therefore they are called 'men,' for their level is close to the level of human comprehension."[9] It should be noted that a mystical introduction to a rational satire is intended to prepare the reader for rational dialogues which take place in Heaven; this reader is one who is emotionally prepared to accept the existence of a close link between the two worlds. The satirist utilizes the world-view of his target audience for his own purposes. In this work Mises adopts some of the satirical methods of Isaac Erter, who published in 1823 his satirical work *Moznei Mishkal*, which is written as a "nocturnal vision."[10] Erter the rationalist did not view himself as a seer of visions, Heaven forbid,[11] but rather chose, for an understandable reason, to impart to his work a visionary, mystic nature.[12]

Kin'at ha-Emet consists of four main sections: the "Word to the Reader" by Mises, writing as the editor (pp. 3-20); three imaginary-scholastic conversations between Maimonides and the author of *Sefer Mirkevet ha-Mishneh* (pp. 21-152); interpretive notes and references

---

[8]*Kin'at ha-Enet*, p. 3. The following citations are from the 1828 edition.

[9]See: Maimonides, *Mishneh Torah*, Laws of the Fundamental Principles of the Torah 2:7. See also *Tanhuma*, *Vayeshev* 2: "'A man came upon him' [Gen. 37:15] – the reference here is not to a man, but rather to Gabriel, as it is written, 'the man Gabriel' [Dan. 9:21]."

[10]First printed in *Bikurei ha-Itim* (1822), pp. 166-169. See: Isaac Erter, *Ha-Tzofeh le-Bet Yisrael* (Watchman for the House of Israel), *Mahbarot le-Sifrut* (Tel Aviv: 1952), pp. 9-17. There is a marked influence by Mises upon Erter's works written after 1828. Regarding this, see: Joseph Klausner, *Historiya shel ha-Sifrut ha-Ivrit ha-Hadashah* (The History of Modern Hebrew Literature II (Jerusalem: 1937), p. 330.

[11]See: *ibid.*, *Tekhunat ha-Tzofeh* (The Nature of the Watchman), p. 8: "And I have not set my face as flint to say to my people, I am among the prophets, and to impart the splendor of heavenly seers to myself....I am not a seer, not one who sees visions, rather I watch for you, O House of Israel."

[12]All his satiric work follows the format of *Moznei Mishkal*. See: Klausner, *ibid.*, p. 326.

for these conversations by the editor, and the appendix *Likutei Perahim*, which contains passages taken from "the books of the Sages of Israel" (pp. 153-198) against the belief in demons and spirits, sorcery, and reincarnation. These sections complement one another, and together form the satirical work of Judah Leib Mises. The last section is, in practice, a source of information for both the imaginary conversations and the conclusions of the editor.

I. The Point of View of the Editor-Satirist in "A Word to the Reader"

In general, the point of view of the editor-satirist is external, for the editor is not included among the characters taking part in the work, which permits him to arrive at some sort of "objective" analysis, evaluation, and judgement. This is especially true regarding ideological satire.[13] Mises, in the guise of the editor, after the mystical introduction, proclaims the foundation stone for his world-view, bolstering it with a citation from the author of *Novelot Hokhmah:* "The light of intelligence is from the God who graces man with knowledge, and the father of truth will not bequeath us falsehoods. The light of religion is also received from God; is it possible that God will contradict His words [?]"[14] Alongside this declaration, which avers the credibility of the arguments which will follow it, we find two biting remarks, one somewhat reserved, and the other quite blunt, which allude to the hostility expected from one portion of the target audience to whom the satire is directed, and to the deprecatory attitude to be expected from another part of the same audience: (a) "the truth will not, in fact, find favor in the eyes of man, and only the Lord Himself will love it";[15] (b) "I have learned of the folly of a sect of the newcomers who have just arrived, who call themselves by the name '*maskilim,*'...who have decided to say that words of wisdom are to be found only in the books written in the

---

[13]This is how Boris Uspensky holds (following in the footsteps of Bachtin); he argues that "this position of the alien in the ideological stratum is typical of the satire" of the modern period. See: Boris Uspensky, *Ha-Poetikah shel ha-Kompositzityah* (A Poetics of Composition) (1970), Heb. trans. by Gideon Toury (Tel Aviv: Sifriat Poalim, 1986), pp. 119, 164n.

[14]*Kin'at ha-Emet,* p. 3. See also Joseph Solomon Delmedigo of Crete, *Novelot Hokhmah* (Basle: 1631), p. 6. Mises repeats this fundamental declaration, in a different version, towards the end of his introduction, basing himself on *Kuzari* 1:47 (should be: 69): "Far be it from the Lord to lie, and far be it from Him to engage in what the intelect removes, placing falsehood in its stead." Mises does not cite this passage accurately. See *Kin'at ha-Emet,* p. 16.

[15]*Kin'at ha-Emet, ibid.,* p. 3.

languages of the [non-Jewish] peoples, and in works written by people of whom they have never heard....Therefore I have intentionally brought some proofs from the sages of the [non-Jewish] peoples."[16] Mises wants to justify his reliance upon non-Jewish sources "whose authors did not intend in their statements and in their researches to oppose the opinions regarding matters touching upon the religion of our people," even from a presumed halakhic point of view, and he directs his words to the believers: "We should consider what is written in these researches ['the words of authors who are not from the Children of Israel'], for regarding them it was said: 'Non-Jews speak innocently, and in a matter not related to the body of the case at hand, they are believed.'"[17]

It is in this manner that the editor-satirist "methodologically" justifies the accumulation of citations, which, in actual fact, is only a common scholastic-satiric stratagem. Mises' point of view as a satiric editor is double-faced. It expresses an attitude of courting the reader, along with one of arrogant haughtiness. The editor-courter desires to introduce into the reader's mind the awareness that the aggressive attack on Hasidism and on the belief in demons and spirits does not contain a speck of heresy,[18] but rather is intended to preserve and

---

[16]*Ibid.*, pp. 3-4. Regarding the attitude of Mises, the extreme rationalist, towards the maskilim who fanatically adhere to the books of non-Jewish scholars, see: Rafael Mahler, *Ha-Hasidut veha-Haskalah* (Hasidism and Haskalah) (Merhavia: Sifriat Poalim, 1961), pp. 57, 81.

[17]*Ibid.*, p. 4. See: BT Git. 28b: "And as for your question, why in such an instance [if the report comes] from a Court of idolators she is not allowed to marry again, seeing that it is a recognized principle with us that [the word of] an idolator speaking without ulterior motives is to be accepted, [the answer is that] this applies only to a matter in which they themselves have not participated, but where the matter is one in which they themselves have participated, they are prone to indulge in falsehood." See also: Git. 19b, Yev. 121b, B. K. 114b. See: Maimonides, *Mishneh Torah*, Laws of Divorce 13:11-14; *Shulhan Arukh, Even ha-Ezer* 17:14-16, and *Pit'hei Teshuvah* and *Ba'er Hetev, loc. cit.* Mises himself reflies upon *Imrei Binah*, section II (should be: III), chap. 2. He did not clarify this vague statement. The reference is to the book *Me'or Einayim* by Rabbi Azariah Min ha-Adumim (Di Rossi) (1511-1578), which is divided into three sections, the third of which is entitled *Imrei Binah*. The book was first published in Mantua in 1574, with a second edition published in Berlin in 1794. It is written in this work (chap. 2, p. 8): "And here the person who reads what we say in the following chapters will find that all the non-Jews...they talk innocently, and have no connection with the matter at hand itself." I assume that Mises possessed the 1794 edition.

[18]*Kin'at ha-Eemet, loc. cit.*: "So that the young men and youth of Israel will know...that the denial of such things is not heresy and a contradiction directed

develop the pure faith, an act of tearing down in order to build. The courting of the reader is one of the outstanding distinguishing marks of a satirical work; the satirist requires the reader as a "partner," and the most delicate relationship is woven, as it were, between them.[19] It is in this sense that we may understand Mises' position as an editor, who desires to draw the reader closer before drawing back the curtain on the main scene in the second section of the work. By way of contrast, his demonstrative attitude of haughtiness vis-à-vis the 'maskilim' reveals that the target of his satiric attack is composed of two heterogeneous groups.

The editor-publisher does not only focus on the group of his opponents; he also assumes an educational role, a public mission, directed towards the masses, for "the masses also have the right to learn by means of the intellect, especially if they know from experience that confused knowledge causes much damage." He therefore views himself, as every educated person with national responsibility, "obligated to teach the truth, according to his knowledge and the limits of his intelligence, to his brothers lacking in knowledge, in simple language."[20] Mises therefore sees himself as belonging to the group of maskilim loyal to Jewish tradition in the spirit of the halakhah, and joins, in his own way, the struggle of the Orthodox rabbis who fought against the spread of false beliefs, on the background of the joint struggle of the maskilim and the rabbis against Kabbalah, Sabbatianism and its offshoots, and Hasidism in the eighteenth and nineteenth century.[21]

II. The Point of View of the Editor-Satirist in "A Conversation in the World of Souls"

Mises could adopt an external point of view in "A Word to the Reader," which is not the case in the body of the work, in the long dialogues between Maimonides and the author of Mirkevet ha-Mishneh. In actuality, these dialogues are only the conversations of sages who possess very similar views, and who bring each other up to

---

against the religion of God, and from them untill now the Sages of Israel have not believed in them [demons, sorcery, and reincarnation]."

[19]See: Dorothy B. Coleman, Rabelais (Cambridge University Press, 1971), p. 101: "In satire the author-reader conspiracy is a delicate balance."

[20]Kin'at ha-Emet, ibid., p. 9.

[21]See: Shmuel Werses, Haskalah ve-Shabta'ut Toldotav shel Ma'avak (Haskalah and Sabbatianism: The Story of a Controversy) (Jerusalem: Zalman Shazar Center for Jewish History, 1988). For Mises' part in this struggle, see ibid, pp. 113-114.

date. The author of *Mirkevet ha-Mishneh* tells Maimonides about the waning of "the pure faith" and the development of demonism among the Jewish people. He places the full responsibility for this on "One person lacking in knowledge named Israel ben Eliezer, who is called *Baal Shem* by the masses; his forefathers were among the poorest of the people who lived in one village in the state of Poland (a place of darkness and folly),...also when he became a man, he was lacking and deficient in all words of Torah and knowledge, and he did not understand a single teaching in the Talmud, and certainly not in the Bible."[22] The editor appends a marginal comment to this blunt statement: "Do not wonder, gentle reader, at the words of the author of *Mirkevet ha-Mishneh* ('and certainly not in the Bible') because in most cases, even the learned, who possess great knowledge of the Talmud, do not understand a single Biblical passage properly."[23]

The character of Maimonides contains a quite instructive innovation. He is depicted as a superintellectual, amazingly up-to-date, for he tells his friend about "the sage Copernicus"...who proved with decisive signs that the earth revolves in 24 hours around its axis, from west to east, and within the course of a whole year it travels around the sun."[24] Maimonides therefore accepted the heliocentric theory of Copernicus the Pole. It follows from his statement that Poland is "a place of darkness and folly" only for Jews.[25]

Furthermore, Maimonides is not described as a rigid scholastic who adheres to his views, and who is not willing to reexamine them, but rather as a brave scholar who is willing to reject his views in the light of scientific progress, and is not deterred from continual self-criticism. Mises puts in his mouth the admission, "I also admit without shame that I have erred in many matters because I held too strongly to the philosophical ways of the sage Aristotle...and I did not thoroughly research his conclusions with my intellect...and this caused me to deduce and decide upon the confused opinion that there are spheres in the world which contain separate intelligences,...how I wonder at

---

[22]*Kin'at ha-Emet*, First Conversation, p. 22.
[23]*Ibid.*
[24]*Ibid.*, p. 29.
[25]In a marginal comment, *ibid.*, Mises finds it necessary to provide informative details about Copernicus, "who was born in the year 1473, in the city Torun in the state of Prussia. This sage studied in university in the city of Cracow." Regarding the image of Mainonides in Mises' work, see: Yehuda Friedlander, "Mekomah shel ha-Haskalah be-Sifrut ha-'Haskalah'" (The Status of the Halakhah in the Literature of the *Haskalah*), *Mekhkarei Yerushalayim be-Makhshevet Yisrael* (Jerusalem Studies in Jewish Thought) 5 (1986), pp. 349-362.

myself now, how could I have believed in such vanities then!"[26] Maimonides is removed from the intellectual world of the Middle Ages, and is fashioned for the nineteenth century *maskil* as the ideal modern scientist.

An instructive, clear example of Mises' observation point as the editor-satirist is to be found in his formulation of the statement by the author of *Mirkevet ha-Mishneh*, who asks Maimonides: "Why have almost all the other nations, who also in early times were imprisoned in the bonds of foolishness, thrown off from themselves its traces, and every day they proceed and succeed in the ways of wisdom...while the majority of our people sinks daily in the pit of folly?"[27] This statement is (with minor changes) the statement made by Mises himself in the introduction to his essay, "Concerning the Reason for the Lack of Human Wisdoms in the Members of Our People," which was published in *Ha-Tzefirah* (ed. Meir ha-Levi Letteris) in 1824: "Every educated person who sees where wisdom has burst forth in these days among the [non-Jewish] peoples, and how lacking it still is among the Israelites, will want to know the reason for this, why the other nations, who were imprisoned in the bonds of foolishness, have now thrown over its traces and every day they proceed and succeed in the ways of wisdom...while the people of Israel sinks daily in the pit of folly and ignorance."[28] Mises does not bother to conceal this fact, and refers the readers of *Kin'at ha-Emet* to his essay.[29]

In short, the editor-satirist is quickly revealed as identifying with the character he depicts. Furthermore, he is embodied in it.[30] Mises, as the editor-commentator-satirist, does not adopt the point of reference of the characters he describes, but rather creates them as fictitious characters, in accordance with an outline he has drawn from the beginning.

---

[26]*Kin'at ha-Emet, ibid.*, pp. 61-62.

[27]*Ibid*, Third Conversation, p. 119.

[28]*Ha-Tzefirah*, First Issue (only issue published), p. 54. He signed this article with his own name, and did not adopt the guise of a "editor."

[29]In a marginal comment, *Kin'at ha-Emet, ibid.*, p. 119: "This article has recently been published in the book *Ha-Tzfirah*, but because I added to it, and put certain matters in it, therefore I will not be deterred from printing it a second time." We have before us the editor attesting to the fact that he is an author.

[30]See: Uspenski, p. 56.

III. Maimonides and the Author of Mirkevet ha-Mishneh: between Routine and Innovation

The manner in which Mises fashions the image of Maimonides as an example for the maskilim of his generation is not innovative, but it does contain an additional (or intensified) aspect in addition to the aspects that had been stressed before him, by the Berlin *maskilim* at the end of the eighteenth century.[31] The influence of Aaron Wolfsohn of Halle upon Mises is quite pronounced.[32] Mises' innovation is expressed mainly in the manner which he chose to describe Rabbi Solomon of Chelm in his satire as one of the supporters of the *Haskalah*, and especially as a vigorous opponent of Hasidism and its influence upon the masses. Rabbi Solomon of Chelm died in 1781, 46 years after the Baal Shem Tov revealed himself in 1735, while *Sefer Mirkevet ha-Mishneh* was published in 1751, only sixteen years after the Baal Shem Tov revealed himself. Mises apparently was deeply impressed by Rabbi Solomon of Chelm's introduction to his book, and especially by the following description:

> And some of them [the 'congregation of the learned']who are empty of all knowledge, and are small and meagre. They have not struggled with mystical knowledge,[33] nor with the Gemara, Rashi, and Tosafot. He is very cunning. The sound of wailing he will raise, leaping over mountains, and with prayers and supplications, with song and rejoicing, and with sounds and melodies. He changes [the tune] ten times, and his acts are strange. He dresses in white, and a cord of blue at the corner, like On son of Peleth[34] (see *She'ilot u-Teshuvot Panim*

---

[31]See: Shimeon Baraz, "Toldot Rabbeinu Moshe ben Maimon Zikhro le-Virkhat Netzah" (The History of Our Master Moses ben Maimon, May His Memory Be an Everlasting Blessing), *Ha-Me'assef*, 1786, pp. 19-27, 35-47; F. Lahover, "Ha-Rambam veha-Haskalah ha-Ivrit be-Reshitah" (Maimonides and the Beginning of the Hebrew Enlightenment), *Moznaim* 3, issue 4-5 (1935), pp. 539-546; J. H. Lehmann, "Maimonides, Mendelssohn and the Me'asfim: Philosophy and the Biographical Imagination in the Early Haskalah," Leo Baeck Institute Year Book 20 (1925), pp. 87-108; Friedlander, *Mekomah shel ha-Halakhah*.

[32]See: Friedlander, *Perakim*, pp. 121-143.

[33]Kabbalistic teachings.

[34]See: Yehuda Friedlander, "Av ve-Toladah - bein Pulmos le-Satirah (Al Nezed ha-Dema le R. Yisrael mi-Zamosc)" (Between Polemic and Satire: Israel of Zamosc's Nezed Ha-Dema'), *Migvan*, Studies in Hebrew Literature in Honor of Jacob Kabakoff (Lod: Habbermann Institute for Literary Research, 1988), pp. 330-332.

Me'irot, part II, query 152),[35] and the sighs break half a man's body,[36] and they move to and fro with their hands, and he moves as someone moving the trees of the forest. His hair stands on edge (see query 113 in the Responsa of Menaham Azariah...),[37] and other such things which our forefathers could not imagine, we have seen with our own eyes. And these are the outstanding qualities of our time. And even though he has not read and not learned, he shall be named "wise" and called "our master."[38] And the more a person engages in movements and manners, he is praiseworthy and distinguished in the mouths of child and women. And they hasten as shock-troops, before the meagre and beggarly in intelligence. They will tell some of his praise before him:[39] O the pious, O the humble![40]...And no one gives thought that his ambush is set for him in his heart.[41]...And the entire world is not

---

[35]See: Rabbi Meir Eisenstadt, Responsa *Panim Me'irot*, section 2 (Sulzbach: 1733), p. 95. Eisenstadt sharply attacks the people during his time who wanted to wear white garments on the Sabbath: "Since several Torah scholars now walk about in black garments on the Sabbath, therefore if one person in a thousand wants to say, 'I will fulfill the words of the Kabbalists who wrote that it is an obligation to walk around in white garments on the Sabbath,' there is no haughtiness greater than this, and he deserves to be banned, unless he is known for his piety and for the fact that all his actions are for the sake of Heaven...and in our times we must fear arrogance; especially in our times due to our many sins, the low are above, standing in the place of the great ones...for haughtiness has increased; every person says, 'I am great and pious.'"

[36]According to BT Ber. 58b: "Sighs break half a man's body...and Rabbi Jonathan says, Even a man's entire body." See also: BT Ket. 62a.

[37]See: Rabbi Menahem Azariah of Fano, Sefer She'eilot u-Teshuvot Bei'urim u-Perushim (Book of Responsa, Explanations, and Commentaries) (Jerusalem: 1963), pp. 239-241. The book was first printed in Venice in 1600. Menahem Azariah vigorously opppsed shaking the body during prayer.

[38]In contrast with BT B. M. 85b-86a: "Samuel Yarhina'ah shall be called a sage, and not master [*rabbi*]." The derisive message is clear: Samuel was not called "master," but now every ignorant person who does not read or learn merits both titles of "sage" and "master."

[39]According to BT Eruv. 18b: "Partial praise of a person is stated before him, while full [praise] is not stated before him."

[40]According to BT Sanh. 11a: "When the last prophets, Haggai, Zechariah, and Malachi, died, Divine inspiration left Israel[.] Once they were dining in the upper chamber in the house of Guriah in Jericho, and a heavenly voice descended upon them from Heaven: 'There is one here who is worthy to have the Divine Presence desend upon him (as Moses), but his generation is not deserving of this.' The Sages looked at Hillel[.] And when he died, they said about him, Here is the pious one, here is the humble one, the disciple of Ezra." Samuel ha-Katan also merited this title after his death. See *Loc. cit.*

[41]Following Jer. 9:7: "Their tongue is a sharpened arrow, they use their mouths to deceive. One speaks to his fellow in friendship, but lays an ambush for him in his heart."

considered as anything in his eyes, He buts northward and westward.[42] I see in the clear glass.[43]...And *damim* in both senses ["blood" and "money"] is permitted. And in the innermost chambers, he does whatever is in his power, because he is all-powerful....And whatever you see before you he will take, for we were created only to serve him, with his soul, and with his might, and with his wealth, when it gives its color in the cup.[44] And now lay Your hand upon his might,[45] or only a portion of his honor; his majesty has turned into corruption,[46] and he will surely blaspheme You to Your face[47] with poured out wrath. The best of them is like a prickly shrub, and the most upright, worse than a barrier of thorns.[48] And I have not attacked all of them, God forbid, rather I found only one man in a thousand[49] whose thought is desirable, without any ulterior motives. They are the survivors who invoke the Lord;[50] I fear them....The All-Merciful requires their hearts.[51] And their banner over me is love.[52]

Mises thought, and accepted, that this passage (excluding the ending) was directed against the Hasidism and the Baal Shem Tov, and was glad to view Rabbi Solomon of Chelm as an authority supporting him in his struggle.[53] The picture which is drawn here

---

[42]Following Dan. 8:4: "I saw the ram butting westward, northward, and southward. No beast could withstand him, and there was none to deliver from his power. He did as he pleased and grew great."

[43]Following BT Yev. 49b: "All the prophets looked in a dim glass, but Moses looked through a clear glass."

[44]Following Prov. 23:31: "When it gives its color in the cup."

[45]Following Job 1:11: "But lay your hand upon all that he has and he will surely blaspheme You to Your face." See also Job 2:5.

[46]Following Dan. 10:8: "For my majesty was turned in me into corruption."

[47]See n. 45, above.

[48]Following Michah 7:4: "The best of them is like a prickly shrub."

[49]Following Eccl. 7:28: "I found only one man in a thousand."

[50]Following Joel 3:5: "But every one who invokes the name of the Lord shall escape; for there shall be a remnant on Mount Zion and in Jerusalem, as the Lord promised. Any one who invokes the Lord will be among the survivors."

[51]Following BT Sanh. 106b: "The Holy one, blessed be He, requires the heart." See: Rashi, *loc. cit.*, cap. "Revuta le-miva Ba'ei": "The All-Merciful requires the heart."

[52]Following Cant. 2:4: "And his banner of love was over me." See: Cant. Rabbah, *loc. cit.*: "The Holy One, blessed be He, said, 'And their banner over Me is love.'" The statement by Rabbi Solomon of Chelm is quoted, with minor deletions, from the "Introduction of the Rabbi-Author," p. 6.

[53]One of the complex issues occupying the researchers of Hasidism is: Did Rabbi Solomon of Chelm refer to the Hasidism of the Baal Shem Tov, or to the Hasidic groups that preceded the Baal Shem Tov, who were prevalent in the Jewish communities of Eastern Europe? Gershom Scholem discussed this question extensively in his essay, "Shetei ha-Eduyot ha- Rishonot al Havurot

serves Mises as a source of inspiration for the fashioning of the character of Rabbi Solomon of Chelm as a fierce opponent of Hasidism. The latter does not, of course, mention the Baal Shem Tov in his introduction. Mises, however, in his description of the first meeting between Maimonides and the author of *Mirkevet ha-Mishneh* in Heaven, is the one who puts biting words against the Baal Shem Tov in the mouth of the latter: "A person of meagre knowledge," "lacking and empty of all Torah scholarship and wisdom," a rural person and ignorant," "possessing a deceitful heart," "proud, pursuing honor, and very desirous to acquire a name in the land as one of the great ones," "in this manner the Baal Shem Tov stole the heart of the Children of Israel," etc.[54] The author of *Mirkevet ha-Mishneh* tells Maimonides that the Baal Shem Tov instituted three practices among his followers which are highly regarded "in the eyes of the ignorant, who lack knowledge": immersion in the ritual bath every day, "even when there is ice," "to engage at length in many new prayers, which have been recently composed by a madman, of confused mind, a dreamer whose imagination is greater than his intelligence," and the study of books which are called by the masses "the wisdom of the Kabbalah," books full of "closed, stupid, and confused matters."[55] These three practices are intended, according to the author of *Mirkevet ha-Mishneh*, to refute the report that had come to the attention of the Baal Shem Tov "that some scholars will call him a sorcerer, and will believe that by means of this sorcery he will heal the sick and perform wonders,"[56] and thereby delude people. In other words, the author of *Mirkevet ha-*

---

ha-Hasidim veha-Besht" (The Two First Testimonies on the Relation between Chassidic Groups and the Ba'al -Shem-Tov), *Tarbiz* 20 (1949), pp. 228-240. Scholem surveys the different opinions which were prevalent before him, and reaches the conclusion that Rabbi Solomon of Chelm referred to the popular Hasidim who preceded the Baal Shem Tov and the remnants of Sabbatianism. This is also the opinion presented by Avraham Brik in his essay, "R. Shlomo Helme, Ba'al Mirkevet ha-Mishneh" (Rabbi Solomon of Chelm, the Author of *Mirkevet ha-Mishneh*), Sinai 61 (1967), pp. 168-184. Rafael Mahler holds that "the author also included here, along with the followers of the Ba'al Shem Tov, who appeared during his time, Sabbateans, whom he censures greatly, as well as Hasidim who preceded the new Hasidism: 'These are the survivors' whom he singles out for praise." See: Rafael Mahler, *Divrei Yemei Yisrael Dorot Aharonim* (History of the Jewish People in Modern Times) (Merhavia: Sifriat Poalim, 1960), second ed., vol. 1, book 3, p. 190. Cf. Mahler, *ibid.*, book 4 (1962), pp. 25-26.

[54]*Kin'at ha-Emet*, pp. 22-26.

[55]*Ibid.*, pp. 23-26.

[56]*Ibid.*, p. 23.

Mishneh explains to Maimonides the Hasidic practices of the Baal Shem Tov as a camouflaged intensification of the plague of demonism which had spread throughout the Jewish communities in Poland. This had led, within a short time, to flatterers and deceivers to assemble around the Baal Shem Tov; they had "also begun to write amulets for the sick, against infertility, and to bless Jewish women, to adjure demons and angels (according to them)," and "Whoever knows how to read in a book will pursue the knowledge of the Kabbalah; and almost all the people will derive pleasure from the tales regarding demons and the history of the deceivers and the fools, and from their power over the spirits."[57]

As the editor-satirist, Mises places these statements, which he put in the mouth of the author of *Mirkevet ha-Mishneh*, next to a citation from Rabbi Jacob Emden (1698-1776) denouncing Hasidism.[58] He

---

[57]*Ibid.*, p. 27. The claim regarding the link between Hasidism and demonism is already raised in the editor's "Word to the Reader": "And a greater evil than this is that the sect of the Ba'al Shem Tov-ists which has recently come into existence and which has spread throughout the camp of Israel is based on this belief, for only the people who believe in demons and sorcery, and the derivatives of these things, will sanctify the great ones and leaders of this sect" (*ibid.*, pp. 6-8).

[58]See: Rabbi Jacob Emden, *Sefer Mitpahat Sefarim* (Altona: 1768), section 2, p. 31: "I writhed to hear that now a new sect of Hasidim has recently come into existence in Volhynia, Podolia. And some of them have come to this state as well. They are occupied only with the book of the Zohar and the Kabbalistic books. And they prolong their prayer for half the day, much more than the early pietists, who would tarry only one hour in prayer, but in addition to this according to what was related to me, they engage in strange and disgraceful movement. They strike with their hands and sway to the sides, with their heads thrown back, and their faces and eyes pointing upward....And you wonder whether they would do so before a king of flesh and blood, who would cast them to the ground untill their limbs would break apart....In truth, if I would see one who does these things which our forefathers, of blessed memory, the true pietists and great appearance. [Following BT B. K. 81b: "Who is this with a great appearance before us."] I would cut their thighs with iron instruments [i.e., I would ban them, following BT, *ibid.*: "Had you not been Judah ben Kenoso, I would have cut your joints with an iron saw" See Rashi, *Loc. cit.*, cap. "Be-Gizra de-Parzela"; cf. *He-Arukh*, c. v. "Gazar"]. Incidentally, I will further mention here that these Hasidim-fools still do not know what has caused them to err, for they rely upon what is to be found in writing and in print, without knowing its subject, root, and source." See: *Kin'at ha-Emet*, p. 23. Mises does not cite this passage accurately. It is of interest to compare the statement by Rabbi Jacob Emden with the passage in Responsa *Panim Me'irot* (n. 36 above), and to that of Rabbi Solomon of Chelm in his introduction. Rabbi Jacob Emden

apparently did this to strengthen his own arguments with a supporting statement by one of the leading scholars of the time. As far as we are concerned, it ca·ı be said that this citation (as is the case for similar citations in other places in *Kin't ha-Emet*) may teach regarding Mises' method of assembling the raw materials from which he created the fictional characters in his satiric work. The spiritual image of Rabbi Solomon of Chelm, as it is reflected in the introduction to the conversations in Heaven, contains a certain coloration from the spiritual image of Rabbi Jacob Emden, regarding their views on Hasidism and Kabbalah. Rabbi Solomon of Chelm is portrayed to us as a forceful and dominant personality; however, matters are completely different in the continuation of the book.

The character of Rabbi Solomon of Chelm in Mises' satire is meant, from the outset, to serve as a secondary character, as a pupil-colleague of the central character, Maimonides, which is how the former is fashioned in most instances. Rabbi Solomon's questions regarding the source of the belief in demons and sorcery and the degree of the validity of this belief in Judaism are a didactic means enabling Maimonides to deliver his message, as planned by Mises. Rabbi Solomon's response-agreement is assured from the outset, and is frequently accompanied by questions on points requiring further clarification. We shall examine the following passage as an example of this method:

> The author of *Mirkevet ha-Mishneh:* I was pleased by your opinion regarding the source of the belief of the masses in the existence of good and evil spirits, because you proved it with intellectual proofs which can hardly be refuted. But what can be said regarding many verses written in the Torah and in the books of the prophets which mention an angel, the Adversary, or demons? And what shall we do with the statements by the Sages regarding the angels, demons, and sorcery?[59]

Maimonides' response, which is based on his interpretative method in the *Guide of the Perplexed*, can be encapsuled in the following statement, which is not acceptable to Orthodox rabbis, but which is in concert with the philosophy of the *Haskalah:*

> But if we were to say that any of the Sages truly believed in spirits and in matters derived from them, such as sorcery, we nevertheless cannot bring a proof from them regarding the truth of their existence, for we are not to believe in and maintain matters which the Sages did not

---

undoubtedly refers here to the Hasidism of the Ba'al Shem Tov, for this passage was published 32 years after the Ba'al Shem Tov revealed himself.
[59]*Kin'at ha-Emet*, pp. 38-39.

receive at Sinai,[60] but which they rather wrote and expounded as it appeared to them according to their intelligence, or as they had heard from people who told them these things, or as they had heard and received these opinions from their sages and teachers, who believed these things without investigation and analysis, and because of a lack of experience, as we know that Socrates believed in spirits.[61]

And indeed the author of *Mirkevet ha-Mishneh* responds, as is to be expected, with a reservation:

Although your words are based on common sense, and therefore cannot be refuted, they nevertheless are difficult to accept, for if the belief in spirits were a false belief, it would have been proper for our holy Torah to enjoin the Israelites not to believe in such matters.[62]

Maimonides' response in Mises' satire expresses, in unequivocal language, a *maskil*-critical-modern position, both regarding the world of thought and beliefs of the Sages, and regarding that of Socrates. The very juxtaposition of the Sages and Socrates in the same plane of reference was scandalous in the eyes of the Orthodox rabbis, who maintained unshakable faith in the Sages, viewed the wisdom of the Sages as the embodiment of the Divine spirit, and shrank from any contact with "Greek wisdom."

There is nothing new, as was stated above, in this fashioning of the character of Maimonides in Mises' work, which is not so regarding the description of the response of Rabbi Solomon of Chelm. His reservation is neither a matter of principle nor methodological. The "counter-argument" he raises is more of a request for an additional explanation than a dissenting opinion. He is bothered by the fact that the Torah did not enjoin against the belief in spirits. He wishes to accept Maimonides' explanations on this subject, and in the end he does accept them, in the continuation of the conversations.[63] In short, Rabbi

---

[60]Excluding the expositions, regarding which it is stated in JT Meg. 4:1: "Scripture, and Mishnah, and Talmud and aggadah – even what a senior disciple will teach before his teacher has already been stated to Moses at Sinai."

[61]*Kin'at ha-Emet, ibid.*, pp. 45-46. In *Likutei Perahim* Mises collects sources from Maimonides' writings according to which he fashioned his spiritual character. See: *ibid.*, pp. 156- 161.

[62]*Ibid.*, pp. 46-47. Rabbi Solomon repeats his question on p. 156: "I greatly wonder why the Torah has not enjoined us against this belief, as it has enjoined us against other follies, as, for example, idolatry and sorcery?"

[63]*Ibid.*, pp. 48, 54, 63, 78, 105-106, and 119. At the conclusion of the conversations, Rabbi Solomon of Chelm thanks Maimonides: "A thousand thanks to you, my friend! You have revived my spirit with your learning! You have quenched my thirst to hear rational statements from you! The mask of folly has been

Solomon of Chelm does not represent the Orthodox rabbis in *Kin'at ha-Emet*, but rather the moderate (or "true," in Mises' terminology) *maskilim*.[64]

Rabbi Solomon of Chelm's adherence to the view of Maimonides regarding the beliefs in demons, spirits, and sorcery therefore overshadows the description of his militant opposition to Hasidism and its derivatives, which consists of a complementary chord (one possible translation of mirkevet mishneh) to Maimonides' opposition. Mises adopts a fine means for the purpose of his satire, wanting thereby to continue, as it were, the path chosen by Rabbi Solomon of Chelm in his own book. Rabbi Solomon writes at the end of his introduction to *Mirkevet ha-Mishneh:* "I called it by the name '*Mirkevet ha-Mishneh'*...in order to ride [*lirkov*] upon the throne of my swift cloud, the top of the palm tree, and go up on the roof of the tower, and to be dependent from a great tree...and be steadfast as the witness in the sky, that my intent and thought is not to exalt myself with my work, and to reveal my treasure-house."[65] In his satire, Mises comes and fashions the character of Rabbi Solomon as a character secondary to that of Maimonides. Rabbi Solomon of Chelm therefore continues his faithfulness to Maimonides in Heaven, in the spirit of the activity he had begun during his lifetime.

IV. Maimonides and the "Editor" (Judah Leib Mises) in Their Condemnation of False Beliefs

The basis assumption in the collection of Maimonides' arguments in *Kin'at ha-Emet* against the various manifestations of demonism in the faith of Israel is that the authoritative rule of the Sages is to be accepted only in matters pertaining to halakhah. The "words of Haggadah (= aggadah)," including "many false matters" are drawn in part from the non-Jewish sages. In order to confirm this claim, Maimonides brings three supporting passages from the Sages: "And they already said by themselves (JT Nazir),[66] they do not refute an

---

removed from my face, and my eyes have been opened to see what I could not have imagined." See: *ibid.,* p. 152.

[64]"A Word to the Reader," p. 6.

[65]*Sefer Mirkevet ha-Mishneh,* p. 7.

[66]The parenthetical comment is supposed to be that of the editor, of course, and it is incorrect. JT Naz. 7:2 states merely: "Is the legal status of expositions that of a matter of faith? Rather, learn out and received reward," i.e., expositions are merely Scriptual supports. See the explanations of the author of *Korban ha-Eidah* and *Penei Moshe, loc. cit.* This sentence was paraphrased in *Shiltei ha-Giborim* by Rabbi Joshua Boaz ben Simon Baruch, on Alfasi, A. Z. 6a:

exposition,[67] and they do not ask questions on aggadah,[68] and our Rabbis said, They may not rely upon aggadah.[69] And they also said: Is an exposition a belief?"[70]

The editor-satirist illustrates these general statements in lengthy marginal comment with four amusing examples of the influence of the superstitions of the non-Jews upon the Jewish Sages, commenting in a

---

"And they further stated in the Talmud of Eretz Israel [JT], in chap. 7 of Nazir[:] 'For are the expositions a matter of faith? Learn out and receive reward.'" See: *Likutei Perahim,* p. 185. For the purposes of his satire, Mises intentionally omitted several sentences from the beginning and from the end. It is stated, *loc. cit.:* "And since I saw the insolent ones of our people mocking and scorning the words of the Sages, and teach them to deride our Torah, I have come to interpret the matter of exegesis...and it was stated, regarding the one who derides their words, 'But they mocked the messengers of God and taunted His prophets.'" The other expressions in this passage from *Kin'at ha-Emet* are not from the Talmud, but rather appear in the literature of the Geonim and Rishonim. See nn. 67-69, below.

[67]See Rabbeinu Isaac ben Judah ha-Levi, *Pane'ah Raza,* ed. Amsterdam 1767, *Bereshit* 7a: " They do not refute an exposition." The author was one of the Tosafists. The work was written at the end of the thirteenth century, and first published in Prague in 1607. See: A. Zions, "'Paneach Raza,' by Isaac ben Judah Halevi," Diss. Yeshiva University 1974. Maimonides could not, of course, have cited *Pane'ah Raza,* but in Mises's satirical work he is current to the nineteenth century....

[68]See: Maimonides, *Guide of the Perplexed,* the end of the introduction: "And for this they said that they do not raise questions on aggadah." Cf. *Guide of the Perplexed,* ed. Yoseph Kapah, (Jerusalem: Mossad ha-Rav Kook, 1972), introduction, p. 15: "And therefore they say that they do not raise questions on aggadah." Rabbi Kapah comments on this expression in a note, *loc. cit.:* "I do not know its source." See also: *Zikaron la-Rishonim ve-gam la'-Aharonim,* ed. Albert (Abraham Elijah) Harkavy, part 1, fourth pamphlet, (Berlin: 1887), par. 354, p. 179: "...and these are all expositions and aggadot, and we do not raise questions on them, for our Rabbis have taught, 'They do not raise questions on aggadah.'" Harkavy comments in a note, *loc. cit.:* "I do not know the place of this wording; perhaps the reference is to the famous teachings censuring aggadah in the JT Shab., Maas., etc." Cf.: *Midrash ha-Gadol,* Gen., ed. Mordecai Margaliot, (Jerusalem: Mossad ha-Rav Kook, 1947), p. 18; *Entziklopedyah Talmudit,* c. v. *"Aggadah,"* second ed., vol. 1, (1973), pp. 129-132.; Yitzhak Heinemann, *Darhei ha-Aggadah,* third ed., (Givatayim: Magnes Press, Hebrew University, and Massada, 1970), pp. 187, 191, 257-258.

[69]See: Rabbeinu Abraham of Narbonne (called Rabad II; the son-in-law of Rabad, Rabbi Abraham ben David of Posquieres), *Sefer ha-Eshkol,* section 2, (Halberstadt: 1868), p. 47: "And Rav Hai Gaon was asked what is the meaning...and he replied...that we do not base oueselves upon aggadah at all."

[70]*Kin'at ha-Emet,* p. 46, See n. 66, above.

festive tone: "The educated person will judge and draw inferences from this regarding the rest."[71] Let us examine one of these: Mises relates to his readers that "The Romans believed that the dreams a person dreams after midnight are true; see Satire X by the poet Horace, which is almost a teaching in Berakhot 55b: 'Three dreams are fulfilled, and they are: the dream of the morning....'"[72]

Mises the editor-satirist here binds together two different realms. A clear distinction must be made between, on the one hand, Maimonides' sharp opposition to all those who interpret the aggadot of the Sages literally, for "they are the most foolish of humans, and more errant than the beast; and their minds have already been filled with the madnesses of the old women,"[73] for they do not understand the rhetorical-allegorical garb of the expositions of the Sages, and, on the other hand, the "non-Jewish" source of this literary garb, which in itself is not invalid. Mises' intent as a satirist is not, however, to discuss the ways of interpreting Rabbinic exegesis, and he does not, of course, invalidate influences from non-Jewish culture. His entire intent is to castigate the ridiculous image of the fools who take the stories of spirits and demons at face value, and who, to make matters worse, are also influenced by superstitions which even the non-Jews have already rejected.[74] All this serves as an introduction to his central argument, that the Hasidism of the Baal Shem Tov is the continuation of this tradition of folly. Furthermore, those who believed in demons and spirits in past generations were sincere in their belief, which is not so regarding the various *ba'alei shem* (miracle workers), including the Baal Shem Tov, who "made themselves as men of God and boast that they are very close to Him and to the spirits...and in order that their false words will be accepted by Israel, these sanctifiers have made a covenant with flatters from among the lowest classes, who are filled

---

[71]*Kin'at ha-Emet*, ibid.

[72]*Ibid.* See: BT Ber. 55b: "And Rabbi Johanan said: Three [types of] dreams are fulfilled: A dream of the morning, and a dream which his fellow dreamed, and a dream which was interpreted within a dream, and according to one opinion, also a dream which was dreamt twice, as it is written, 'As for having had the same dream twice....'" See also: Horace, *Complete Works*, Satires, Book 1, 10 (New York: Modern Library, 1936), p. 38: "Romulus himself appeared to me in the early morning hours when dreams are true."

[73]*Igerot ha-Rambam, Igeret o Ma'amar Tehiyat ha-Metim* (Treatise on Resurrection), ed. Mordekhai Dov Rabinovitch (Jerusalem: Mossad ha-Rav Kook, 1977), p. 346. Cf. *Hakdamot le-Perush ha-Mishnah* (Introductions to the Interpretation of the Mishnah), ed. Rabinovitch, (Jerusalem: 1961), intr. to Helek, pp. 117-119; *Guide of the Perplexed* 3:43. See: Heinemann, pp. 2, 197.

[74]See pp. xxx and nn. 27, 28, above.

with deceit and falsehood...and who practiced customs which arouse amazement among those lacking wisdom, such as wearing a hairy mantle and engaging extensively in prayers and fasting, and similar practices.[75]

According to Maimonides, these acts of deceit led, in the final analysis, to unbridled competition among the *ba'alei shem*, and on the pretext of trespassing, "they cast aspersions on each other, and they wanted to cause them to be hated by the people...those among the people who believed one deceiver did not believe a second one; they even pursued him and made efforts to destroy him." Here as well the editor-satirist hurries to write a marginal comment which imparts contemporary significance to Maimonides' statement: "And this is how the leading Baal Shem Tov-ists act in our times, when it is known to any person who is aware of their actions, how each one speaks insolently about his fellow who resides close to his city and trespasses his bounds."[76] Mises' comment was undoubtedly influenced by Joseph Perl's satiric description of the struggle between the court of the Rabbi of Zalin and that of the "Dishpaler" in *Megaleh Temirin* (1819).[77]

Hasidism, as the reflection of demonism, is therefore the central axis in Mises' satire. It serves as the connecting link between the beginning of the opposition to Hasidism in the writings of Orthodox rabbis and the satire of the *maskilim* in the nineteenth century.

---

[75]*Kin'at ha-Emet*, pp. 48-49.
[76]*Ibid.*, p. 52.
[77]See, e.g.: *Megaleh Temirin*, letters 62-64, 82, 127, 129, 133, 136, 138-141, 144-145, 151, et al.

39

When a Rabbi is Accused of Heresy

R. Ezekiel Landau's Attitude Toward R. Jonathan Eibeschuetz in the Emden-Eibeschuetz Controversy[1]

Sid Z. Leiman
Brooklyn College

Toward the end of Moshe Aryeh Perlmuter's study of R. Jonathan Eibeschuetz' attitude toward Sabbatianism,[2] the author lists a series of problems that he admits he cannot solve. Included on the list as especially perplexing was the enigmatic relationship between R. Jonathan Eibeschuetz and R. Ezekiel Landau. The passage reads:[3]

לא נפתרה השאלה בשל מה ולמה היו לו להרב יהונתן
תומכים וסניגורים בין הרבנים הבלתי שבתאיים, וכן
שאלת היחסים התמוהים שבינו ובין הרב יחזקאל לנדא.

Perlmuter, who basically was persuaded that Eibeschuetz was a Sabbatian, could not fathom why so many leading rabbis defended Eibeschuetz. That Landau, who was a notorious anti-Sabbatian, defended Eibeschuetz, was simply incomprehensible to Perlmuter.

In fact, the problem of the relationship between Eibeschuetz and Landau has proven to be enigmatic on other grounds as well. The Emden-Eibeschuetz controversy, which was initiated on that fateful Thursday morning, February 4, 1751, when R. Jacob Emden announced in

---

[1] To Marvin Fox, mentor and colleague, whose scholarship and demeanor imbue academe with כבוד הבריות and כבוד התורה.
[2] M. A. Perlmuter, ר' יהונתן איבשיץ ויחסו אל השבתאות, Tel Aviv, 1947.
[3] Ibid., p. 316.

180 Hasidism: Messianism in Modern Times

his synagogue in Altona that an amulet ascribed to the Chief Rabbi –
Jonathan Eibeschuetz – could only have been written by a Sabbatian
heretic, did not cease with the death of Eibeschuetz in 1764. Emden
continued to wage the battle against Eibeschuetz' memory, and against
his descendants and disciples until his own death in 1776. Nor did the
controversy end then; it simply entered a new phase, namely a
scholastic one. With the rise of *jüdische Wissenschaft* and the
publication of studies by scholars such as Graetz,[4] Kahana,[5] Scholem,[6]
and Liebes,[7] the Emden-Eibeschuetz controversy has attained an
immortality and a notoriety that one suspects will not soon be
exhausted. *Jüdische Wissenschaft*, especially as represented by the
aforementioned scholars, has tended to condemn Eibeschuetz. Rabbinic
scholars – R. Reuven Margalioth[8] is typical – have tended to vindicate
Eibeschuetz. Interestingly, both groups adduce Landau as proof of their
positions, and this is the real enigma of the relationship between
Eibeschuetz and Landau. Graetz,[9] for example, considered Landau to be
an implacable enemy of Eibeschuetz, and therefore concluded that
Landau's attitude itself was proof that Eibeschuetz was a Sabbatian. In
striking contrast virtually every rabbinic defense of Eibeschuetz – the
most recent one was published in Bnei Braq in 1981[10] – stresses the fact

---

[4]H. Graetz, *Geschichte der Juden*,[3] ed. by M. Brann, Leipzig, 1897, vol. 10, pp.
339-524. Cf. S. P. Rabbinowitz' critique of Graetz' account of the controversy in
H. Graetz, דברי ימי ישראל, ed. and trans. by S. P. Rabbinowitz, Warsaw, 1899 [photo-
offset: Jerusalem, 1972], vol. 8, pp. 455-528 and 614-636.
[5]D. Kahana, "אמת ליעקב" 6 (1875) 232, 281-288, 338-344; "מהר"י אייבשיץ: זכאי או חייב" השחר
השחר 5 (1899) 256-261, 327-332, 524-529, and 6 (1899) 137-143, 337-343. Cf. his
magnum opus: תולדות המקובלים השבתאים והחסידים,[3] Tel Aviv, 1927, vol. 2, pp. 20-64, 129-
145.
[6]Many of Scholem's studies treat aspects of the controversy. Among those
most directly concerned with the controversy are his review of M. J. Cohen,
Jacob Emden: A Man of Controversy in קרית ספר 16 (1939) 320-338; לקט מרגליות, Tel
Aviv, 1941; "על קמיע אחד של ר' יהונתן אייבשיץ ופירושו עליו" תרביץ 13 (1942) 226-244; and
"Eybeschuetz, Jonathan" in *Encyclopaedia Judaica*, Jerusalem, 1971, vol. 6,
columns 1074-1076.
[7]Y. Liebes, "מחבר ספר צדיק יסוד עולם" 1 דעת (1978) 73-120; "מיתוס שבתאי: מיתוס יסוד צריק ספר"
"משיחיותו של ר' יעקב עמדין ויחסו לשבתאות" 159-173; (1978-79) 2-3 דעת הנביא השבתאי ר' ליבלי פרוסניץ
"כתבים חדשים בקבלה שבתאית מחוגו" 49 (1979-80) 122-165 and 52 (1983) 359; תרביץ
"של ר' יהונתן אייבשיץ מקרי ירושלים במחשבת ישראל" 5 (1986) 191-348; and cf. below, note 24.
[8]R. Margalioth [Margulies], סיבת התנגדותו של רבינו יעקב מעמדין, Tel Aviv, 1941;
להקטגוריה שנתחדשה, Tel Aviv, 1941; "לתולדות אנשי שם בלבוב" סיני 29 (1951) 378-388.
[9]H. Graetz, "Ezechiel Landau's Gesuch an Maria Theresia gegen Jonathan
Eibeschütz," *MGWJ* 26 (1877) 17-25.
[10]Y. S. Feder, תולדות הדורות, Bnei Braq, 1981, vol. 3, pp. 131-133.

that he was vindicated by no less a rabbinic scholar, and anti-Sabbatian, than Landau himself.[11]

What follows is an attempt to resolve the enigma alluded to above, and to present a fuller, more accurate, and more persuasive account of Landau's attitude toward Eibeschuetz than has previously been made available in the literature. We shall examine, however briefly, the primary sources, as well as the anecdotal evidence. Although modern scholarship ordinarily (and rightly) puts little or no stock in anecdotal evidence, it will become obvious as this presentation unfolds why an exception is justifiable for the purposes of this discussion.

It is important to note at the outset – together with Scholem[12] – that whatever our conclusions regarding Landau's attitude toward Eibeschuetz may be, they by themselves cannot prove Eibeschuetz' guilt or innocence regarding Emden's charge that Eibeschuetz was a Sabbatian. Thus, on methodological grounds we must reject Graetz' view that Eibeschuetz was a Sabbatian simply because – according to Graetz – Landau considered Eibeschuetz to be a Sabbatian.[13] On the same methodological grounds, we must reject every rabbinic defense of Eibeschuetz which bases itself on the fact that Landau vindicated Eibeschuetz.[14] Our focus, then will be on Landau's perception of Eibeschuetz rather than on the realities of Eibeschuetz' alleged Sabbatian leanings.

There is no evidence that Landau and Eibeschuetz ever met. When the Emden-Eibeschuetz controversy erupted in 1751, neither Landau nor Eibeschuetz had published any of the works that would later become landmarks of rabbinic scholarship. Nonetheless, both were widely known and well connected in rabbinic circles. Certainly, Landau had heard of Eibeschuetz. Long before 1751, Eibeschuetz had earned an international reputation for himself. Gems from his mouth appeared in print as early as 1729 in Judah of Glogau's קול יהודה, a popular anthology of the best rabbinic lectures (more accurately: חדושים) of 1729. Such anthologies were commonplace in the 18th century and were frequently reprinted.[15] Eibeschuetz' lectures at the *yeshivoth* of Prague and Metz

---

[11]Typical are the accounts in Y. Kamelhar, מופת הדור, New York, 1966, chap. 2, p. 5 [first edition: Munkacz, 1903]; Z. Lipsker, "דגלנו "תולדות הגאון רבי יחזקאל סגל לנדא 7 (1927), n. 4, p. 13, n. 5, pp. 12-13, and n. 6, p. 13; R. Margalioth, סיבה הדברות של רבינו יעקב מעמדין, p. 13; and T. Y. Tavyomi, אמרי טל, Tel Aviv, 1954, p. 106.
[12]G. Scholem, "ציון "פרשיות בחקר הדבועה השבתאית 6 (1941), p. 100.
[13]H. Graetz, "Ezechiel Landau's Gesuch," (see above, note 9), p. 25.
[14]See above, notes 10 and 11.
[15]Thus, four editions of קול יהודה appeared during the lifetime of Eibeschuetz. The most recent reissue is: New York, 1983. For the titles of other such

were assiduously recorded and widely distributed.[16] His former
students occupied pulpits throughout Europe.[17] It is inconceivable that
Landau had not read or heard about Eibeschuetz' Torah teaching by
1751. It is conceivable, however, that in 1751 Eibeschuetz had not yet
heard of Landau, who was 23 years younger than Eibeschuetz.[18]
Conceivable, but not likely, for in 1751 Landau was a rising star on the
rabbinic scene. In 1734, at the age of 21, Landau was appointed *dayyan*
at Brody, a major center of Torah scholarship.[19] Nine years later he
was elected rabbi of Yampol, a small but distinguished settlement in
Volhynia.[20] In the 1740's both Landau's and Eibeschuetz' names
appeared prominently on the approbation pages of various rabbinic
works. In 1752, at the height of the controversy, Landau and
Eibeschuetz crossed paths for the first time. In a valiant attempt to
bring the controversy to a close, Landau addressed letters to all the
involved parties and to the leading Jewish authorities throughout
Europe.[21] In them, he called for an immediate cessation of hostilities,

---

anthologies, see D. L. Zinz, גדולת יהונתן, Piotrkow, 1930-34 [photo-offset: Tel Aviv,
1968], p. 212; and cf. M. Piekarz, בימי צמיחת החסידות, Jerusalem, 1978, pp. 30-31.
[16]Virtually all major collections of Hebrew manuscripts contain copies of
Eibeschuetz' lectures as recorded by his students. Many have been published.
See, e.g., the bibliography listed in N. Ben-Menahem, ed., חוברת לדוגמה,
Jerusalem, 1964, pp. 13-24. For recent samplings, see J. Eibeschuetz, [ed. by E.
Hurvitz] "הסברות על מסכת ביצה" 71-75; (1981-84) 2 העמק "חידושי הגאון רבינו יהונתן אייבשיץ זל"
(Scheider שם עולם "חידושים והסברות למס' חולין פרק ראשון ושני" 7-29; (1984) 8 קובץ יגדיל תורה
Memorial Volume), Wickliffe, Ohio, 1985, pp. 71-101; חידושי רבי יהונתן על מס' ברכות,
Jerusalem, אבן ציון: ספר זכרון לבן ציון הכהן כהנא "בדין מצוה מחמת מיתה"; 1986,
1987, pp. 134-135.
[17]For a partial listing, see D. L. Zinz, *op. cit.*, pp. 264-283.
[18]Assuming the conventional date of birth assigned to Eibeschuetz – 1690. See,
however, Y. Y. Greenwald, הרב ר' יהונתן אייבשיץ, New York, 1954, pp. 44-49 and notes.
[19]See, e.g., N. M. Gelber, עדים ואמהות בישראל) = תולדות יהודי ברודי, vol. 6), Jerusalem,
1955.
[20]Landau's Yampol is not to be confused, as it often is, with Yampol in Podolia.
For Volhynian Yampol, and for the rabbis who resided there, see A. L. Gellman,
הנודע ביהודה ומשנתו,[3] Jerusalem, 1970, pp. 2-3 and 161-165.
[21]The letter was published separately by Emden (in full) and by Eibeschuetz (in
abridged form). Emden's version appeared in פתח עינים, Altona, 1756;
Eibeschuetz' version appeared in לוחת עדות, Altona, 1755, pp. 41b-43a [photo-
offset: Jerusalem, 1966, pp. 102-105]. A comparison between the two published
versions and the unexpurgated text, as it appears in manuscript form at Oxford
in Joseph Praeger's נחלי אש, yields interesting (but not startling) results regarding
the accuracy of Emden's and Eibeschuetz' transcription of primary sources. I
plan to publish those results, together with an accurate transcription of the full
text of Landau's letter, as a separate study. Precisely because of the general
unavailability of the full text of Landau's letter, rabbis and scholars have been
misled in their assessment of Landau's attitude toward Eibeschuetz. Aside

and proclaimed that due respect be accorded to Emden and Eibeschuetz by all. Landau basically vindicated Eibeschuetz by depicting him as one of the greatest rabbinic scholars of the generation. Landau ruled that, henceforth, anyone who would slander Eibeschuetz in any way would immediately be placed under the ban. On the other hand, Landau admitted that if not for the fact that the amulets were ascribed to Eibeschuetz, he would have concluded that their author could only have been a Sabbatian. Landau suggested the possibility that either he – Landau – had misread them, or else they were partially falsified between the time Eibeschuetz had written them and the time they were shown to Emden. In any event, all the amulets were to be returned to Eibeschuetz and were to be withdrawn permanently from circulation. Moreover, Eibeschuetz was proscribed from writing and distributing amulets ever again. No less embarrassing for Eibeschuetz was the stipulation that since numerous allegedly Sabbatian works – aside from the amulets – were circulating under Eibeschuetz' name, Eibeschuetz had to publicly condemn all those works by title and place their author under the ban.

In effect, Landau provided Eibeschuetz with a graceful exit out of the controversy. Emden's forces had threatened Eibeschuetz with a דין תורה. Indeed, unless Eibeschuetz was prepared to defend himself before a Jewish court-of-law, he would be defrocked and placed under the ban. Thus, Eibeschuetz had been painted into a corner by the leading rabbinic authorities in Germany – either an appearance in a Jewish court-of-law or the ban – when out of left field, or, more precisely, Yampol, Landau came to his rescue. Landau's compromise, while personally welcomed by Eibeschuetz and by many of the moderates involved in the controversy, failed. It failed because Emden's forces rejected the compromise out of hand. They refused to cease hostilities, demanding nothing short of total capitulation. Indeed, Emden's sustained effort at character assassination of Eibeschuetz probably has only one parallel in the annals of Jewish history, namely, Emden's sustained effort at the character assassination of Landau. It will come as no surprise that Emden – somewhat guardedly – accused Landau of being a Sabbatian.[22] And that was among the nicer things he had to say about Landau.

Precisely because Landau's effort was intended as a compromise it is difficult to assess just what it tells us about Landau's attitude toward Eibeschuetz. As indicated, Eibeschuetz' supporters and detractors cited

---

from the references cited above, notes 10 and 11, see the egregious account in A. L. Gellman, *op. cit.*, pp. 19-21 and 166-169.

[22] E. G., פתח עינים, p. 13a. Cf. Emden's ספר התאבקות, Altona, 1769, pp. 147b-148b.

Landau's effort as proof of their view of Eibeschuetz. We shall refrain from further analysis of Landau's missive until we have had the opportunity to examine the remaining evidence.

In 1756, during the Ten Days of Penitence, Moses Brandeis, a cantor in Prague, slandered Eibeschuetz' name. The matter was brought to the attention of Landau, now Chief Rabbi of Prague. He immediately convened a rabbinical court and Brandeis was anathematized. The court ruled that he could no longer lead services; moreover, for a full year he must take his seat in the mourner's section of the synagogue. His penance would be completed earlier only if Eibeschuetz expressly sends a note to Landau indicating that he forgives Brandeis' indiscretion. Within eight weeks of the court's ruling, Eibeschuetz sent a note to Landau on behalf of Brandeis. The court reconvened and rescinded its ruling, with the proviso that should Brandeis ever again slight Eibeschuetz, he would never again be allowed to lead services in Prague or, for that matter, anywhere else.[23] Now it may be that Brandeis was not much of a cantor; and after listening to him lead a service any rabbi would have sought a means of placing him under the ban for at least a year. Nonetheless, no historian could be faulted for viewing this episode as clear evidence that Landau defended the honor of Eibeschuetz.

Our sources are silent until late in 1759 when a *yeshiva* student in Hamburg addressed an urgent appeal to Landau, informing him that Eibeschuetz' son, Wolf, and other Kabbalists in Wolf's entourage, were secret adherents of Sabbetai Zevi.[24] In his reply to the student, Landau indicated that he was sending a letter directly to Eibeschuetz, and ordering him to admonish his son and to expel all heretics from his community. Should Eibeschuetz refuse to comply,

או במקום חלול השם לא אחלוק כבוד לרב, ואעשה כל מה שבכחי.[25]

Landau goes on to advise the student that if he and other students at Eibeschuetz' *yeshiva* could arrange to study elsewhere, they should do

---

[23]S. H. Lieben, "Zur Charakteristik des Verhältnisses zwischen Rabbi Jecheskel Landau und Rabbi Jonathan Eibenschitz," *Jahrbuch des Jüdisch-literarische Gesellschaft* 1 (1903) 325-326. Cf. Bamberger's corrections in *JJLG* 4 (1906) 342-343.

[24]ספר התאבקות, pp. 51a-52a. For Wolf Eibeschuetz, see Y. Liebes, 148-(1982) 57 קרית ספר "חיבור בלשון הזוהר לר' וולף בן ר' יהונתן אייבשיץ על חבורתו ועל סוד הגאולה" 178, 368-379 and the literature cited there. Add to Liebes' bibliography: Y. Y. Greenwald, תולדות גדולי הדור : בית יהונתן, Maramarossziget, 1908, p. 27 (which blunts somewhat Liebes' criticism of Greenwald at p. 153, note 30); H. Sofer, שו"ת מחנה חיים, מהדורא תליתאה, Jerusalem, 1970. אורח חיים, סימן פ; and A. J. Schwartz, דרך הנשר ותורה אמת, Satumare, 1928, pp. 58-59.

[25]ספר התאבקות, p. 52b.

so. Eibeschuetz' response to Landau is not extant, but from a letter addressed by Landau some six months later to the rabbi of Frankfurt,[26] we know that Eibeschuetz had in fact responded to Landau and indicated that he would acquiesce to Landau's demands. Regarding his son Wolf, Eibeschuetz noted that he had initially been moved by a divine spirit, but that it was now unclear whether Wolf was under the influence of pure or impure forces. No further correspondence or personal contacts between Landau and Eibeschuetz are recorded in our sources.

In 1762, Eibeschuetz – now old and worn – decided that he wanted to spend his remaining years far away from Emden, preferably in Prague, the city of his youth. Eibeschuetz, however, had left Prague in 1742 during the War of the Austrian Succession. Worse yet, he left Prague in order to assume the rabbinate in Metz, a city belonging to the enemy forces, namely France. Eibeschuetz was suspected of cavorting with the enemy and was banned from all Austrian lands. Through the Danish embassy, he petitioned Maria Theresa for the right to visit and ultimately settle in Prague. A copy of a letter purportedly sent to Maria Theresa by Landau, in response to Eibeschuetz' petition, was discovered in the archive of the Jewish community of Prague, and published by Graetz in 1877.[27] It is a devasting letter which states unequivocally that Eibeschuetz was a Sabbatian, that he had been placed under the ban by the leading rabbis in Germany and Italy,[28] and that Jewish law prohibits Landau and Eibeschuetz from residing together in the same city. The letter allegedly bears Landau's signature in Latin letters and in Hebrew, though the former signature was subsequently crossed out. The publication of this letter generated no small controversy between *jüdische Wissenschaft* enthusiasts who supported, and rabbinic scholars who denied, its authenticity.[29] The rabbinic scholars argued:

---

[26]*Ibid.*, p. 106a-b.

[27]H. Graetz, "Ezechiel Landau's Gesuch" (see above, note 9). For an abridged Hebrew version of Graetz' article, see H. Y. Gurland, "עדות נאמנה ביעקב" אור הבקר 2 (1877) 345-347.

[28]Graetz, *ibid.*, p. 19, expressed surprise at the mention of the "leading rabbis of Italy" as having placed Eibeschuetz under the ban, a fact otherwise unknown to him. But see Emden, שפת אמת ולשון זהורית, Amsterdam, 1752 [photo-offset: Jerusalem, 1971], pp. 34-35.

[29]See, e.g., G. Klemperer, "Das Rabbinat Prag: Jecheskel Landau," *Pascheles' Illustrierter israelitischer Volkskalender* 32 (1884) 94-96 [reissued in English as "The Rabbis of Prague: Ezekiel Landau," *Historia Judaica* 13 (1951) 60-61]; E. Duckesz, אוה למושב, Cracow, 1903, pp. 41-42 (Hebrew section), pp. XIX-XXII (German section); D. Simonsen, "Eine ungerechtfertigte Anklage gegen Graetz," *Allgemeine Zeitung des Judenthums* 68 (1904), part 3, p. 31; J. Cohn, "Zur 'Rechtfertigung' des Herrn Prof. Graetz," *Israelitische Monatsschrift*, 1904, n. 2, p. 5-7; J. Hirsch, "R. Ezechiel Landau, Oberrabbiner in Prague, und seine

Why would Landau have signed the copy rather than the original? Why was the signature in Latin letters crossed out? Why can no one locate the original? How do we know that the letter was actually written by Landau and sent to the Austrian chancellery? The facts are, however, that although the original letter and (apparently) the copy discovered in Prague no longer exist, an examination of official Austrian records in 1919 established beyond cavil that on April 3, 1762 Eibeschuetz was denied permission to settle in Austrian territory. Moreover, attached to the record of this ruling was a note which read:

> Ezekiel Landau, Jewish chief Rabbi of Prague, petitions that Jonathan Eibeschuetz' request that he be permitted to return to Prague, be denied.[30]

More importantly, a photograph of the letter that was discovered in the archive of the Jewish community of Prague is extant. The photograph, published some 50 years ago, apparently has gone unnoticed since then. A comparison of the signature on the photograph with other extant copies of Landau's autograph leaves no question about the authenticity of Landau's signatures on the document published by Graetz.[31] In sum, while we cannot be certain that the text of the letter discovered in the archive of the Jewish community of Prague was actually sent to the Austrian chancellery, it was certainly signed by Landau. Moreover, there can be no question that Landau did in

---

Zeit," *Freie Jüdische Lehrerstimme* 7 (1918), n. 3-4, pp. 32-35, n. 5-6, pp. 53-57; S. Wind, "בצרון "לברור "לבדור היום של הגאון ר' יחזקאל לנדו לדגאון ר' יהונתן אייבשיץ" 6 (1945) 211-217; and S. Adler, "הצופה, "אגרת מוו"פת של העודע ביהודה נגד ר' אייבשיץ" July 10, 1964 = ד'תשכ'א אב חשכ'ד.

[30]J. Mieses, "Beiträge zu Jonathan Eibeschuetz' Biographie," *Mitteilungen für jüdische Volkskunde* 21 (1919) 29-30.

[31]See S. Adler, "Ochrana cti moderními prostředky," *Věstnik Židovské obce Náboženské v Praze* 5 (1938) 100-102. Adler claimed that both signatures on the copy were forged, basing himself on a sampling consisting of one authenticated Landau signature in Latin letters, and two genuine copies of Landau's Hebrew signature. An examination of a larger sampling of Landau's signatures, however, establishes the authenticity of the signatures on the Prague document beyond cavil. Thus, e.g., Adler claimed that two rows of dots that appear on Landau's genuine Hebrew signature were lacking from the Hebrew signature on the Prague document. In fact, they are lacking from many other authenticated samples of Landau's Hebrew signature. See, for example, the document with Landau's Hebrew signature published in כרם שלמה 9 (1986), number 2, p. 47 (the original of which can be examined at the Schwadron autograph collection at the Jewish National and University Library in Jerusalem). Indeed, the Hebrew signature on that document ends with an elongated curlicue (visible only on the original document; it was not reproduced accurately in כרם שלמה) whose closest – and almost exact – parallel is the elongated curlicue at the end of the Hebrew signature on the Prague document.

fact petition the Austrian chancellery not to allow Eibeschuetz to return to Prague.[32]

On September 18, 1764 Eibeschuetz died in Altona. The news spread quickly and eulogies were delivered in Jewish communities throughout Europe. In Prague, Landau eulogized Eibeschuetz, and a portion of the eulogy was preserved and published.[33] It was hardly a typical rabbinic eulogy. To begin with, Landau offered an apology to those who might express surprise at Landau's delivering a eulogy over someone he was known to dislike. Landau admitted openly that he and Eibeschuetz were enemies. At one point, Landau said:

> What can I say: If I list his virtues some will find what I say to be impressive, and others will destroy my pleasant words. So I say to you: If you want to hear from me the extent of this man's virtues, look at the lengthy letter that I wrote some 14 years ago. See how elaborate was my praise of him! But all this is not necessary. Just as one cannot deny the brightness of the sun at mid-day, so too it is impossible to deny the greatness of his Torah and good qualities. He was a great preacher; there was none like him. He dealt kindly with all humans, especially his enemies. He taught Torah to thousands of students, especially in the city of Prague. It is proper to eulogize; it is appropriate to cry.

Clearly, Landau had nice things to say about Eibeschuetz. Yet what we have here is probably unique in the history of eulogies delivered by rabbinic scholars over other rabbinic scholars. One of the greatest rabbinic authorities of all time, Landau, not only apologized for delivering a eulogy over another great rabbinic authority, Eibeschuetz, but found it necessary to justify why he was delivering a eulogy at all!

So much, then, for the hard evidence on Landau's attitude toward Eibeschuetz. We have deliberately suppressed two pieces of evidence, which we shall return to after we examine the anecdotal evidence. Careful historians, as indicated, do not put much stock in anecdotal evidence, and rightly so. Nonetheless, when properly controlled and weighted, the anecdotal evidence can sometimes provide insights that would have eluded us on the basis of the primary sources alone. Sensitive matters, after all, are not often reduced to writing by the *dramatis personae* themselves. We all say things that we would never

---

[32]Especially noteworthy is the fact that Landau's opposition to Eibeschuetz' return is recorded in our sources even prior to 1877, the year Graetz published the then recently discovered copy of Landau's petition. See G. Klemperer, "Rabbi Jonathan Eibenschütz," in W. Pascheles, ed., *Sippurim*, Prague, 1856, vol. 4, p. 330; cf. S. H. Lieben's personal communication to J. Hirsch in the latter's "R. Ezechiel Landau" (above, n. 29), p. 54.

[33]E. Landau, דרושי הצל״ח, Warsaw, 1884 [photo-offset: Jerusalem, 1966], pp. 46b-47a. Correct Friedberg, בית עקד ספרים, Tel Aviv, 1951, vol. 1, p. 245, who mistakenly dates the first edition to 1899.

put in writing. The anecdotes that follow were first heard in Prague, mostly by *yeshiva* students who studied there during the fifty years following the death of Landau in 1793. These anecdotes were reduced to writing by these same students or their disciples, and published in a variety of sources emanating from mid-nineteenth century Prague. We wish to underscore the fact that none of these anecdotes derives from Emden or from Emden circles (the primary repository of anti-Eibeschuetz sentiment), nor are they 20th century fantasy.

1. When news of Eibeschuetz' death reached Prague, Landau refused to eulogize him. His wife implored him to deliver a eulogy, but his mind was made up. Finally, by means of a ruse she got her way. She called in the beadle and ordered him to announce in the marketplace and throughout the streets that the Chief Rabbi will deliver a eulogy for Eibeschuetz that same afternoon, immediately following the *minḥah* service. The beadle did as he was bidden. When he appeared beneath the window of Landau's study, Landau was startled by the announcement. He was about to expose the impostor, when his wife entered the study and, with a smile, admitted that she had arranged for the announcement. Since the decree had been issued, she added, it could no longer be rescinded.[34]

2. Landau eulogized Eibeschuetz from the pulpit, but the audience felt that Eibeschuetz was not being accorded his due. Landau was interrupted by a prominent member of the Prague Jewish community who shouted: "Rabbi, you will have to speak with greater enthusiasm! Don't forget who Rabbi Jonathan was!"[35]

3. A student who studied at the Prague *yeshiva* between 1829 and 1832 reported the following tradition concerning Landau. Despite his opposition to Eibeschuetz' amulets and mystical learnings, Landau recognized that Eibeschuetz was a profound talmudic scholar. He once said: Rabbi Jonathan's Sabbatian tendencies would hardly trouble me, if not for the fact that he is such a great ולמדן![36]

4. Two students reported that they once entered Landau's study and saw him pouring over a volume by Eibeschuetz, which he hastily

---

[34]Kamelhar, *op. cit.*, p. 22, n. 7, who heard it from Dr. S. J. Fischer, Chief Rabbi of Prague. An earlier version appeared in print in 1884. See G. Klemperer, "Das Rabbinat Prag: Jecheskel Landau" (see above, note 29), pp. 100-102, who heard it from Dr. M. Hirsch, then Chief Rabbi or Prague who, in turn, heard it from his teacher.

[35]Klemperer, "Rabbi Jonathan Eibenschütz" (see above, note 32), p. 344.

[36]Klein, "Zuschrift an Herrn Moses Mendelson in Hamburg," *Literaturblatt des Orients* 33 (1848), column 526.

pushed aside as he noticed them enter, saying *"Er ist doch ein Schebs gewesen!"*[37]

In brief, if the anecdotal evidence is to be believed, it was no secret in Prague that Landau considered Eibeschuetz a Sabbatian. If so, how do we account for Landau's vindication of Eibeschuetz in 1752? Would Landau have vindicated Eibeschuetz if, in fact, he was persuaded that Eibeschuetz was a Sabbatian? How do we account for Landau's severe reprimand of Cantor Brandeis in 1756? Graetz[38] suggested that historical development accounts for the conflicting evidence regarding Landau's attitude toward Eibeschuetz. Graetz explained that until 1760 Landau was convinced that Eibeschuetz was innocent of the charges levelled against him by the Emden forces. In 1760 or thereabout, Landau chanced upon new evidence that persuaded him that Emden was right after all, hence the letter to Maria Theresa. One suspects, however, that not so much historical development as conceptual analysis may best account for all the evidence. But first, let us turn our attention to the final pieces of evidence, alluded to earlier, that bear directly on Landau's attitude toward Eibeschuetz.

The first piece of evidence derives from a letter addressed by an East European rabbi to his son, who at the time was attending Eibeschuetz' lectures at Altona. The letter was written in the summer of 1751, some six months after the outbreak of the controversy. In it, the distraught rabbi indicated that he was aware of the controversy surrounding Eibeschuetz and therefore was issuing a plea to his son that he abandon Eibeschuetz' *yeshiva* and return home. The rabbi did more than implore; he spelled out the dire consequences of coming under the influence of the wicked. At one point the rabbi wrote as follows:[39]

כי ביום שמוע שמעתי מהרב מהור"ר ר' יחזקאל מק'ק יאמפלי
ותרגז בטני וממש שעיני נזלה מים ואוי לאזנים ששומעות
כדבר הזה ויש לי חרטה גדולה על זה שאתה לומד אצלו
שלא תתחבר ותלמד דרכו חס ושלום דרכי שאול יורדת אל
חדרי מות ... ובאם שתשוב לביתך לקוח עמך שנים או שלשה
קמיעות וראה שלא יתחלפו רק שתדע שהיא בודאי אמת
מכתיבת ידו או העתקה מכתיבת ידו כדי לידע האמת וגם
הרב מק'ק יאמפלי גם כן בקש במטותיה בעבור זאת.

[37]Klemperer, "Rabbi Jonathan Eibenschütz" (see above, note 32), p. 345. For evidence that Landau's library included a book by Eibeschuetz, see below, note 47.

[38]H. Graetz, "Ezechiel Landau's Gesuch" (see above, note 9), pp. 24-25.

[39]פרח עינים, p. 14b.

It would appear, then, that as early as summer 1751, i.e., almost a full year prior to Landau's vindication of Eibeschuetz, an East European rabbi heard an earful from Landau, enough to warrant an urgent plea that the son withdraw at once from Eibeschuetz' *yeshiva*. Moreover, Landau requested that the son, on his return to Eastern Europe, bring with him amulets written by Eibeschuetz, either originals or genuine copies. At the very least, Landau suspected Eibeschuetz and sought to examine the evidence first hand.

Turning to the final piece of evidence, some background information is necessary in order to appreciate its full import. R. David Oppenheim, Chief Rabbi of Prague prior to Landau, died in 1736. For reasons which need not detain us here, no successor was appointed. Instead Eibeschuetz, who frequently served as acting Chief Rabbi during Oppenheim's lifetime, was elected *Oberjurist*, i.e., President of the בית דין of Prague, but was denied the office of *Oberrabbiner*, i.e., Chief Rabbi of Prague.[40] Eibeschuetz served Prague with distinction until he left to assume the rabbinate of Metz in 1742. Indeed, no Chief Rabbi of Prague was elected until early in 1751, when prior to the outbreak of the Emden-Eibeschuetz controversy R. Aryeh Leib of Amsterdam was elected Chief Rabbi of Prague.[41] With the outbreak of the controversy, R. Aryeh Leib, who was Emden's brother-in-law, joined the leadership of the anti-Eibeschuetz forces. When R. Aryeh Leib's stance in the controversy became evident, the appointment to the post of Chief Rabbi was rescinded. R. Aryeh Leib, who had not yet left Amsterdam, unpacked his bags and continued to serve as Ashkenazi Chief Rabbi of Amsterdam until his death in 1755.[42]

The most distinguished member of the anti-Eibeschuetz forces was neither Emden, nor R. Aryeh Leib, but rather R. Jacob Joshua Falk, the זקן הדור, Chief Rabbi of Frankfurt am Main, and author of the פני יהושע: Falk's uncompromising stand during the controversy ultimately led to

---

[40]See R. Zerah Eidlitz, אור לישרים, Jerusalem, 1972, דרוש ב׳, p. 29:

שנודע לכל שטרם נסיעתו מפה היה ממלא מקום
אב בית דין שהרביץ תורה והפס ישיבה וכל הבית
דין מורה שה מחכמין לוביה ושמחו לראש עליהם.

Cf. G. Klemperer, "The Rabbis of Prague: David Oppenheim," *Historia Judaica* 12 (1950), p. 152; and his "The Rabbis of Prague: Ezechiel Landau," *Historia Judaica* 13 (1951), pp. 76-77.

[41]S. H. Lieben, "Handschriftliches zur Geschichte der Juden in Prag in den Jahren 1744-1754," *Jahrbuch des Jüdisch-literarische Gesellschaft* 2 (1904), pp. 292-295, 320-322, 327-330. Cf. Emden, שפת אמת ולשון זהורית, pp. 45 and 47.

[42]See the previous note. Cf. Emden's eulogy of R. Aryeh Leib, שאגת אריה, Amsterdam, 1755, p. 6b, where he alludes to the Prague debacle.

his being deposed from the Frankfurt rabbinate.[43] After his deposition, Falk resided in Worms, from where he directed the campaign against Eibeschuetz. In 1753, at Worms, Falk addressed a letter to R. Aryeh Leib of Amsterdam, which was published by Emden in 1756.[44] The letter is dated ‏ראש חודש אדר שני תקי"ג‎, i.e., it was written approximately one year after Landau had circulated his famous letter vindicating Eibeschuetz. Falk's letter reads in part:

> I was informed by the scribe who arrived from Frankfurt that persistent rumor has it that the rabbi of Yampol [Landau] has been appointed Chief Rabbi of Prague. I dismissed the rumor out of hand since not a hint of such an appointment has been heard anywhere in the communities surrounding us, not even among the wicked ones [i.e., the pro-Eibeschuetz faction] in Mannheim....You too would have heard about it. So I concluded that it was an outright lie. If I thought for a moment that it was true, I would include in the broadside we are about to publish an account of the *first letter* addressed by the rabbi of Yampol to all rabbis and *geonim* wherein he admitted that despite the fact that Eibeschuetz' abominations were well known to him, he beseeches all of us to take pity on the *honor of his Torah*, and to take into account the *profaning of God's name* that had occurred. In the light of these considerations he asked that we partially overlook Eibeschuetz' sins and treat him with leniency. So he wrote me in a lengthy letter; no doubt he wrote you the same. Now there appears to be more to the rumor than I thought, for yesterday I received a letter from Poland in which it is stated that the rabbi of Yampol openly announced that he was appointed Chief Rabbi of Prague. Moreover, he compounded his villainy by influencing the Chief Rabbi of Lvov to refrain from contributing yet another missive to the controversy, claiming that such action would be detrimental to his appointment to the Prague rabbinate. Landau found it necessary to wield his influence, for the Chief Rabbi of Lvov had convened an assembly of rabbis who were about to place Eibeschuetz under the ban and circulate letters to that effect throughout Europe and especially in Germany. Landau was explicit in justifying his intervention to the Chief Rabbi of Lvov: his appointment to the Prague rabbinate was due to Eibeschuetz' extraordinary efforts on his behalf....After searching diligently through my correspondence, I located the *first letter* sent by the rabbi of Yampol. Indeed, he denounces Eibeschuetz at length.

Falk's letter was published by Emden during the lifetime of Eibeschuetz, Landau, and many of the other rabbis mentioned in it. It is highly unlikely that the letter was forged by Emden; no document

---

[43]In general, see M. Horovitz, *Frankfurter Rabbinen*,[2] ed. by J. Unna, Jerusalem, 1969, pp. 125-166. (Significant material relating to the Emden-Eibeschuetz controversy was omitted from the Hebrew version, ‏רבני פרנקפורט‎, Jerusalem, 1972, pp. 90-109.) Cf. D. L. Zinz, ‏עטרת יהושע‎, Bilgoray, 1936 [photo offset: New York, 1982].

[44]‏פתח עינים‎, pp. 13b-14b.

published by Emden has been proven to be a forgery. Quite the opposite: to the extent that modern scholars have been able to verify their content, the documents published by Emden were not only authentic, they were ordinarily published with great precision. It is especially unlikely that Emden would have published a forgery that could so easily be exposed. We shall discount the hearsay about Landau's activity in Poland; Falk may have been misinformed by his informant. But what remains incontrovertible is Falk's testimony about Landau's negative attitude toward Eibeschuetz *prior* to the publication of his famous letter of vindication in 1752.

In the light of all the evidence, it would appear that Landau was entirely consistent in his view of Eibeschuetz. He was persuaded that Eibeschuetz was, and continued to be, a Sabbatian. Some will suggest, perhaps, that we ought to distinguish between "suspicion" and "certainty" of guilt. It may be that Landau suspected Eibeschuetz of Sabbatianism, but was not convinced of his guilt. Falk's letter, the letter to Maria Theresa, and the anecdotal evidence indicate otherwise. Moreover, Landau's disciple and successor, R. Eleazar Fleckeles, preserves a tradition that he heard from his teacher regarding suspected Sabbatians. He writes:[45]

לפי הקבלה אשר בידי מאת מורינו הגאון האמתי:
באנשים מצורעים הרעים האלה לא נכשל אדם מעולם
בעון חושד בכשרים, כי מי שחושדין בו יש בו.

Thus, Landau was persuaded that Eibeschuetz was a Sabbatian. He was also persuaded that Eibeschuetz was one of the greatest masters of Torah of his generation. Landau's primary concern was with כבוד התורה and חלול השם. The former was to be maintained; the later was to be contained. These key terms – כבוד התורה and חלול השם – appear and reappear throughout Landau's famous letter of 1752, as well as in Falk's summary of Landau's first letter.[46] It was clear to Landau that Emden's approach of total exposure of, and capitulation by, Eibeschuetz, only aggravated the problem. The controversy had brought כבוד התורה to low ebb. חלול השם was rampant. Rabbinic authority was being ridiculed by Jew and Christian alike. Landau's solution was to drive Eibeschuetz' alleged (or: real) Sabbatianism underground. So

---

[45]שו"ת תשובה מאהבה, Prague, 1809 [photo offset: New York, 1966], vol. 1, ח' סימן. This was Fleckeles' rephrasing of a teaching he had received from Landau. Landau's formulation, preserved *ibid.* at סימן קב, is less striking but the import is the same.
[46]The terms כבוד התורה and חלול השם are displayed prominently throughout Landau's writings. See especially דרושי הצל"ח, p. 43b דה' לשון הרע, and cf. Landau's reply to the *yeshiva* student in Hamburg (see above, note 25).

long as Eibeschuetz would publicly denounce Sabbetai Zevi and the Sabbatian writings ascribed to him, including the amulets, Landau was satisfied that Eibeschuetz would be identified publicly only by his Torah teaching, which was great indeed.[47] Once Eibeschuetz was publicly cleansed of his Sabbatian connections, anyone who spoke ill of this Torah giant was dishonoring the Torah itself. Hence Landau's swift action against Cantor Brandeis.

It was a brilliant attempt on Landau's part;[48] it failed[49] only – as indicated above – because Falk, Emden, and R. Aryeh Leib of

---

[47]Consistent with Landau's approach is the fact that he was a subscriber to the first edition of Eibeschuetz, אורים ותומים, Karlsruhe, 1775-77. See B. Brilling,"Israel Eibenschuetz as a Collector of Subscriptions," *Studies in Bibliography and Booklore* 6 (1964), n. 4, pp. 142-149. Moreover, Landau cites a passage from Eibeschuetz' אורים ותומים in his ציון לנפש חיה לסדר נזיקין, Jerusalem, 1959, p. 112 (cf., however, the editor's introduction).

[48]For a somewhat similar attempt, see the letter of R. Mordecai of Dusseldorf in Emden's שפת אמת ולשון זהורית, pp. 59-60. R. Mordecai foresaw much that would transpire, and warned the Emden forces early in the fray that any frontal attack on Eibeschuetz was doomed to failure. He stressed the fact that Eibeschuetz was articulate, bold, and influential in governmental circles. In effect, he advised the Emden forces to adopt a strategy not unlike Landau's, one that would provide Eibeschuetz with a graceful exit. Apparently his advice was accorded the same reception as Landau's; his name never appears again in the literature of the controversy. On R. Mordecai of Dusseldorf, see B. H. Auerbach, *Geschichte der israelitischen Gemeinde Halberstadt*, Halberstadt, 1866, pp. 74-76.

[49]Although Landau's efforts failed at the time, ultimately his approach would prevail. Eibeschuetz' place among the giants of Torah scholarship for all generations (see the comments of R. Meir Simḥa of Dvinsk cited by Tavyomi, *op. cit.*, p. 103), and not among the scoundrels, as the Emden forces would have preferred it, if not largely due to his legitimization by Landau, has certainly followed the general contours established by Landau. Eibeschuetz followed Landau's prescription: he withdrew from circulation whatever amulets he was able to retrieve; he wrote no more amulets after the outbreak of the controversy (we have Emden's testimony to that effect); he publicly renounced all Sabbatian amulets or writings ascribed to him. His reputation would rest on his exoteric Torah teaching; virtually all his published work is in this area, and it is precisely his exoteric works that are printed and reprinted again and again. In contrast, his esoteric teachings would have no appreciable effect on later generations. Indeed, they remained underground after his death, as during his lifetime, until *jüdische Wissenschaft* would resurrect them (e.g., שם עולם, Vienna, 1891 and Liebes' forthcoming edition of ואבוא היום אל העין). If Landau's approach continues to prevail, as we suspect it will, the efforts of modern Jewish scholarship in the esoteric realm will have little or no impact on the traditional (i.e., *halakhic*) Jewish community.

Amsterdam were relentless in their pursuit of Eibeschuetz.[50] From their perspective, Landau had engaged in a cover-up, and hardly for the respectable reasons mentioned above, i.e., concern for כבוד התורה and חלול השם. Rather, Landau had sold his soul for the rabbinate of Prague. As R. Aryeh Leib of Amsterdam had learned from bitter experience, no one could serve as Chief Rabbi of Prague without Eibeschuetz' support. According to the Emden forces, Landau paid for that support by providing Eibeschuetz with a graceful exit from the controversy. This accounts, of course, for Emden's venomous attitude toward Landau.[51] *Emden knew that Landau knew;* if despite his knowledge Landau insisted on supporting Eibeschuetz, it could only be viewed as a cover-up.

Religio-moral imperatives and expediency sometimes move in the same direction. When a particular action is at once morally compelling and expedient, motivations need to be examined if judgments are to be made about character. Certainly, one suggestive interpretation of the facts is that Landau felt morally compelled to make an attempt at bringing the controversy to a close. That is proved expedient may well have been a welcome fringe benefit. Obviously, Emden felt otherwise.

---

[50]The rationale of the Emden forces for rejecting Landau's compromise is poignantly argued in a broadside published by R. Aryeh Leib of Amsterdam in 1752. It reads in part:

I know full well that scholars of your stature are aware of the truth. You seek to rehabilitate him. But you are rehabilitating his body and public image at the expense of his spirit and soul! Our approach differs. We too seek to rehabilitate him, but we seek to rehabilitate his soul....In sum, such scholars as yourselves understand the essence of the matter. But you prefer to take pity on him and, as a facade, claim that your actions are for the sake of heaven, in order to reduce strife within the Jewish community, and in order to prevent profaning of God's Name among the nations. Quite the contrary, by your inaction God's Name is profaned among the nations and impurity increases among the Jews.

Although not addressed to Landau, it captures the essence of the rejectionist approach to a compromise such as the one put forward by Landau. See Joseph Praeger's נחלי אש, vol. 2, pp. 36-37.

[51]Emden's final act of vengeance against Landau (aside from the nasty comments in פתח עינים and ספר התאבקות; see above, note 22) came in the elections for Eibeschuetz' successor in 1764. Landau was among the candidates for the post. Fully aware of Emden's less than friendly attitude toward the previous incumbent rabbis of Altona, Hamburg, and Wandsbeck, the communal leaders sought to nip any future controversy in the bud by allowing Emden to select Eibeschuetz' successor from the list of finalists. Emden welcomed the opportunity with no small measure of delight. Landau, of course, didn't get the job. Cf. E. Duckesz, *op. cit.,* p. 53.

Part Fourteen
THE MODERN AGE: PHILOSOPHY

40

The Character and Status of the Concept of History in Three Twentieth Century Systems of Judaic Thought: Cohen, Rosenzweig, Lévinas

Wendell S. Dietrich
Brown University

In this essay,[1] I propose to describe, analyze and interpret the character and status of the concept of history in three major twentieth century systems of Judaic thought. The first system is that of the Marburg neo-Kantian Judaic thinker from the time of the turn from the nineteenth to the twentieth century, Hermann Cohen. Cohen's system finds mature expression in his *Religion of Reason out of the Sources of Judaism*. The second is that of the German Judaic thinker, Franz Rosenzweig, whose *The Star of Redemption* is the premier work of systematic Judaic thought in the twentieth century. The third system is that of the contemporary French philosopher, Emmanuel Lévinas, whose two major works *Totality and Infinity: An Essay on Exteriority* (1969) and *Otherwise than Being or Beyond Essence* (1981) are becoming increasingly well known in the English-speaking world.

---

[1]I should like to express my appreciation to the seminar on "History, Historiography, and Religion," Department of Religious Studies, University of Pennsylvania, and to the Colloquium of the Jewish Studies Program, University of Washington, to whom I presented earlier versions of this paper. That such matters are now treated in American universities is in itself a vindication of Marvin Fox's life work in establishing Judaic Studies as an academic discipline.

Modern systems of Judaic thought characteristically give a novel conceptual articulation to classic themes of Judaic thought and these classic themes are presented in new constellations derived from various sources. In systems of thought of the type I interpret here, the Judaic elements are an independent variable and they indeed give a characteristic cast to the whole system. However, the conceptual schemes employed are worked out through critical appropriation of concepts from certain modern philosophical schemes. And some of the elements of the modern Judaic systems come over from such modern philosophical schemes.

Most important in this connection are the schemes of Kant and Hegel, schemes which themselves express significant features of modernity and the modern Western experience of history. The Judaic systems interpreted here are unintelligible without taking into account interpretations of history in the Kantian and Hegelian modes. That means both history as a locus of emancipation (Kant and Hegel) and a locus of catastrophic events (Hegel). Moreover, insofar as these Judaic systems take specifically into account the modern experience of the Jewish people, that means that attention is paid both to the emancipation of the Jewish people and their emergence into the common life and history of the West (Cohen, Rosenzweig, Lévinas) and also to the catastrophic events of World War I (Rosenzweig) and World War II and the Holocaust (Lévinas).

With these considerations in view, I turn to a more precise specification of the character and status of the concept of history in the systems of Cohen, Rosenzweig and Lévinas.

In the mature system of Hermann Cohen, human history as the sphere of moral action and locus of social interaction between groups and institutions is a central element. This is so despite the fact that, as a Marburg neo-Kantian elaborating a postulatory system oriented toward the logical correlation of concepts, Cohen is hostile to the historicist tendencies of late nineteenth century German thought, including the Heidelberg historicist neo-Kantianism of Ernst Troeltsch.[2] To view the matter from a slightly different angle, Cohen assigns to history a prominent place in his system and assigns to what occurs in that sphere a very positive valence while at the same time framing the sphere of history at the outset by the ideality of the universal moral imperative and, as goal, by the ideality of Messianic humanity never fully realized in history.

According to Cohen, there are three interconnected ideal concepts or postulates which the contemporary Judaic thinker can derive from the

---

[2]See Dietrich, 1986.

sources of Judaism by a process technically known as "idealization." These three postulates are: the one, unique God, in his transcendent ethical ideality; unitary human history; and the ideal goal, never to be fully attained, of a unified Messianic humanity. These postulates are to be commended to mankind as an appropriate basis for a religion of reason in modern Western civilization. Indeed these concepts, in Cohen's judgment, constitute a sounder religious basis for a continuingly "emancipatory" society in the West than the traditional resources of Christian religion.

Further, in Cohen's view, the universally valid criterion by which change and development in the sphere of human groups and institutions is to be judged is the criterion of justice. Justice is specified first of all in terms of major effort in rectifying disproportions of social power in modern industrial society. (Cohen is a neo-Kantian revisionary Marxist.) Indeed, poverty not the threat of death is the principal obstacle to human flourishing.

The criterion of justice is further specified in terms of fostering human emancipation. This emancipatory process has begun in the break from status oriented, hierarchically structured pre-modern societies of the type which Toennies called "community" *(Gemeinschaft)*. The older, "community"-type of social organization was, according to Cohen, traditionally supported by mythical world-views focussed on other-worldly individual salvation and fateful enmeshment of humanity in the sins of the fathers. Modern Enlightenment and post-Enlightenment society has emancipated itself from the fateful grip of the past. In modern society, one finds the constant construction and reconstruction of situations in which emancipation can continue. In such modern society, one finds a new sense of this-worldly human solidarity and a sense of the openness of the historical future. The ideal of a unitary Messianic humanity functions as a permanent, never to be fully actualized, goal. This ideal goal keeps under critical judgment the achievements of any social group or national state.[3]

These critical postulates – the one unique God, unitary human history, and the goal of Messianic humanity – initially appear in human history in the prophetic faith and ethos of Biblical Israel. The function of the people Israel has been and will continue to be an instrumental one: to carry these ideas through human history, while now also contributing them as the religious basis of modern civilization as a whole.

I now turn to a subordinate but critical issue in the interpretation of Cohen's thought. What for Cohen and his school of Marburg neo-

---

[3]Dietrich 50, 59.

Kantians is the relation between the notion of history previously sketched and the practice of that modern critical scientific discipline developed in the universities called historical science? In my judgment, it is characteristic of the formulation of this neo-Kantian system of Judaic thought in its original socio-cultural matrix that such an issue should be prominent. (It is conceivable that the permanently valid features of the system could be preserved and restated without major attention to this issue.)

It is often alleged in present-day interpretative literature – and this allegation was pressed very hard by members of the Heidellberg Southwest Baden neo-Kantian school like Windelband and Rickert – that the Marburg neo-Kantians display a fatal methodological weakness in their performance as historians. In principle, Marburg neo-Kantians, so it is said, fail to make a distinction between the "nomothetic" interest of the natural sciences in describing general regularities in the cosmos on the one hand and the proper interest of the historical sciences on the other in that picture-making "ideographic" operation involved in presenting historical individuality.[4] In actual performance, this abstract formalism of the neo-Kantians distorts, so it is alleged, the presentation of the history of philosophical thought. Moreover in the case of Cohen in particular, it is contended, this abstract formalism distorts his handling of the data of religion.

Now admittedly Cohen, who is principally a systematic thinker, is also heavily preoccupied in his historical inquiries with the history of ideas and the history of philosophic systems in the West. This is related, I think, to the fact that, despite his revisionary Marxist recognition of the role of material interests in determining social interaction, Cohen assigns a causative role to certain key ideas in human history. But in my judgment, his presentation and appraisal of such thinkers as Maimonides is massively learned and sophisticated and not notably distorted by Cohen's ultimate interest in drawing forth from the history of philosophy permanently valid ideas.

Nor does Cohen, in the process of idealization, gravely distort the data of Judaic religion. Admittedly, Cohen is intent on vindicating prophetic ethical monotheism and he assigns to Biblical prophetic belief and ethos a role of unsurpassable primacy. Moreover, Cohen takes over as his own that version of the data of the Biblical phase of Judaic religion very recently formulated in Wellhausen's total reconstruction of the history of the religion of Israel. But, I interpret this as a daring and imaginative appropriation of the results of historical-critical scholarship for philosophical purposes. No other

---

[4]Dietrich 51, 56.

Judaic thinker of the nineteenth or early twentieth century even attempted, to say nothing of effectively carrying off, so bold a maneuver.

I turn finally to another feature of Cohen's system as a whole: the role of the people of Israel and the world-historical significance of Israel's "mission" in human history. I have already indicated that for Cohen the instrumental function of the people Israel has been and will continue to be to carry the ideas of the one unique God, unitary human history, and the Messianic goal of history through history, while now contributing these ideas as the religious basis of modern civilization as a whole. That means that the historical role and function of the people Israel is always construed in relation to the history of mankind as a whole.

At this point in his system, Cohen gives distinctive and in many ways definitive formulation to a major preoccupation of Judaic thinking in nineteenth century Germany and America. Whether on the part of individual systematic thinkers like Steinheim, Samuel Hirsch and Formstecher or on the part of major figures in the *Wissenschaft des Judentums* movement (especially Geiger and Graetz), a principal item on the nineteenth century agenda of Judaic thought is the "invention" of Judaism as prophetic ethical monotheism. Integral to this invention is the notion of the world historical significance of the people Israel and Judaism.

That is, in these versions of Judaic thought, the people of Israel and its history is interpreted in relation to a universal horizon, a universal horizon initially sketched by the prophets of Israel. In playing its instrumental role in relation to humanity as a whole, the people of Israel carries out its "mission" as an exemplary chosen people, a "priestly nation." To that theme, Cohen gives definitive, if distinctive, formulation.

I offer no final appraisal of the validity of this prophetic ethical monotheistic vision of the realization of history as an ethical process and the concomitant view of how the people Israel and its history matter for the history of the whole of humanity. I do contend that such a view is one of the permanently valid options for the modern reinterpretation of Judaism. And, without overdramatizing the matter unduly, I register my profound admiration for the way in which Cohen refuses to let the people Israel subside into isolation and self-preoccupation.

In treating the problem of the character and status of the concept of history in the Judaic religious system of Franz Rosenzweig, I turn initially to a section of *The Star of Redemption* until recently neglected and inadequately interpreted. I have in view the section on "Messianic Politics" in the third, concluding, portion of *The Star*.

This exposition of "Messianic Politics" is deeply informed by Hegel's reading of the history of the nations as a history which is a history of force and slaughter yet is simultaneously to be interpreted as a historical theodicy. (Recent Francophone Rosenzweig scholarship, especially the work of the Francophone Israeli scholar Stéphane Mosès,[5] stresses this point.) Recall that Rosenzweig's first major scholarly work was a subtle and erudite treatment of "Hegel and the State." In the section on "Messianic Politics" in *The Star*, Rosenzweig, building on his earlier analysis of Hegel, acknowledges and assesses the deadly import of Hegel's claims on behalf of the totalizing reality of history and its inevitably developing social and cultural dynamisms. Indeed, Rosenzweig judges the fratricidal strife of World War I to be the expression of the nationalistic Messianic rivalries of the Christian nations in an increasingly secular Western culture.

Precisely as a witness against these totalizing dynamisms of Western culture, Rosenzweig interposes the social reality of the Jewish people, in his famous phrase, "beyond history" in eternity, already "with God." (I follow here the interpretation of Stéphane Mosès.) Thus, one of the axes on which *The Star of Redemption* turns is the history of the nations as a history of force and slaughter in relation to the people Israel as the eternal people "beyond history." But in order to appraise this aspect of Rosenzweig's thought more accurately, it is necessary to look at some other aspects of the system of *The Star*.

That means reverting to the first section of the work where Rosenzweig sketches a duality of man as "personality" and as meta-ethical "I." According to Rosenzweig, man as "personality," even in the Kantian sense of ethical personality, has a fate; man as personality is tied up with man as a historical-political being. According to Rosenzweig, the individual in Kant's scheme is not adequately protected; the law of morality is formulated as the law of a universally valid act. Thus freedom, which is, according to Kant, the miracle in the midst of the phenomenal world, lapses back, with the post-Kantians, into the phenomenal world. Kant himself serves as godfather to Hegel's concept of universal history.

So Rosenzweig seeks a meta-ethical and meta-historical point of standing. Such a point of standing is secured in recognizing the individual self, individuated by having to die.

But in the first section of *The Star*, Rosenzweig is simply establishing analytically and abstractly one of the three irreducible

---

[5]See Mosès 1982, 1985.

"elements" of reality: the meta-ethical, meta-historical self. (The other two are the world and God.) Thus, one must move on into Book II where, in the reality of "revelation," the various elements come into relation with each other. This relating of the elements is established and verified in and through the narrating of what has been and stating what is the case about reality, specifically by focussing on God's self-disclosure to man on the model of the self-disclosure of lover to beloved in a "love stronger than death."

But even this narrating and statement is, in its own way, abstract and does not present the whole of reality. Thus one must press on to the third book of *The Star*, the place where, as I have already indicated, one first comes upon the axis of the history of the nations as a history of force and slaughter and the people Israel as "beyond history." In this connection, it is useful to recall a well-known and sometimes misunderstood aphorism of Rosenzweig's that salvation comes not from "history" – I claim now history interpreted in Hegelian terms – but from "religion."

Religion in the fully articulated sense of *The Star* is a symbolic mode of experiencing time which does not focus on the timefulness of the historical process but breaks through it in two directions: to eternity in the present and also the future, grasped not as historical continuation but symbolically in a radically utopian way. (I follow, insofar as I understand him, Stéphane Mosès once again.)

With this conception of religion in view, one may recall once again Book II of *The Star* and the still partially abstract narrating of the dialogue of revelation between God the Lover and the human beloved. The reality of such revelation is in fact only fully established and verified in the social reality of the two concrete historical religious traditions of Judaism on the one hand and Christianity on the other. In both Judaism and Christianity as social historical realities God as ultimate reality is revealingly present in the world until the moment of truth's final verification.

But, in Rosenzweig's view, the differences between Judaism and Christianity as social historical religious realities must be clearly specified. In fact, the definition of religion I have just presented – religion as symbolic mode of experiencing time which does not focus on the timefulness of the historical process but breaks through it in two directions: to eternity in the present and also to a radically utopian grasp of the future – is keyed normatively to Judaism, the "eternal people," beyond history, already with God in eternity.

In the light of these considerations one can profitably look at some of the details of Rosenzweig's account of Judaism as the eternal people beyond history.

As even the most casual reader of Rosenzweig is bound to notice, Rosenzweig contends in the final section of *The Star* that the Jewish people now lack the standard appurtenances of nationhood: a distinctive land, a living language and an ever-evolving system of law. The Jewish people, dispersed among the nations, no longer is tied to a particular geographical space; its language is immobilized in its unchanging liturgical form; its law is a law of sacred obligation which quite properly strikes both Jew and Gentile alike as remote from the present.

Furthermore, Rosenzweig contends that the life of the Jewish people is primarily oriented by liturgical time, by the cyclical and spiralling round of festivals of creation, revelation and redemption, culminating in the festival of the people which is both most individual and most universal, Yom Kippur. Moreover, to undergird this notion of liturgical or sacred-calendrical time, Rosenzweig insists that more deeply ingredient in human reality than any involvement in a realm of historicized totality is participation in a kind of vital organic time of flourishing and decay, read in a vitalistic fashion.

But if the life of the Jewish people is primarily oriented by liturgical time, Judaism for Rosenzweig is not only a religious communion in the nineteenth century sense of that notion but also an ethnic reality. In fact, Rosenzweig deliberately chooses to give renewed prominence to Judaism as ethnic collectivity in which membership is transmitted by generation from generation to generation through matrilineal descent.

Thus, Judaism, according to Rosenzweig, is archetypically an eternal religious ethnic reality. In contrast to Christianity's spatializing of time and its promotion of the organic growth of the body of Christ and the extension of the sphere of the Christian nations, Judaism, according to Rosenzweig, normatively surmounts time, in Stéphane Mosès' very subtle formulation, internally from generation to generation by reference to "eternity." This "eternity" is at the same time a fundamentally metahistorical situation in which religious experience permits participation in the lived reality of redemption outside of time and also a "utopic" tension toward the future. So the Jewish vocation is, in Mosès' phrase, to "suspend time without abolishing hope."

To put this another way, one could say with Mosès that intrinsic to Rosenzweig's conception of Judaism is a "political refusal." But this political refusal cannot possibly refer to an other-worldly asceticism in the pre-modern style or a confinement of religion to the private as distinct from the public sphere in the sense of some nineteenth century German Jewish theoreticians and public figures. Rather, Rosenzweig specifies this political refusal in relation to those totalizing dynamisms of nineteenth and twentieth century social and cultural life fired by Hegelian historicist readings of history and expressed in the nationalistic Messianic rivalries of Christian nations. This is the political refusal of the Jewish people who by their very social existence make a social-ethical witness against all modes of what we have learned to call totalitarianism. (Incidentally, this reading of Rosenzweig permits Mosès to contend that Rosenzweig, who is conventionally read as anti-Zionist or at most non-Zionist, could, if he were redoing his system today, accommodate, as one modality of the historical actualization of the ethnic reality of the Jewish people, a modern political presence, i.e., the State of Israel.)

To round out my description of the character and status of the concept of history in Rosenzweig's system, I allude to the problem of Rosenzweig's periodization of the history of Western civilization, a civilization which is also Christian civilization. Judaism, Rosenzweig claims, does not suffer successive and differentiated epochal development in its existence. The Church and Western civilization, on the other hand, do pass successively from the Petrine to the Pauline and now to the Johannine epoch. In the Petrine epoch, the Church is characterized by the love of the missionary who goes out extensively into the world to convert the pagan nations, creating in the political sphere a Christian Empire and also the religious institutions of the visible body of Christ. Indeed this duality of state and Church sets up one of the characteristic tensions of Western civilization. But throughout the Middle Ages the Church failed to come to grips with the paganism in its own soul. Paganism was repressed but not truly converted; hence the dualism of faith and reason in Medieval scholasticism.[6] A new phase of Christianity is initiated, after the revival of paganism in the Renaissance, when the Pauline Church of the Reformation promotes, in contrast to the Petrine Church, the Christianizing of the believer's inward soul through faith alone. In this period reality is split into the pure inwardness of faith and the world of Christendom organized by the secular authorities. Since 1800, Rosenzweig insists, the world has been increasingly secularized; but the possibility has emerged of a new Johannine epoch for the Church. The Johannine epoch is an epoch not of love or faith, but of hope. Rosenzweig does not have in view here, as is sometimes supposed, a kind of Free-Masonry of the spirit, the fellowship of elite religious individuals. The Johannine epoch is an epoch in which the social identity of religious communions still matters. In this new epoch

---

[6]See Altmann 1958.

Judaism is for the first time free to interact with Christianity on equal terms instead of being hauled into court to give an account of itself in disputations organized by Christian authorities.

It is in this context that one should look at the differentiated yet interconnected assignments which Christianity and Judaism receive in Rosenzweig's scheme. Christianity has, according to *The Star*, an extensive mission to the pagan nations, to Christianize them, bringing them to the Father through the Son. Judaism, on the other hand, already with God, may become, it would seem, ever more preoccupied with the intensity of its own life. Nathan Rotenstreich, among others, has even suggested[7] that, in contrast to the role of exemplary mission to the nations which nineteenth century Judaic thinkers assigned the Jewish people, the Jewish people has, in Rosenzweig's scheme, no mission.

Certainly, Rosenzweig stresses the intensity of Jewish life and it is Christianity which has an extensive mission. Is Rosenzweig to be interpreted as breaking completely with the nineteenth century Judaic vision of the realization of history as an ethical process and Judaism's instrumental role within that process? Rosenzweig indeed lacks Cohen's stress on the prophetic universal criterion of justice which judges critically all historical actualization, including the life of the Jewish people as religious communion and ethnic reality. But there is a universal horizon in Rosenzweig's thinking about the Jewish people. Rosenzweig's view of Judaism does not simply mandate a retreat into religious isolation. The Jewish people and the history of mankind are bound together and what happens in one sphere matters, in myriad ways, for what goes on in the other. Indeed, I have argued, intrinsic to Rosenzweig's interpretation of the social reality of the Jewish people is an element of social-ethical protest against the totalitarian dynamisms of nineteenth and twentieth century society and culture.

I turn finally to the thought of Emmanuel Lévinas. To some it may appear unwarranted to treat Lévinas' thought comparatively in a study of systems of modern Judaic thought. After all, Lévinas is usually regarded as a phenomenologist whose enterprise began in interpretation and critical appropriation of Husserl and Heidegger. More important, Lévinas' system can certainly be properly read as an interpretation of the human situation which issues finally in a universally pertinent "ethical metaphysics." Is Lévinas in any sense a Judaic thinker? The full answer to that question is a matter of great complexity which, in my judgment, is still being worked out on the frontiers of Lévinas interpretation. For the purposes of this essay, I call

---

[7]See Rotenstreich 1978.

attention to these preliminary considerations. First, Lévinas asserts emphatically that Rosenzweig's *The Star of Redemption* is one of the major sources of his own thought, especially in *Totality and Infinity*. Secondly, from a typological point of view Lévinas' thought conforms in many respects to that ethical monotheism worked out in the great tradition of nineteenth and early twentieth century Judaic thought. Moreover, especially in the concluding sections of *Otherwise than Being*, one finds increasing articulation of classic themes of Judaic thought about God and the world, even themes from the Judaic mystical thought of the medieval period.

What then can one say about the character and status of the concept of history in Lévinas' thought? In my judgment, Lévinas in *Totality and Infinity* has taken over wholesale Rosenzweig's reading of the deadly import of Hegel's claims for the totalizing reality of history and its inevitably developing social and cultural dynamisms. That is at least one of the important things Lévinas means by his cryptic observation in *Totality and Infinity*:[8] "We were impressed by the opposition to the idea of totality in Franz Rosenzweig's *Stern der Erloesung*, a work too often present to be cited." What Rosenzweig had to say about that fratricidal strife of World War I, fired by Hegelian historicist readings of history and expressed in the nationalistic Messianic rivalries of the Christian nations, Lévinas applies by extension to totalitarianism and the destruction of European Jewry in the Holocaust. Thus, in contrast to the positive valence given to the sphere of history in Hermann Cohen's scheme, Lévinas' twentieth century "ethical metaphysics" assigns to the sphere of history, initially and as an indispensable presupposition, a negative valence.

To put it another way: if Lévinas initially reads history in a Hegelian fashion as a history of force and slaughter, he emphatically does not read that history of force and slaughter simultaneously, as Hegel does, as theodicy. Rather, the principal energy in Lévinas' execution of his project is devoted to securing a meta-historical point of standing from which such unfolding dynamisms of history can be resolutely resisted. This point of standing is secured in the recognition of the "visage" of the other as the other confronts one with the commanding declaration "Thou shalt not kill" and challenges one to acknowledge the radical superiority of the claim of the other over obligation to self. In fact, it is this meta-historical moral experience which gives specific content to the acknowledgement of the Transcendent One whose enigmatic presence is discerned formally in

---

[8]Lévinas 1969:28.

connection with that awareness of the infinite which is part of the constitution of human being.

Further, in adducing the idea of infinity as a formal constituent of human being, Lévinas is seeking something analogous to the meta-ethical, meta-historical "I" of the first section of Rosenzweig's *The Star*. But this idea of infinity is purely formal and when it is filled out the content is moral experience shaped by the commanding declaration "Thou shalt not kill" and by the acknowledgement of the radical superiority of the claim of the other over preoccupation with fulfillment of the self. Lévinas' point of standing for resistance to the totalizing dynamisms of modern history has an explicitly moral component. Here Lévinas differs from Rosenzweig's adducing, in his strategy of resistance, of the individual who has to die and the eternal people Israel.

At this juncture, it becomes important to ask whether Lévinas has an explicit "doctrine" of the people Israel and their world-historical significance, comparable to Rosenzweig's doctrine of the eternal people. Despite the presence of a number of provocative *aperçus* on the topic, principally in what one may call his "Jewish writings," I think the answer is No. In Lévinas' system, the reality and historical experience of the Jewish people is only obliquely in view. There is indeed not even anything as explicit as Cohen's instrumental notion of the function of the people Israel as bearers of the ideal postulates of the one God, unitary human history, and ideal humanity.

But if the reality and experience of the Jewish people is only indirectly invoked in *Totality and Infinity* and *Otherwise than Being*, that reality and experience is nonetheless powerfully present. And it is present primarily as resistance. Such resistance does resemble Rosenzweig's view of the eternal people as a sign of resistance to the totalizing Messianic dynamisms of history. But, Lévinas suggests, such resistance was in fact historically expressed, as Rosenzweig did not anticipate, in the Holocaust where the Jewish people is victim. Lévinas, in his Jewish writings, is not unaware of that resistance expressed in a tremendous display of political and social will in the establishment of the State of Israel. But this datum is not systematically adduced. Nor is establishment of the State of Israel joined to the Holocaust as the second term of a myth of death (holocaust) and resurrection (establishment of the State of Israel) of the Jewish people. For Lévinas, acknowledgement of the reality and historical experience of the Jewish people as victim in the Holocaust is cast as a universally valid warning against granting to history and its dynamisms, read in a Hegelian way, the primacy assigned in the first half of the twentieth century.

But Lévinas' work is not exclusively given over to warnings about history's totalizing dynamisms. There is in Lévinas' thought something comparable to the importance assigned by Cohen to history as the sphere of the interaction of groups and institutions. (I claim only a typological similarity between Cohen and Lévinas, not a direct historical influence of one thinker on the other.) Lévinas has worked out a rather extensive social and political theory.

Lévinas takes a long cautionary look at the devastations of the totalizing dynamisms of nineteenth and twentieth century history and then deliberately faces in another direction. Acknowledging these shattered ruins, he recommends that mankind begin, with patience and self-restraint, to construct and reconstruct. Lévinas' social and political theory deliberately stresses, especially for Western societies but with the implication of the universal validity of such recommendations, the establishment of social and political institutions strictly limited in their scope and power. (I follow on these points, the thorough and thoughtful analysis of Roger Burggraeve whose highly selective preoccupations in interpreting Lévinas coincide with my own.)

In the historical sphere, mankind, holding off that outbreak of violence that is always threatening, arranges a reasonable peace, a non-aggression pact, a social contract.[9] Free subjects appropriately found a rational and generally valid order and they give it form and shape by ordinances, written laws and institutions. External authority must be assigned the power of sanction in order to maintain these laws and institutions. But the securing of human rights is a principal motivation for establishing social-political order and the state provides each person with the legal means to protect his rights.

Within the sphere of the social contract, social equality is the goal. But, with respect to the ultimate rationale of the social order, Lévinas wants to push further. He reverts again to the commanding presence of the One who declares "Thou shalt not kill" and to a humanism of the subject infinitely responsible for the lot of the other. Especially with the history of the Jews in the twentieth century in mind, Lévinas alludes to a "humanism of the oppressed," indeed even a "humanism of the suffering servant." Acknowledgement of human vulnerability and indeed giving the self as hostage for the other is the ultimate ground of social and political order.

Thus, cautionary awareness of the devastation of totalizing historical dynamisms is one of the two roots of social and political theory in Lévinas' system. (The other root, as I see it, is stated in terms of a phenomenological analysis of the self in a relation of

---

[9]See Burggraeve 52, 53.

responsibility to the other, now pressed by the presence of the third person out into the realm of the impersonal and thus the social and political.)

In the systems of Judaic thought of Cohen, Rosenzweig and Lévinas, the concept of history is a systemic indicator. To grasp that concept's location, the positive or negative valences assigned to it, its relation to other concepts is to understand something important about these systems and indeed about modern and contemporary Judaic thought.

Works Consulted

Altmann, Alexander

1958 "Franz Rosenzweig on History." In Alexander Altmann (ed.), *Between East and West: Essays Dedicated to the Memory of Bela Horovitz*, 194-214 East and West Library.

Burggraeve, Roger

1981 "The Ethical Basis for a Humane Society according to Emmanuel Lévinas." *Ephemerides Theologicae Lovaniensis* 57, 5-57.

1985 *From Self-Development to Solidarity: An Ethical Reading of Human Desire in Its Socio-Political Relevance according to Emmanuel Lévinas.* Center for Metaphysics and Philosophy of God, Institute of Philosophy (Leuven). Peeters.

Cohen, Hermann

1972 *Religion of Reason out of the Sources of Judaism.* Simon Kaplan (trans.). Frederick Ungar.

Dietrich, Wendell S.

1986 *Cohen and Troeltsch: Ethical Monotheistic Religion and Theory of Culture.* Brown Judaic Studies 120, Scholars Press.

Lévinas, Emmanuel

1961 *Totalité et Infini: Essai sur l'Extériorité.* Martinus Nijhoff.

1965 "Franz Rosenzweig: Une pensée juive moderne." *Revue de théologie et de philosophie,* 3e série, no. 15, 208-221.

1969 *Totality and Infinity: An Essay on Exteriority,* Alphonso Lingis (trans.). Duquesne University Press.

1974 *Autrement qu'être ou au-delà de l'essence.* Martinus Nijhoff.

1976 "'Entre deux mondes.'" In *Difficile liberté: Essais sur le Judaisme.* Deuxième édition refondue et complétée. Albin Michel, 235-260.

1981 *Otherwise than Being or Beyond Essence.* Martinus Nijhoff.

1982 "Préface." In Stéphane Mosès, *Système et Révélation.* Editions du Seuil, 7-16.

Mosès, Stéphane
1976 "La critique de la totalité dans la philosophie de Franz Rosenzweig." *Les Études philosophiques,* no, 3.
1982 *Système et Révélation: La philosophie de Franz Rosenzweig.* "Préface" by Emmanuel Lévinas. Editions du Seuil.
1985 "Hegel pris au mot: La critique de l'histoire chez Franz Rosenzweig." *Revue de métaphysique et de morale,* 90:3, 328-341.

Rosenzweig, Franz
1971 ET *The Star of Redemption,* William Hallo (trans.). Holt, Rinehart, Winston, Reissued Notre Dame Press imprint 1985.
1979 et seq. *Franz Rosenzweig: Der Mensch und sein Werk: Gesammelte Schriften.* Martinus Nijhoff, Band 1.1; 1.2; 2; 3; 4.1; 4.2

Rotenstreich, Nathan
1979 "Die Verschiedenheit der Religionen: Judentum und Christentum in den Systemen Kants, Cohens und Rosenzweigs." In Rudolf von Thadden (ed.). *Die Krise des Liberalismus zwischen den Weltkriegen.* Vandenhoeck and Ruprecht.

41

Heschel's Critique of Kant

Lawrence Perlman
Vassar College

I. Introduction

In the history of modern religious philosophy, there are several books from the non-Jewish world which have had a continuing and important effect on many Jewish philosophers. Two of those books are undoubtedly, Kant's *Religion Within the Limits of Reason Alone* and *The Critique of Pure Reason* (hereafter referred to as The Critique). In *Religion Within the Limits of Reason Alone* Kant argues that religion is essentially a matter of looking upon moral duties as if they were divine commands. This does not represent an attempt to gain knowledge of a supersensible Subject or Object but is a way of representing morality that happens to find its most true expression in Christianity. When Christianity does not correspond with this religious morality it is because it has been corrupted by insignificant elements from Judaism.[1] This Kantian attitude toward knowledge of a supersensible Subject or Object and its role for religion is a combination of Kant's ideas expressed both in The Critique and in *Religion Within the Limits of Reason Alone*.

These Kantian ideas have dominated much of the attention of religious thinkers in the last two centuries.[2] It is my contention that these two basic Kantian ideas, the rationality of morality and the

---

[1] I. Kant, *Religion of Reason Within the Limits of Reason Alone*, trans., T. Greene and H. Hudson, (New York: Harper and Row, 1960), p. 155.

[2] For a modern theistic critique of these Kantian ideas see, J. Stout, *The Flight from Authority*, (Notre Dame: University of Notre Dame Press, 1981), pp. 217-227.

impossibility of a positive knowledge of God, stand in total opposition to the philosophy of religion and Judaism advocated by Abraham Heschel. One of the keys to understanding Heschel's philosophy is this critique of Kant's position. Heschel's philosophy of Judaism is premised on two contrary positions. According to Heschel there is an act of intuition which yields knowledge of a Supreme Subject and that knowledge is not strictly moral within the limits of reason alone, but is prescriptive within an intuitive framework. Within Heschel's formulation of the problem, this religious knowledge is not cut off from so-called external trappings of religious life such as ceremonies and rituals and logically transcendentalized, but is embedded in these divinely prescribed actions.

It is my contention, that Heschel devises a description of intuition to counter that of Kant because he asserts that Judaism is unthinkable without knowledge of a divine Subject that is included within religious actions and institutions. The overriding concern of this paper is the fact that this Kantian description of religious knowledge and hence of intuition is the main reason for Kant's and many others' rejections of the possibility of revelation from a Personal Supreme God to man. Consequently, one of Heschel's major challenges is the articulation of this issue and its impact on Jewish thought. Heschel's criticism of these ideas is directed precisely at the removal of these obstacles. Therefore I propose to explain Kant's position, examine Heschel's criticism of these Kantian positions and compare the positions to those taken by Heschel.

II. Kant's Description of Intuition

Kant's doctrine of consciousness uses a threefold distinction to analyze the process whereby awareness of meaning is possible. His critical teaching is best understood from a functional point of view, as the association of the forms of sensibility, the categories of understanding and the ideas of reason. These three aspects of thought operate together and not in isolation vis a vis consciousness. Unfortunately, Kant deals with them singularly and then cooperatively only in terms of his schema.

In the Transcendental Analytic (B34), sensibility is defined as the "the capacity for receiving representations through the mode in which we are affected by objects." As such, Kant holds that sensibility is the source both of objects and intuitions, which necessarily imply one another. In his desire to create to create logical values by means of his critical philosophy, Kant moves on to the forms of sensibility which enable him to interpret facts in terms of a schema of intelligibility.[3] These forms of sensibility, being universal and not accidental to human knowledge, at once admit of the transcendental relation of an object to its appearance. The admittance of the transcendental nature of these forms leads to the assertion of the a priori conditions of the form of intuition because this act of thought contains nothing but relations. It is upon this rock that Kant erects the notion that synthetic a priori judgments are possible due to the universal and necessary imposition of the form of the mind which is completely detached from the matter of experience.

The second of the tripartite aspects of consciousness is labeled the understanding by Kant. It is in direct consequence to the mind's receiving representations (sensibility) that it can produce representations from within itself. This spontaneous activity characterizes the understanding. As opposed to sensibility where objects are given, in the understanding, objects are thought. Kant emphasizes the absolute unity of the understanding as the birth place of the a priori concept. Again, Kant distinguishes the sensible which rests on affects from the conceptual which rests on functions. These concepts are functions of unity which bring various representations under one common representation. The act of judgment now becomes central. The understanding, as distinguished from sensibility which has an immediate relationship to objects, does not have such a relationship and can only operate as functions of unity via judgments. The required connections which are embedded in the a priori sensibility of the manifold of the transcendental aesthetic, are referred to by Kant, as the act of synthesis.

This act of synthesis, according to Kant, is a result of the power of imagination and without it we would have no knowledge whatsoever. But, before we can obtain knowledge properly so called by Kant, the synthesis must be brought to concepts by the categories of the understanding. Kant's transcendental logic, as contrasted to general logic, is interested in bringing to concepts, the pure synthesis of representations and not in bringing different representations under one concept (B104). The transcendental deduction, (an a priori relation of concepts to objects), takes place at this juncture. It is the kernel of all critical philosophy. The categories of the understanding, totality, causality etc..., left undefined by Kant, act as the modes of knowledge (a priori) which contain the necessary unity in respect of all possible appearances.

---

[3]J. H. Randall, *Aristotle*, (New York: Columbia University Press, 1960), p. 54.

The four groups of the categories, quality, quantity, relation and modality, logically fix and exhaust the faculty of the understanding. In combination with the forms of sensibility and the manifold of sense, the categories yield the consciousness of an empirical order, which can be interpreted in accord with universal laws.[4]

The third aspect of consciousness is reason. As an intellectual faculty, according to Kant, reason is more abstract than understanding. It is with the ideas of reason that the criteria distinguishing between truth and falsity come into existence. In this way, the ideas of reason are not constitutive of the mind, but are regulative in that they render the mind dissatisfied with the chaotic and haphazard representations of experience. Since only the ideas of reason are capable of producing the criteria of truth and falsity, the ultimate distinction of appearance and reality falls upon them. Kant is emphatic in holding that reason is not in immediate relation to an object. Reason has the faculty of understanding as its object with its own ideas and does not create concepts but only orders those found in the understanding. The manifold of the concepts of the understanding are ordered by the ideas of reason because reason posits a collective unity for the categories of the understanding which are otherwise only capable of distributive unity (B671-672).

Reason's positing of a collective unity in conjunction with the categories of the understanding aids us in clarifying the purpose of reason. Reason exists so as to enable us to deduce the particular from the universal. In simple terms, Kant is saying that reason must have a pure concept of water, even though no such thing exists, so that we may determine that something is or is not water.

This is a seminal point in Kant's description. If Kant can hold that the understanding has unity and is the spontaneous source of knowledge, he must make clear how such a judgment or determination of logical value is carried out. Kant must produce evidence that a priori knowledge is applicable to the objects of experience.

Kant attempts to do this by focusing the transcendental judgment on the schematism. The schematism must be able to subsume an object under a concept. It must secure the application of empirical intuitions, which are contained in sense, to the categories, causality for example, which can never be objects of sense. The transcendental schema must be pure, that is, contain nothing which is empirical if it is to perform its correct mental task.

---

[4]N. Kemp Smith, *A Commentary to Kant's Critique of Pure Reason*, (New York: MacMillan Press, 1979), p. liii.

To assure the purity of the schema Kant assigns the intuition of time. Time is at once present in the connections of all representations and is constitutive of the unity of the categories – thereby being universal. Kant links this universal procedure of the schema to the imagination. This enables Kant to claim that the synthesis of the imagination aims only at the unity in the determination of sensibility (B 179). Thus, Kant is able to say of this "third thing" (the schema), that it is nothing more than an a priori determination of time in accordance with rules. Hence, the schema is the critical provision which justifies the employment of pure concepts of understanding for synthetic judgments and upon it all critical knowledge rests. It acts as a cohesive bond, permeating the transcendental doctrine of elements, unifying them and indeed, determining their validity.

Two considerations must be made of Kant's use of the schema. First, the problem it was to have solved must be elaborated and second, there is a decided absence of a key Kantian concept. Space, the pure form of which necessarily underlies all outer intuitions, is not mentioned by Kant in relation to the schema. I believe that by investigating the second consideration first, we will come to an important realization about Kant's description of the problem to which the schema is the desired resolution.

In his discussion in the transcendental aesthetic, Kant describes space and time as the only pure forms of sensible intuition. Regardless of our acceptance or rejection of this thesis, nowhere does Kant realize that *only together* are space and time pure forms. Intuition of an object could not take place if space and time were considered singularly or independently as the means of an object being represented to us. The concreteness and depth of any object assumes the correlation of time and space as forms of intuition within the Kantian structure. If we considered them singularly or independently we would be assuming that objects of experience were statically present and not dynamically present. Indeed they would be flat representations which, regardless of acceptance or rejection of the doctrine as a whole, is not possible or true.

I think that the underlying problem with this position is to be found in Kant's conception of the imagination and how it functions. For, if we were to consider all his other definitions correct and his other functions correctly described, *we would still be unable to imagine the wholeness and undissolved presence of any given object or event*, as I indicated above. This is due in large part to the negligent treatment of the correlation of time and space in the transcendental aesthetic, in comparison to their treatment vis-à-vis the schema of the transcendental analytic.

As Kant forgoes any references to space in the doctrine of the schema we are led to the conclusion that this absence creates an irreconcilable split in the imagination. This unbridgeable gap in turn leads us to reconsider the problem to which the schema was the supposed solution. If the schema, in its attempt to supply an image for a concept, cannot unify the imagination, then Kant's doctrine of consciousness cannot operate sufficiently. As Norman Kemp Smith points out,[5] the schema, as mediator between category and intuition is misleading due to the implication of the illustration that Kant uses (B176). In describing the problem of the merger of intuition and category, Kant uses as an example of the subsumption of an object under a concept, that of a plate and the geometrical concept of the circle. Roundness is the common bond of thought and intuition. The interpreted relation (correlation), is of a class concept and its particular. This would be correct if we were to deny that strictly speaking all content was intuitive. Seeing that we cannot deny this, we must conclude that the interpreted relation of intuition (sense data) and category is a correlation of matter and form. It is then quite correct to hold that form and content, in their interdependence, mutually elicit in the imagination any particular thought or image.

This mutual interaction is the downfall of Kant's use of intuition throughout the Critique. Kant has tried to give an account of the valid conditions of truth that is consistent with formal laws of understanding and reason. It has been doomed to failure because the creative aspect of the imagination must always resist the attempt to limit its activity through rules and universal procedures. The correlation of form and content cannot be fully and exhaustively described through rules. There must always remain, in any use of the imagination, an aspect of indeterminacy.

An investigation of Kant's description of imagination will, I think, yield these incompatabilities in his thought. The imagination is responsible for the fact of synthesis (B103). Imagination is supposed to connect the appearances spontaneously. This mode of imagining is further broken down into two functions. The first is reproductive which is the completion of the whole of the object (of which we see only part) and the second is the productive imagination which combines experience into a simple connected whole. This combination is a transcendental operation previous to experience and not subsequent to it. Herein lies the source of Kant's mistaken assumptions.

According to Kant's division of the imagination, all complementary acts of the imagination are either reproductive and based on past

---

[5]Smith, pp. 335-336.

experiences or productive and based on what precedes experience. It is necessary for Kant to supply us with a notion of imagination that is congruent to experience and thought, so that he can prove the validity of synthetic a priori truths via schematization. But, precisely at this point, his doctrine of intuition gets in the way.

In a seemingly unimportant footnote, Kant tells us something important about the relationship of imagination and intuition.

> For should we merely be imagining an outer sense, the faculty of intuition, which is to be determined by the faculty of imagination, would itself be annulled.[6]

Here Kant shows his true self. While he begins the Critique with the forthright statement that intuition is in immediate relationship to objects and supplies whatever mode or means of knowledge we have of them (A19), he later converts the whole originating function and makes it subservient to the faculty of imagination. Throughout the Critique Kant has assumed that only what is objective is intuited. This has led him to define his idea of intuition as being sensible, in purely passive terms always resting on objective affections. Accordingly for Kant, intuition does not have a non-sensible conformity but only the capacity to require that objects conform to it. Kant cannot hold both positions, that intuition conforms to objects and objects conform to intuition. To assume this complementary nature of intuition would rid Kant of the problem of schematization and run counter to something unspoken throughout the Critique. An outstanding example of this unspoken assumption may be found in Kant's discussion of the logical form of judgments which consists in the objective unity of the apperception of the concepts.

> Only in this way does there arise from this relation a judgment, that is, a relation which is objectively valid, and so can be adequately distinguished from a relation of the same representations that would have only subjective validity – as when they are connected according to laws of association. In the latter case, all that I could say would be, 'If I support a body, I feel an impression of weight'; I could not say, 'It, the body, is heavy.' Thus to say 'The body is heavy' is not merely to state that the two representations have always been conjoined in my perception, however often that perception be repeated: What we are asserting is that they are combined 'in the object,' no matter what the state of the subject may be.[7]

---

[6] I. Kant, *The Critique of Pure Reason*, trans., N. Kemp Smith, (New York: St. Martin's Press, 1965), p. 246.
[7] Kant, p. 159

Here the pitfall is clear. To ascribe to an object a combination that exists necessarily, is to contradict all previously held critical principles. First, an object as an object of experience presents necessarily, according to Kant's critical principles, a contingent truth to the subject. Second, and more fundamental, when one attributes to an object any combination of quality and quantity, one implies that this combination is grounded in external objective relations of space and time, which, is contrary to Kant's views of space and time as a priori forms of intuition that precede all thought.

This problem is not unnoticed by Kant. Only two pages further Kant intimates something is unresolved.

> But in the above proof there is one feature from which I could not abstract, the feature, namely, that the manifold to be intuited must be given prior to the synthesis of understanding and independent of it. How this takes place, remains here undetermined. For were I to think an understanding which is itself intuitive (as, for example, a divine understanding which should not represent to itself given objects, but through whose representation the objects should themselves be given or produced), the categories would have no meaning whatever in respect of such a mode of knowledge.[8]

Kant's only alternative so stated, would have been to assume that the categories, vis-à-vis a different idea of intuition would have either no meaning or purpose or another meaning for scientific discovery or perhaps would have to be resituated within his system vis-à-vis their function and objective validity and meaning. So, it seems, while unwilling to challenge his idea of the categories in association with the content of experience, Kant, also unwillingly held to his first understanding of intuition. But, as I will show, he came to have other doubts about intuitive understanding.

In his discussion of the noumenon (B307), Kant explains two facets of intuition. First, he asserts we may mean by noumenon, not an object of our sensible intuition. This abstraction from our mode of intuiting describes a negative condition. Kant adds that if we understand by noumenon an object of non-sensible intuition, we in turn are in possession of a special mode of intuition which is intellectual but of which we don't understand its possibility. Since this does not fit into the structure of critical thinking, it cannot be accepted as part of our faculty of knowledge. Kant is satisfied to explain only the negative sense of noumenon. He goes on to explain in a footnote, that while he cannot prove that sensible intuition is the only mode of intuition, it is so for

---

[8] Kant, p. 161.

us.[9] In agreement with this, Kant has shown that our idea of "the thing in itself" cannot be specified but has an ineffable character. But Kant stops here. The ineffable character of "the thing in itself" never prodded him to subject his idea of intuition to further analysis. Of course, he very wisely deals with the possibility of a Divine Object affecting our intuition and rejects it, but he never considers that intuition participates with (or is congruent with) a Supreme Subject. Such a Supreme Subject would in fact determine intuition on the one hand, but on the other hand would require that the intellect make complementary associations that would overcome the problem of a priori concepts combining with sense data. This consideration would restore a truly critical position as regards the inseparability of form and matter, structure and content.

If we are to take seriously the claim that intuition is knowledge that has immediate relation to objects, then intuition itself cannot be purely objective as Kant's defense of the categories suggests it must be. Primarily this means that truth cannot only be the agreement of knowledge with its object, but must also mean the coherence of the understanding with its subject (and as such admits that the understanding is not merely discursive but is also intuitive). This thesis declines the continually suggestive and seductive option of philosophy to give intuition a synthetic role. The undissolved nature of intuition must be guarded, not by requiring its objectivity alone, but rather by focusing on the "presense" of objects to the mind. Some forms of rationalism and empiricism seem to include a distrust of intuition, when they formulate associative ideas of intuition. Without concern for presence these ideas of intuition urge the destruction of their own immediate character. This is the result of Kant's overly scientific view that the categories only have meaning when applied to sense data and must lose their meaning when applied to intuitive knowledge which is non-sensuous. This error is clear in Kant's discussion in the Transcendental Analytic where he states;

> everything in our knowledge which belongs to intuition – feeling of pleasure and pain, and the will, not being knowledge, are excluded – contains nothing but mere relations; namely of locations in an intuition (extension), of change of location (motion), and of laws according to which this change is determined (moving forces). What it is that is present in this or that location, or what it is that is operative in the things themselves apart from change of location is not given through intuition.[10]

---

[9] Kant, p. 270.
[10] Kant, p. 87.

If we were to assume that knowledge was totally devoid of pleasure pain and will, then the understanding could not admit of intuition for it would have to retain its discursive character. But if knowledge can admit of the complementary nature of the a priori and of experience, then it must also include feeling as a determinative factor. Presence is not merely reducible to idea. On account of its ineffable quality, a Locating Subject could incorporate these "mere relations" and provide a context for the human subject whose reason is also fused with emotion. As such, understanding is not a mere mental event but because of the role of intuition described complementarily, is an existential event. It must be willed. Experience cannot, as Kant would have it, only represent contingent truths. For even Kant's basic assumption about the possibility of experience cannot dissolve the fact of experience itself, when it seeks necessary and universal knowledge.

III. Heschel's Rejection of Kant

Heschel's remarks about certain Kantian positions are interspersed throughout his writings. They do not appear in any systematic fashion nor do they follow any of Kant's arguments as Kant presented them. Heschel's descriptions of these Kantian ideas appear when they serve as foils to his own description of consciousness, morality or religion. Since Heschel's use of other thinker's ideas serve his own kerygmatic purpose and style, he never enters into a discursive argument with his interlocuters.

This mode of presentation creates an obvious problem. It is virtually impossible to reconstruct, in its entirety, Heschel's criticism of each Kantian position. As a result, I have isolated one Kantian position, the use of intuition vis-à-vis transcendental judgments and the role of consciousness, and Heschel's reaction to this position. Significantly, Heschel's response to this Kantian position determines his attitude toward any transcendental judgments about religion.

Heschel's response to Kant's view of religion and consciousness is present from the beginning of his philosophy of Judaism. In an obvious allusion to Kant's magnum opus on religion, *Religion Within the Limits of Reason Alone*, Heschel informs the reader of his outright rejection of Kant's basic position.

> We must therefore not judge religion exclusively from the viewpoint of reason. Religion is not within but beyond the limits of mere reason. Its task is not to compete with reason but to aid us where reason gives

only partial aid. Its meaning must be understood in terms compatible with the sense of the ineffable.[11]

This passage sets a basic tone of Heschel's treatment of Kant. If, as Heschel says in response to Kant, religion is not within but beyond the limits of mere reason, then the use of intuition must be the vehicle which alludes to that transcendent character. This point is made throughout Heschel's works in many different ways. The following serves as the most concise statement of the transcending character of intuition. It is connected to a discussion of transcendent meaning in *Who Is Man?*

> It is not by analogy or inference that we become aware of it. It is rather sensed as something immediately given, logically and psychologically prior to judgment, to the assimilation of subject matter to mental categories; a universal insight into an objective aspect of reality, of which all men are at all times capable; not the froth of ignorance but the climax of thought, indigenous to the climate that prevails at the summit of intellectual endeavor.[12]

Heschel's use of intuition is clear. His reference to the "assimilation of subject matter to mental categories" is the aspect that needs clarification. This elucidation is made by Heschel, but in another entirely different context. In *Man Is Not Alone*, Heschel criticizes the God of the philosophers as opposed to the God of the prophets. In a long passage that is worth quoting, Heschel begins his critique in the vein cited above and curiously centers it on Kant.

> The speculative arguments are either cosmocentric or anthropocentric. To the cosmological argument for the existence of God, the design and reality of the universe are the point of departure. Its question is: What is the ultimate cause of all that exists? The principle of causality serves as the ladder on which the mind climbs up to a supreme being; He is looked for as an explanation for natural events, as a scientific solution to a problem. Similarly, Kant's moral argument for the existence of God starts from moral premises. If morality is to be more than an empty dream, the union of virtue and happiness must be realized. Now, experience shows abundantly that in the empirically known system of nature there is no dependence of happiness on virtue. The union must therefore be effected for us by a supreme power, not by us. Thus, it becomes a postulate of morality that there is an absolutely wise and holy supreme being. The essential weakness of these arguments lies in the fact that their point of departure is not a religious but a cosmological or an anthropological problem. But there is also a unique religious situation, in which the mind is primarily concerned not with the problems of nature and man

---

[11]*God in Search of Man*, p. 20.
[12]A. Heschel, *Who Is Man?*, (Stanford: Stanford University Press, 1978), p. 77.

– urgent and important as they are – but with God; not with the relation of the world to our categories but with the relation of the world to God.[13]

Although Heschel's criticism openly mentions the moral nature of Kant's argument for the existence of God, the impetus of his real criticism, as he hints, lies elsewhere. All of the cosmological or anthropological arguments, as Heschel claims, begin "with the relation of our world to categories." Kant is the example par excellence of this type of thinking and is cited here to that end. According to Heschel, Kant's use of causality and natural experience misses the point of a religious understanding of consciousness and overlooks all of the problems I cited at the conclusion of Part II.[14] Yet, Heschel has not shown the depth of his disagreement.

In another passage, Heschel overtly makes the connection between his criticism of Kantian consciousness and his own treatment of religious intuition. He is totally unambiguous about the origin of the problem and the basis of his criticism.

In other words, our belief in the reality of God is not a case of first possessing an idea and then postulating the ontal counterpart to it; or to use a Kantian phrase, of first having the idea of a hundred dollars and then claiming to possess them on the basis of the idea. What obtains here is first the actual possession of the dollars and then the attempt to count the sum. There are possibilities of error in counting the notes, but the notes themselves are here.[15]

This rejection of Kant's ontology originates in Heschel's understanding of Kant's transcendental judgments. As I noted in the second section of this paper the use of reason with the categories of the understanding enables us to deduce the particular from the universal. In simple terms, Kant claimed that reason must have a pure concept of water, even though no such thing exists, so that we may determine that something is or is not water.[16]

Heschel clearly rejects this Kantian use of transcendental judgments. The abstract rational unity that Kant claims exists for the understanding, is null and void for Heschel. According to Heschel the only spontaneous source of knowledge, exists because of man's ability to

---

[13]*Man Is Not Alone*, p. 53.
[14]For a thorough treatment of Heschel's use of consciousness see my forthcoming book to be published by Scholar's Press, *Heschel's Idea of Revelation*.
[15]*Man Is Not Alone*, pp. 84-85.
[16]See above, p. 6.

intuit the ineffable,[17] which is based on a personal relationship with God. Heschel, although he does not spell out in detail his rejection of Kant's transcendental judgment, clearly thinks that Kant's mental categories get in the way of intuition. In Heschel's eyes, Kant's attempt to clarify how such a judgment or determination of logical value is carried out is doomed to failure because he cannot produce evidence that a priori knowledge is applicable to the objects of experience. Nor can Kantian intuition indicate the presence of meanings in other than logical terms.

Kant's attempt to produce the hierarchical nature of thought and its limitations is severely flawed in Heschel's eyes because it cannot sufficiently allude to the role of intuition which is existential and depends on some situational aspects.[18] It is within this context that Heschel's phenomenological descriptions of awe and wonder for example, provide the epistemological counterpoint to this Kantian detachment.[19] This is not a mere theoretical point for Heschel. In practical terms, as Heschel made clear in an appendix to *The Sabbath* occasioned by a misunderstanding of his concept of rest, space and time function interdependently as intuitional concepts in a way they do not for Kant.[20] And for Heschel, this is not a mere subjective representation. There is an objective continuum with human actions.

> Not things but deeds are the source of our sad perplexities. Confronted with a world of things, man unloosens a tide of deeds. The fabulous fact of man's ability to act, **the wonder of doing,** is no less amazing than the marvel of being. Ontology inquires: what is **being?** What does it mean to be? The religious mind ponders; what is **doing?** What does it mean to do? What is the relation between the doer and the deed? between doing and being? Is there a purpose to fulfill, a task to carry out?[21]

---

[17]"If our basic concepts are impregnable to analysis, then we must not be surprised that the ultimate answers are not attainable by reason alone. If it is impossible to define 'goodness,' 'value,' or 'fact,' how should we ever succeed in defining what we mean by God? Every religious act and judgment involves the acceptance of the ineffable, the acknowledgement of the inconceivable." *God in Search of Man*, p. 103.

[18]The section on "Situational Thinking" in *God in Search of Man*, pp. 5-6, makes this abundantly clear.

[19]For a complete description of this phenomenological attitude see my dissertation, "Abraham Heschel's Idea of Revelation, Phenomenologically Considered."

[20]A. Heschel, *The Earth is the Lord's* and *The Sabbath*, (New York: Harper and Row, 1966), pp. 103-117.

[21]*God in Search of Man*, p. 285.

It is the objective nature of space and time as elements of man's practice that contribute to Heschel's critique of transcendental judgments.

In a passage closely following the Kantian one quoted above, Heschel, in a somewhat poetic, but no less meaningful philosophical manner speaks of the existential function of intuition vis-à-vis thought.

> We have no power to reach the climax of thought, no wings upon which to rise and leave all dangers of distortion behind. But we are at times ablaze against and beyond our own power, and unless human existence is dismissed as an insane asylum, the spectrum analysis of that ray is evidence for those who look for it.[22]

The theoretical and the practical uses of intuition in Heschel's philosophy of religion and his philosophy of Judaism indicate Heschel's profound respect for the use of reason but his ultimate rejection and refutation of Kant's (and for that matter, anyone who advocates a similar strategy) assertion that transcendental judgments can penetrate the meaning of religion. The evidence of God's presence is of a phenomenological and existential nature, never to be categorized in pure concepts nor to be confused with empirical limitations. And religion is as much a rational as a non-rational response to that evidence.

---

[22]*Man Is Not Alone*, p. 85.

42

Ararat and Its Fortress: Excerpts from the Rawidowicz-Margulies Correspondence[1]

Benjamin Ravid
Brandeis University

Simon Rawidowicz (1896-1957) was at the time of his passing Philip Lown Professor of Jewish Philosophy and Hebrew Literature and first chairman of the Department of Near Eastern and Judaic Studies at Brandeis University. Rawidowicz was known for his scholarship which centered around Saadia, Maimonides, Mendelssohn, Krochmal and the role of interpretation in Jewish thought, as well as for his ideological writings on the relationship between the Land of Israel and the Diaspora.[2] As a result of his deep commitment to

---

[1]I wish to thank Mr. Alexander Margulies for making available the correspondence from which the following excerpts from the letters of Rawidowicz are taken, and Mr. Samuel J. Goldsmith of London for his great encouragement and help in identifying certain realia. Also Ms. Sylvia Fuks Fried and Prof. Howard Adelman for their perceptive comments.

Hebrew and Yiddish words originally written in Hebrew characters have been underlined, and omissions within the text of the excerpts indicated by [...]. Certain minor changes in spelling and punctuation have been made, and also translations of certain words and lines in Hebrew, Yiddish and German as well as a few occasional words of explanation have been provided in square brackets.

[2]For an introduction to the life, scholarship and ideology of Rawidowicz, see "Lehayyav ulektavav shel Shimon Rawidowicz," in S. Rawidowicz, *Iyyunim Bemahashevet Yisrael*, B. Ravid, ed., 2 vols. (Jerusalem, 1969-71), I, 17-82 (Hebrew pagination), published in a condensed English version, "The Life and

227

scholarship and Hebrew creativity, Rawidowicz did not limit himself only to literary activity but also devoted himself to practical matters, including the founding of the Brit Ivrit Olamit in Berlin in 1931,[3] and the establishment of two Hebrew publishing houses, Ayanot in Berlin in 1922[4] and Ararat in London in 1942.[5]

In London, in the early years of World War Two, Rawidowicz met the brothers Benno and Alexander Margulies. In the words of Alexander Margulies some forty-five years later, "My brother Benno was a Maskil in the traditional mould, and kept contact with Jewish scholars and writers. Simon Rawidowicz was one of them. Simon and I shared memories of a period in Germany during the Weimar Republic and until the Nazi upheaval. We hit it off from the word go. During subsequent conversations, Rawidowicz told me that he used to edit *Yalkut*, a Hebrew supplement to an Anglo-Zionist paper, published by the Zionist Federation. It folded up with the beginning of the war. He complained that there was not a single Hebrew word printed in Europe, and that nothing was done to save European Jewish culture from the ruins. I asked what he thought could be done. He had various ideas, among them the idea of a proper Hebrew publication. This, he said, would not only keep Hebrew culture alive but also give an outlet to a number of refugee Hebrew scholars, as well as the few Anglo-Jews who wrote Hebrew, perhaps three or four.

"Rawidowicz wondered whether a fund for such a publication could be established in England while the war was raging. I was never good at fundraising. I am incapable of asking people to part with money even for a good cause. But I don't mind taking financial responsibilities myself for something I believe in. I asked Rawidowicz straight: What is involved in terms of money, assuming the facilities are there. He said there was still a very good Hebrew printer in London, and he named a sum. It was a goodly sum of money but not something beyond

---

Writings of Simon Rawidowicz," in S. Rawidowicz, *Israel: The Ever-Dying People and Other Essays*, B. Ravid, ed. (Rutherford, New Jersey, 1986), pp. 13-50. A bibliography of Rawidowicz's major writings appeared in *Iyyunim*, I, pp. 83-92 (Hebrew pagination), and in an updated version in *Hagut Umaaseh*, A. A. Greenbaum and A. Ivry, eds. (Haifa, 1983), pp. 1-9.

[3]For details, see "Lehayyav," pp. 33-42 (Hebrew pagination); "The Life and Writings," pp. 23-25.

[4]For details, see "Lehayyav," pp. 26-29 (Hebrew pagination); "The Life and Writings," pp. 17-20.

[5]For details, see "Lehayyav," pp. 53-68 (Hebrew pagination); "The Life and Writings," pp. 31-45.

the capacity of myself, perhaps with some help from members of my family and one or two outsiders, if they should be willing.

"I told Rawidowicz to go ahead. This is how it started. We established a non-profit making society with the aim to foster Hebrew literature and to encourage Jewish learning."[6]

9 November 1942

I think that it would be advisable for many reasons to name the Publishing House (or Society): Ararat (The Ararat Publishing Society). [...] Our activities and books should symbolize the top of the mountains of Ararat, which were first seen when the terrible mabul [flood] reached its climax, or rather began to decrease. Please do think it over with your brother.

6 April 1943

I am glad you were interested in the controversy between Lavater and Mendelssohn. What a nice century the 18th one was! People could discuss most burning problems without being sent to a concentration camp etc! How cruel are our times.

He deaseret yeme teshuvah, 5704 [The fifth of the ten days of repentance, 22 September 1943]

Yes, you are fully entitled to a sense of pride over the *Metsudah* [Fortress, the name given to Ararat's Hebrew miscellany]. Pride over money or any material things is surely not a virtue. It is different with spiritual achievements. "Pride" means here that our efforts have encouraged our fellow-men to something, be it an action or "just" an act of faith, of belief in the possibility of doing things in a proper and satisfactory way. "Pride" just indicates our joy over an "echo" reaching us from unexpected corners.

As far as I am concerned, I am glad that Hebrew is the spiritual pioneer in the desert of Anglo-Jewry; also that Hebrew, the tongue of our great and sacred fore-fathers, is regaining its due respect and authority. [...] The revival of Anglo-Jewry, the raising of its spiritual standard will thus begin with the restoration of "derech eretz" to our national language and its literature.

4 November 1943

I have just received the news that you are nursing a cold in Liverpool – ausgerechnet....And this in spite of the fact that you went there on a holy mission: bar mitzvah. Our sages used to say: *Sheluhe*

---

[6]Memoir of Alexander Margulies, April 1987.

mitzvah einan nezokin (those who are discharging a mitzvah, no harm befalls them). Unfortunately, so many things happen which contradict the letter and the spirit of the wise statements of our sages. [...]

To cheer you up – here are two of the *Metsudah*-articles: Parkes's and Kobler's.[7] Both have been here and there "modified" in their Hebrew dress. The one will show you what the "best of the Gentiles" think of us, the other – what the post-1933 "English" Jews have done here – in every respect much, much more than the pre-1933 "English" Jews. I hope both will interest you.

21 December 1943

It is very, very kind and thoughtful of you to suggest the dedication of the *Metsudah* to the memory of my late father-in-law.[8] Yet, as I explained to your brother, since the volume is dedicated to the memory of our hundreds of thousands of Martyrs it cannot be connected with any individual name.

Meine Frau hat hier in einer Library ein Buch von H. G. Wells entdeckt, das heisst: *All Aboard for Ararat!!* (London, 1940, Secker and Warburg), das sogar ein *"Symbol"* hat, das dem *unsrigen sehr nahe kommt!* [My wife discovered here in a library a book by H. G. Wells entitled: *All Aboard for Ararat!!* (London, 1940, Secker and Warburg), that even has a *"symbol"* {logo?} that *comes very close to ours!*][9]

19 March 1944

About 2 1/2 years ago I put myself at the disposal of my opponents for 8 consecutive weeks at the Anglo-Palestine Club. Although the series of my lectures was arranged by Mr. [Sol] Temkin [Deputy General Secretary] of the [British] Zionist Federation, various officials of 77 and 75 Great Russell Street pressed on Mr. Temkin to stop it after the second lecture. Mr. Temkin said to me: "I told them, if my Zionism cannot stand any critical analysis, so what is the good of it?" I remember, [Sir Leon] Simon told me in those days that it was said at a meeting of the Education and Organization Committee of the Federation that this series was one of the finest activities of the

---

[7]The two articles, both published in Hebrew in *Metsudah* 2 (1943), are J. Parkes, "The Jews in England," pp. 64-75, and F. Kobler, "Achievements of the Jewish Refugees in England, 1933-1943," pp. 223-230.

[8]On Alfred Klee, the Berlin lawyer and Jewish communal and Zionist leader, see *Encyclopedia Judaica*, s.v.; *Metsudah* 3 (1943), pp. 426-428; "Lehayyav," p. 31 (Hebrew pagination); "The Life and Writings," pp. 20-21.

[9]On Rawidowicz's wife, Esther Eugenie Klee-Rawidowicz, see "Lehayyav," pp. 31-33 (Hebrew pagination); "Life and Writings," 20-21.

Federation in recent years, and he laughed at it with as much bitterness and irony as he did publicly when your brother said that the *Metsudah* had already exercised some influence in this country.

Well, not all danger is outside. The greatest danger for Zionism and Hebrew in this country as in many others lies *within* the ranks of Zionists and Hebraists. Sterile Hebraism without vision, without faith in the Jewish people, without power of initiative is responsible for the very low standard of Jewish education and Hebrew literature in this country. Those responsible for this state of affairs prefer undermining new efforts to "apologizing" for their own life-failure. We, however, have to adhere to our task and to carry it on till more worthy supporters will come with greater vision and more understanding of the main-problem ahead.

28 June 1944

I would like to know how you are, how you and your wife "take" the Hitlerite "Golem" [rockets]. Do you get all the London "warnings?" It is a most exciting experience. Various reports make on me the impression as if it is just the lifelessness of the new device which produces the terrific shock. As long as we know that there is a human living inside the bomber over our heads, we still have some kind of "communion" with our enemy: at least language, speech, life in common. Something might happen. The murderer may change his mind etc. It is the lack of all "community" with that pilotless semi-man bomber, this being exposed to a lifeless, heartless, soulless, feelingless "Golem," which makes us so speechless, feel so hopeless. We understand murder when it is "aimed at us," we can even take it; we lose all patience when confronted with a killing machine let loose, without a certain aim. Much more can probably be said about it. It is man's first experience of this kind – what a foretaste of World War III, etc!

3 August 1944

When one sees Hitler's end nearing and one examines the way this end is coming, one becomes a great believer in *sakhar vaonesh*, reward and punishment. Yet why was it at all possible that such a monster should rise so high and bring so much misery upon man – and destroy about 3 or 4 million Jewish men and women and children? Here it is where a clear reply is wanting. Here we are at loss to understand. Hitler will be punished – and I am so glad about his recent narrow escape: why should he die so easily, and before he and his gang have seen the disaster of the hell they have built to the last? Why should the "good Germans" of 1960 or so be able to say: if the Jews etc. had not killed our Messiah in 1944, he would have made the Germans the masters of the world, for we were not beaten in 1944, not at all, just a stab in the back etc. As an "old Jew" I say about his escape: *gam zu letovah* [this too was for the good]. Satan was spared for something "better," for an end more benefiting to mankind.

On the other hand, how happy one is to witness Churchill's triumph over Hitler, Mussolini etc. For so many years before the war, he was calling in the wilderness, warning, admonishing – and suspected, kept away, ridiculed by his own party and the others. What a comfort it is to see the great warner of 1933 etc. as the great victor in....Yes, there is punishment, there is reward, though we do not always live to see it, though it comes about not in the way we expected it to come.

18 August 1944

I was glad to hear from you. We both agree on Hitler, i.e., on his "escape." But here is also a reply to your question whether there is a precedent in history for the success of an honest man and for the downfall of Satan. There are as a matter of fact two aspects, one of time or timeliness and one of timelessness or eternity. Though it is not easy, we have to view many of the things which matter to us and to our fellow-men from both angles. Time is on the side of Satan. Eternity not. In the long run, no dictatorship, no tyranny survives. But it does prosper in the short run. Man's tragedy is that he lives in time, not in eternity, and he cannot view things from the angle of eternity, sub specie eternitatis, as our great Baruch-Benedictus Spinoza called it. Aber alles hat seine "Zeit." Auch "Ewigkeiten" haben ihre "Zeit." Die Hitler-Ewigkeit, die bisher ca. 11 Jahre gedauert hat, nähert sich zusehends ihrer "Zeit"..., d.h. ihrem Ende. [But everything has its "time." Also "eternities" have their "time." The Hitler-eternity, which has so far lasted around 11 years, obviously approaches its "time," that is, its end]. Well, try to think always of "the long run." It is the only one that really matters. The more you view things, men and events from this angle, the better you will grasp them, the more peace it will bring to your mind.

19 October 1944

Is your wife still without a nurse? It must be a great strain on her. I know it from our little experience. It seems to me that most children do not repay their mothers their due. Their due is one of the things which our Sages used to describe as *devarim sheen lahem shiur* – not given to measurement.

You are absolutely right in your observations. These indifferent and non-interested aloof English or British Jews, many of them could be easily won for Jewish things positive, if they were properly approached and adequately enlightened. It is a pity, Zionism – not only in England – has not found so far the means and ways to open the hearts of these people. Opening their pockets, "capturing" institutions alone will not do. I am glad you are in favour of alloting 50% of the collections for education on the spot. Does Zionism spend on education even 5% of its income? [...]

Recently more reviews and references have been published in Palestine about the *Metsudah* – and very enthusiastic too. Yes, you have done something very good – you may say it to yourself whenever you are on the verge of becoming disappointed at things which displease you. And I am sure, with joined forces we shall erect a stable literary building which will inspire the lecturers, the educators and their audience. We are on the top of the work to be done. You remember the gentleman – excuse me, it was a Sir, but when I knew him and we were friends he was a gentleman... – who told us to climb down, to teach "aleph beth." This, of course, has to be done. But all "aleph beth" has failed in this country because there was no vision of the peak of the educational system, no faith in the gimel, dalet etc. Those who criticise me, most of them are responsible for the present "Tiefstand," low level of Jewish education and Zionist life in this country. They are like the "ganev" in the Jewish story who ganvet sich arain [sneaked in] among the people looking for the ganev, and join in the shouting: chapt dem ganev [grab the thief]....

I am glad to inform you that there are bright prospects for an agreement between us and the Hebraists in the U.S.A. according to which they will buy from us about 200 copies of each *Metsudah* volume. I have been working on it very long, corresponding with various people in N.Y. It will be very good to be sure of a fair distribution in the U.S.A. I consider ca. 200 copies as a beginning.

14 November 1944

First things first. Our first thing is the *Metsudah*. Yes, it is a fat baby; or rather twins. I hope to know very soon the exact number of the pages, well over 400. As a normal volume should consist of 250-300 pages, it is justified to present a volume of ca. 450 pages as a double one: III-IV. Vol. II was ready by Christmas 1943. If Naroditsky [the printer] will make an effort – and he *must* do it, I admonish him *daily* – vol. III-IV will be ready latest by the middle or end of January. When this will be ready, it will be some achievement, even from the merely technical point of view. At present I am working top speed. For years I have not been under such a strain. But I must see it to its proper end. It is, of course, a pity that I must even read three proofs of every line (of 450 pages...), as I have nobody in London whom I could entrust with this work. Well, there is nothing which I would not be ready to do for our *Metsudah* – as long as I can go on in this tempo. [...]

God made me write in a language, the readers of which are so "happy," "satisfied" and complacent that many of them are not too keen to listen. But that language is mine, I am hers, and we shall never part.

4 January 1945

As to the sale [of *Metsudah*] in Palestine – it is partially due to inadequate organization, partly to a "passive boycott" in Palestine as far as Hebrew non-Palestine books are concerned.

3 May 1945

At the moment, the "events" are too good to be true: Mussolini and Hitler dead in one week! Dead? Many sceptics do not believe, Hitler is dead. They have seen Mussolini hanging or lying on his mistress (horrible pictures, especially the latter one!) – but there was no picture of the dead – or gepeigerten – Hitler. Who knows? If a Jew could once re-appear after 3 days – I wish he would have never done so... – why should not an Aryan of the Herrenvolk make his re-appearance after 3 years?...Nevertheless, he is probably no more alive. One of the 4 versions about his death will probably be correct.

And yet there is not much joy in the tents of Jacob. How could it be? For 12 1/4 years we have been praying for this day. But the blows he had inflicted on us, the loss of about 5 million Jews in 2 years or so, have modified us so much that we are no more able of any real rejoicing, even when this most terrible gangster has gone the way of all flesh. Now, when the War will be over – and it is virtually over – we shall begin to realize fully what this Hitler-Period has done to us, everywhere. We have to be grateful that this Hitler-Period did not last a century or so. It might have been so. But even these 12 1/4 years were too, too long.

Well, for the sake of Israel and of our own private unimportant and humble lives, we have to do the best of it: to build, to fortify, to strengthen all that is worthy of it in a life. I feel certain that the foundations which that cruel Hitler-period forced you to lay in this country will be strong and able to resist any "tempest" with which Time may "bless" us – and that you will live in happiness to see the fruit of your efforts in the spiritual sphere. All of us need now some encouragement and strengthening – in the days of the "Katzenjammer" which might follow the V-Day excitement. We have to be on our guard – and think and act accordingly.

21 May 1945

Many thanks for your two recent letters. I fully appreciate your scepticism and anxieties. They are deeply felt by every decent man on God's earth in the year 1945. The manifold explosions of the incessant thunderstorm of 1939-45 have not achieved a lot – as far as the root of things is concerned. The skies are very far from clearing up. New and innumerable clouds are gathering before our eyes. But, all this notwithstanding – no despair. We should strengthen ourselves and not become despondent, though we are deeply disappointed. For great responsibilities lie on us, the worthy or unworthy survivors of the Flood. The darker the clouds in the skies over our heads, the stronger and more powerful must be our efforts to hold our own in this hostile world, to enlarge it, to fortify it, so that those who will come after us may live to see the bright sunshine behind the clouds, of which we were and are robbed. As long as man believes or knows that there is sunshine somewhere, he will be able to carry his burden, to go on carrying, even if he is sure never to enter the "Promised Land." This is man's duty and privilege at the same time.

11 September 1945

You are right, although we have sinned and are sinning very much we deserved a better, more human lot. The Hitler punishment is much too hard. For us alone? No, for the world in general. But "the world" is somewhat responsible for this monster, while we with all our sins and shortcomings and defects are absolutely innocent as far as this great plague, perhaps the greatest in modern History, is concerned. Our fathers would have said: gei un freg kashes auf dem ribono shel olam, auf der Hashgachah!.... [Go question God and his Providence!...] No mortal will ever be able to find some satisfactory answer to this problem of "Why all that?" which haunts us day and night.

8 February 1946

Did you attend some of the sittings of the Inquiry Commission? I read all that was available about them. [...] But we know not the whole of our people's future will be decided [...] by this very Inquiry Commission. The decision lies at home, i.e., with the Jewish people everywhere. All depends on the decisive will of our masses to survive, to get on preserving Jewish values and ideas, fighting for the glory of our so glorious and so poor Israel. Our problem is not – or not only – that of our representation towards the outside world, but chiefly that of our creativeness at home, of our "inner mobilization," of safeguarding our "interior lines" of communication and self-expression. This is which matters most. Are we adequately equipped for this task, on which our survival depends so much?

We need a powerful "Home Office" – which would encourage, inspire, awaken, guide all the forces dormant in our people so as to turn it into a living, really living, community.

4 June 1946 [Erev Shavuot]

From Erev Yom Tov to Erev Yom Tov: I wrote to you last on Erev Pesach....Well, we were on the eve of the festival of Liberation and Liberty as far from Freedom as we are far from Law and Order on the eve of the festival of Mattan Torah, the giving of the Law. Neither Freedom nor Law in our so victorious world. Yet we go from Yom Tov to Yom Tov. Our former "countrymen" used to say: man muss die Feste feiern wie sie fallen....Muss man wirklich? [one must celebrate the Festivals as they occur....Must one really?]

23 January 1948

I shall not "bother" you to-day with a detailed account of my doings here. I had so far a series of very successful lectures in N.Y. (in spite of the snow-mabul) and Chicago. The response is here much, much stronger. Had I invested all my toil, blood and sweat I spent in England – it might have yielded better results. But my heart is still in the far-away Isles, with my family and friends – whom I miss very much.

27 September 1948

Our meeting of 1942 has probably been – apart from our personal friendship – one of the most fruitful meetings in our lives for the benefit of our people and its literature. If you were at the few farewell-gatherings in London and Leeds – and I missed you there so much, – if you could hear what serious, very serious-minded Jews say here, in the New World, of our common Metsudah, you would have surely found very great moral satisfaction. "We have achieved something," as Benno said.

[...] the lahat haherev hamahapechet [the fiery ever-turning sword] begins again to threaten mankind. It is such a shame, such an insult to all of us, to every man, woman and child on God's earth. We do not want bloodshed, we hate war, all of us – and all of us have to do it and are doing it over and over again. So advanced, terrifically advanced in every respect man is, yet he has not learned to live peacefully with his neighbour, to cultivate his life quietly, to grow his children for life and its enjoyments and not for Moloch, the ruthless God of battle and blood. Political regimes come and go, ideologies arise and disappear – and there is no change in man's nature, no improvement. It is needless to say that the threatening and threatened war may put to a superhuman trial the newly born state-baby of Israel. Well, we shall pray this *Rosh Hashanah* for *malkhuyot* – and hope for as little *shofrot*, shofar of war, as possible, for no shofar at all. May [your children] Marcus and Stephen and little Judith live in a happier age than ours – *ase lemaan tinokot shel bet raban* [do it for the sake of the young children]. May the zekhut of our children save us from our follies and their results.

25 December 1948

It is a long time since I have heard from you – and meanwhile it is snowing again – oh, the snow in the New World! – and while prosperous America (God knows how long this is going to last) is celebrating Christmas, we kindle the first candle of our Channukah, thinking of a very remote past and of a not too distant one at the same time. As I said the other day, at a Chicago reception for the Hebrew poet Jak. Kahan, who wrote thirty years ago: *bedam vaesh Yehudah nafla, bedam vaesh Yehudah takum* [in blood and fire Judah fell, in blood and fire Judah will rise], one may establish a State with blood and fire, but to keep it alive, to stabilize it, one needs something else, and much more than *dam vaesh*. Have we enough of this "something else?" We have to make the greatest efforts possible to discover it in us, to revive it, to keep it alive. Meanwhile Ben Gurion and his colleagues argue about the importing of non-kosher meat to Israel – in the day-to-day life of a nation things look quite differently. [...]

Do you like Kobler's book?[10] After years of preparation, patience, etc. – I too invested in it a lot of time and Kopfzerbrechen – Ararat got it. I pray and hope that it should be a great success. It is not unpleasant to note that our *Metsudah* is becoming more and more popular in America. A few Yiddish dailies have published very detailed and complimentary reviews.

16 January 1949

I am glad to tell you that the *Metsudah* begins to be "discovered" by American Jewry. With some patience the *Metsudah* will perhaps become the leading Hebrew forum. In 1948 it was the *only* Hebrew Sammelbuch [miscellany] published on God's earth – imagine, not even Palestine has published one Miscellany of the size and format of the *Metsudah*. I am sending you in a separate cover a few articles about our *Metsudah*. [...] It is interesting: a religious Zionist like Carlebach and

---

[10]F. Kobler, *Letters of Jews Throughout the Ages*, 2 vols. (London, 1952), distributed in the United States under the title *A Treasury of Jewish Letters*.

Yiddishists and Bundists like Niger, Finkelstein, etc., so divergent elements, can identify themselves with the *Metsudah*. Is this not a good omen? According to Ben Uri (Who is he? Why does he hide his name?) the Agudah too admires the *Metsudah*....Herz, was willst du noch? [Heart, what more do you wish?]

21 September 1949

I get so often inquiries – from various countries, camps and individuals – about the *Metsudah*. Its continuation now is as urgent as ever. One needs badly such a free and independent platform. It will be studied in Medinat Yisrael too. *Metsudah* will become – as years go by – a symbol for the Diaspora's will to *survive*, to *create* values for life and thought. The coming volumes will have a still greater echo than the previous ones. Practically, now it will find a better market in the U.S.A. – it will be more saleable, like other goods produced in the Sterling area.

30 October 1949

I get so often so many invitations – from various quarters – to state my views on our contemporary problems. My reply to them: I prefer doing it in our *Metsudah*. As a matter of fact, if the *Metsudah* would not be continued, I would most probably divert my mind from our political problems and cease meddling in these "worldly affairs"....

10 May 1950

Here not much news. I have crowded classes, many many students, one of them [Seymour Fox] gave up medicine to study with me for the next 5 years. Yet I do not feel like having reached my "Promised Land"....This is not the harbour for which I was sailing in the rough seas of my short life.

Last winter, I felt for a few weeks not too well at all. I asked a certain "angel" not to be too hasty, to give me some time for a few things I have still to do – among them Benno's *Metsudah* and a few other *Metsudahs* (one for *your* 50th!! When do you reach this glorious year?) and a few other things. So far he seems to have been sensible....I feel the last few weeks much better. But the thought of the Chicago heat frightens me sometimes – what a climate! Yet, Americans work hard. If the English would have worked as hard, they might have been in a somewhat better position. Yes, the H-bomb is not a great comfort – but it is too terrible to think of. So let us not think of it.

30 July 1950

I was so happy to hear from Benno about Marcus' wonderful progress. He thinks he will be a Jewish scholar. I say: halevai. My father used to say to me: kenen lernen wie a rov, ober kein rov nisht sein.... [be able to learn like a rabbi, but do not be one....] (the second of his advice I have followed, the first one – who knows?). Equally I would say to Marcus, when I live to see him one day, before his Bar Mitzvah: kennen lernen wie a Jewish scholar ober kein professional Jewish scholar nicht sein....It is a "profession" – and this I say in spite of my great moral satisfaction in Chicago, and after I got (a few weeks ago) a call for a top professorship from the Brandeis University (Boston, which I could not accept so far because Chicago does not release me and another offer is "in the Schwebe" [in the air] – and after all these "glicken" I sometimes envy my father that he did not choose a rabbinic career – though he was fit for it – but went into business. Do not tell it in Gath. Business gives a man so much independence – though most business men do not make proper use of it.

Erev Rosh Hashanah, **5711 [17 September 1950]**

I hope you enjoyed your stay in the Holy Land – as well as the [Zionist] Congress, as far as such things are objects of just enjoyment. Am still hoping to hear from you in some detail about your trip and your impressions of the Congress etc. Many people wrote to me, if I were at the Congress I would have been able to play die erste Violine....Knowingly and unknowingly many repeated some of my ideas of the last 20 years. One Mapam delegate is said to have attacked me. I would have liked to hear his arguments. Mapam threatens English and American Jewry with a second Hitler....He is, of course, nicht ausgeschlossen [It is, of course, not impossible]. Satan is not dead. Perhaps now more alive than ever. But woe unto the young state of Israel if American Jewry would come into the clutches of a Hitler II. That these otherwise ideologically so sophisticated gentlemen do not see such an obvious truism is more than surprising. What the zeal for propaganda can make of human beings. Well, as far as the "diagnosis" of our Jewish problem is concerned – as well as the "prognosis" – our *Metsudah* was not a waste. It will grow in stature and value in years to come.

21 November 1951

As to the State of Israel or Zionism – I never based my theories on any political or economic difficulties or crises. I am not – I have never been – pessimistic about Zionism or Eretz Yisrael. I am surprised that so many Zionists are today so disheartened because of the terrific problems involved in the "cause." My line of thought was, and is: all will be good, fine etc., but even when all will be fulfilled, the solution of the Jewish problem will not look the way our official Zionism prophesies or predicts. Dollars no dollars, black market no black market etc. – there lies here a fundamental problem which needs a totally different approach – and practical treatment. [...]

When one loves Jerusalem so much, one has to pay dearly for it. Whenever and whatever one loves – one has to pay. If so, let it be Jerusalem.

8 August 1952

These days, ten years ago, we met first on the eve of Marcus' Brit – and Ararat and *Metsudah* were born. [...] You must be fed up by now with congratulations, droshes, etc. – yet, I would like to express one wish: may the next decade of Ararat (1952-1962) be full of achievement, at least not less than its first decade. We could have achieved more – if the circumstances were a little more favorable than they were, if we had not started under the clouds of war etc., if geography would not have been as "unfriendly" to us as it was, i.e., if "fate" had not brought about the first distance London-Leeds, then the second, still greater of London-Chicago-Waltham, Massachusetts, U.S.A. Considering all these handicaps – we have certainly laid a foundation for something that is capable of growing, increasing in vigour and value as time goes on. May it be given to you to see the *fullest* fruition of the Ararat tree you and your dear Reb Ben-Zion planted with much faith and devotion. I often think of our first meeting in 1942 – and the following ones in the years that follow – and I do thank to whom all thank is due that it was given to us not to fail where so many failed, to establish something which given proper additional strength will stand for a long time to come. Efforts in themselves have never guaranteed results. We often toil and toil – and do not achieve. When results follow efforts, when achievement is granted – we are bound to be grateful – and to pray for more. So do I.

16 September 1952

P.S. Every Jewish paper – including your Mizrachi paper in London – writes now about the Caananites. When I was one of the first who went out – in the *Metsudah* – to draw people's attention to that disease of our youth, the Great Russell Street was going to stone me....

14 October 1952

Every year I "plan" a journey to the Holy Land – and in the end I see that I can not afford it; for I would not like to go by myself but take my wife and son with me. It is a pity that America is so far from Eretz Yisrael. [...]

Yes, you said it very well: "The wind has changed a lot since the old days." Sometimes when I read official Zionist statements by Ben Gurion and dozens of the other leaders of the State and the Zionist movement, I feel as if they have just read our *Metsudah*....They water it down a little, they do not notice the inconsistency between their "new" approach and their previous one. I never wanted to be right. I hoped and sometimes even prayed for being proven wrong by the development of Eretz Yisrael, Zionism etc. But, unfortunately, I was not proven wrong.

Am I happy? We are too "grown up" to ask ourselves such questions....We just want to do our duty. The publication of our *Metsudah* – and of the two volumes of my collected essays on our political problem, which I am preparing[11] – would give me very great satisfaction – and some "compensation" for much grief caused by many of our "friends" – today.

18 June 1953

And how are the other parts of the world you have seen meanwhile? One thought, South African Jews would soon begin to migrate. Has the position improved there?

I hope your allusion to problems of education is just the general feeling of *zaar gidul banim* [the pain of raising sons] which every father had since Adam, whose two sons were not getting on too well- and every Jewish father still more so since our first Father, Abraham. We are all in the same boat. We would like to make our children as happy as possible, or rather even happier than possible. But no man can "make" another man, child or grown-up, happy. Man, it seems, can make only himself happy – unfortunately he was given the gift of making himself unhappy too....So the two tendencies clash too often. Here is where a father's heart trembles, is full of anxiety, fear of the unknown. [...]

Have I no other "worries"? you first asked yourself. Of course, I have. When one man says to another: "Ihre Sorgen möchte ich haben [I should have your troubles]," he often does not see all the implications of the small and seemingly insignificant "Sorgen" of his fellow man.

---

[11]See below, note 15.

We have to stand up for clear thinking about our Jewish problems – or at least somewhat clearer thinking. As you can see, the "Israel" question is *not* a problem of a *name*. It concerns the *soul* of our people. On it depends the formation of the attitude of our children to our past. There is so much involved in it that I could not remain silent, and even went out of my way to put parts of my Essay into English – avodah zarah to a certain extent.[12]

26 August 1953

As the year 5713 is nearing its "peaceful" end, it is good to take stock of all that we did and all that was left undone. The little note on the Ararat Climb [from *The New York Times*] – enclosed herewith – was very "handy." They climb – and we climb. They look for the mountain on which Noah's ark rested, we build a little fortress against the Flood of disintegration and assimilation etc. In 5713 Ararat gave a good account of itself – with the two Kobler volumes, containing letters written by Jews flooded, overflooded by all kinds of *mabul*, and not all of them reached their Ararat....In 5714 Ararat will do still better: it will give three signs of protest against the flood of disintegration, and in the original language of the great *mabul* epic: Dubnov, *Metsudah* (7) and the book by the undersigned.... [...]

P.S. It will interest you that I got last week President Ben-Zvi's essay for the *Metsudah*, and have already corrected it – yes, it needed linguistic editing, never before have I corrected and edited an article by a State President, so, let us say: shehehiyanu. It is "amazing" that the President of the State of Israel sends a contribution to the "anti-Zionist"....[13]

8 August 1954

The first week in August brings me always back to a certain place in England, "the old country" as some call her here, where we first met twelve years ago, after we shook hands in London: to Waddesdon....And to Marcus' "brith." How "time flies" – yes, time flies and does not do in flying as much harm as man does when he takes to flying. Marcus is already a far advanced High School scholar – and the seed which was planted on that memorable weekend in Waddeston has borne some fruit too, and not too sour, I hope....We could have done more, perhaps. Yet we tried to do our best. Under the circumstances we did achieve something. When the flag of Hebrew literature all over

---

[12]"Israel: The People, the State," *Judaism* 2 (1953), 31-40, reprinted in *Israel: The Ever-Dying People*, pp. 182-193.

[13]I. Ben-Zvi, "Contemporary Sabbatians," *Metsudah* 7 (1954), pp. 331-338.

Europe was tragically dragged down, the lights of Hebrew creativity went out in the house of Jacob in Europe, once the citadel and fortress of the Jewish spirit, Ararat lit a new candle, or rather relit the old one. They would never say, in the last Fortress of Europe where Jews could still do something for Torah and Hebrew there was nobody who cared for giving a signal, saving the honour of our spirit. In spite of begrudging nagging by some "friends," the few pages Ararat added and is adding to our literature – they can already be counted in thousands – did make people pause, awakened them to certain needs neglected so much before. If the Jewish Agency, if I am not mistaken, is following in Ararat's footsteps and tries to establish a Hebrew platform in London and Paris – our efforts were not in vain. When Ararat started its work nobody in the Jewish Agency would have shown the slightest interest in such a project, and there would not have been a penny for it.

As I said in my editorial postscript to *Metsudah*-seven, the issuing of a Hebrew book today in the Tefutzot is a great miracle, *nes gadol*. When this will be no miracle any longer, we will have achieved our primary objective.

I hope you will find a spare moment to "blättern" a little in the new *Metsudah*, and to have a look at the mentioned P.S. As we have not issued any *Metsudah* since 1948, this volume had to be a large one, about 700 pages, for about 160 pages of which the poor Editor is to blame, the rest being supplied by 29 contributors. Divided by 6 years it amounts to about 115 pages per year....It was not easy to produce this volume, yet not as heartbreaking as "Dubnov" – which even if its distribution will take longer than expected, will be a credit to Ararat. [...]

Did you partake in the recent [Zionist] Actions Committee Meeting? I saw in an Eretz Yisrael paper that one unnamed Minister of the E. I. Government called the A. C. *kotel maaravi*....This is typical for the irony and disrespect many of "that side" of Zionism – "fulfilled" Zionism – exhibit towards the "other side" of Zionism, Zionism in the Tefutzot.

5 November 1954

I am always glad to hear from you – this applies particularly to your last letter. "Greediness" in the material sphere is not counted among the virtues. Yet it is a very great virtue in the spiritual sphere. The Saying of the Fathers say: *ezehu ashir hasameah behelko* [who is rich, he who is happy with his lot] – in matters of the spirit man should never be sameach behelko, never complacent, should always try to do more, to give more, to take more. Your "greediness" for Ararat's sake is most recommendable. May it never weaken.

Your idea about the Ararat evening is very good. As you suggested, I shall mention here a few points – of course, you may make use of them in any way you like:

Before the mountains of Ararat were seen at the beginning of the decisive hour in World War II, when Hitler flooded all Europe and threatened the rest of the world, Jewish and Hebrew creativity in Europe was totally extinct, as never before in the last 1500 years or so – in the "Fortress" of Europe Ararat was established, as a symbol for our will not to surrender to annihilation, not to give in, to stand up for the Jewish spirit, Jewish learning, survival of our people, etc.

Ararat contribution modest – but sincere, clean, unbiased, not partisan.

The five books of *Metsudah* (7 vols.) represent a very serious contribution to Hebrew literature and Jewish learning. It aroused respect for and faith in the creativity of Jews outside *Eretz Yisrael*. It serves [as] a link of creative Jews all over the world – from the second President of the State of Israel to young sabra writers and veterans in England, America etc. (You could read here Dr. Weizmann's letter to you). *Metsudah* has not its like in Europe or America – in *Eretz Yisrael* it is considered as one of the best publications in Hebrew literature.

Metsudah encouraged Hebrew literary activity in Europe ("Tarbut" in London, "Shvivim" in Paris).

It contains a considerable number of essays and studies of great, even lasting value.

The Dubnov Book[14] is the only Memorial volume to the great Jewish historian, the Martyr-historian, thus far. It reconstructs Dubnov as a great Hebraist, a very fine stylist – in addition to the studies it contains on D's philosophy of history and achievements in Jewish life, from various angles. The book aroused a very great interest.

Ararat is also aware of the many needs in Anglo-Jewish learning. Kobler's two volumes are a beginning of Ararat's work in this field. Maybe an English anthology of the five Metsudot – containing some of the material especially suitable for the English reader – will be prepared at some future date.

In print – soon to be published – is Rawidowicz's book *Babylon and Jerusalem*, of about 500 pages, in which the author outlines a philosophy of the one-ness of man and of Israel (= the Jewish people), examines in the light of his approach many problems in Jewish life between the end of World War II and the present day, discusses some of the fundamental problems arising out of the establishment of the state of Israel etc. In its first chapter, the most comprehensive one, the

---

[14]*Sepher Shimon Dubnov* (London-Jerusalem-Waltham, Mass., 1954).

author develops his thesis concerning the development of Jewish thought which has a special bearing on the spiritual and political problems of our day[15].

Ararat has additional literary plans which will develop in due course. The fact that the "founding fathers" live at present not in one place but in different environments will in time turn out to be an enrichment of Ararat's activities.

The Jewish world – both the Hebrew and the English speaking one – needs very much such an institution.

Ararat's mills grind slowly – it may seem to our friends – but they grind well. Ararat's message is the same as in 1942, the year of its foundation: to encourage spiritual and literary self-expression of the Jew in Chutz-laaretz, to create a center for creative Jews in various fields of learning, to strengthen the foundations on which the "tent of Torah," mahane shekhina, stands, to remind Chutz-laaretz Jewry of its duties towards its own spiritual survival. Thus Ararat supplies Israel with a broad, non-partisan platform that transcends all borders of parties, countries etc. – where the President of the State of Israel and English and American Jewish scholars and essayists can meet and work together for the sake of Torah, learning in Israel.

Ararat has taken out Anglo Jewry from its isolation. The London Metsudah linked up the spiritually active circles of Anglo Jewry with the world: Eretz Yisrael on the one hand, America on the other.

Ararat has worked under very difficult war conditions. It overcame them. So it will overcome other difficulties as well. [...]

P.S. It might interest you: I have sent Ben Gurion an offprint of my article on "Israel" (the name). He answered me in much detail (7 pages). His answer strengthened my conviction that the name "Israel" *cannot* be kept.[16]

---

[15]Rawidowicz changed his initial plan to publish his collected ideological essays and instead decided to reformulate systematically his views. *Babylon and Jerusalem*, 909 pages in two volumes, appeared posthumously in 1957. For a summary of its contents, see "Lehayyav", pp. 63-68 (Hebrew pagination); "Life and Writings," pp. 38-44.

[16]Rawidowicz sent Ben Gurion the Hebrew version published in *Metsudah* 7 (1954), 11-61 (rather than the shorter English abridgement cited in note 12, above). The complete correspondence between Rawidowicz and Ben-Gurion was published in *Babylon and Jerusalem*, pp. 872-909; English excerpts were published in *Perspectives on Jews and Judaism: Essays in Honor of Wolfe Kelman*, A. A. Chiel, ed. (New York, 1978), pp. 355-368, and reprinted in *Israel: The Ever-Dying People*, pp. 194-204.

14 September 1955

Another New Year is around the corner. Maybe the disappearing year has brought some relaxation in the terrific tension of the mighty nations of the earth. Let us hope it was no mutual "lulling" to a "phony" peace, but a real opening to some new effort of a peaceful solution to the central problems of the world. And as one of the chassidic Rabbis said: *rebono shel olam*, you do not want to redeem Israel; you do not want to, for how could we say that you could not? But redeem, bring *moshiah* to the *goyim*, maybe we shall be able to breathe a little....Yes, the more "they" will be peaceful to each other, the more law and order will prevail [....], the more will Israel be able to live in peace all over the world, go on wrestling with its eternal problems since the days of our arch-father Jacob up to our own times.

6 February 1956

I was so glad to learn a little from your recent letter about yourself and the children. While in England, I remember, we discussed from time to time the problem of "politics." Sometimes it seems to me, "politics" shares the fate of "education." Both are such important – really important, not what people usually call "important" – areas of our life, so much depends on them, as a matter of fact almost everything, and both are at most times in most places in the wrong hands. How and why this is so – is probably a very long story, but so it is: the cleanest, noblest men and women ought to have gone into politics – where our life and destiny are shaped. The best minds ought to have shouldered upon themselves the tasks of education. Unfortunately neither of the two areas is very lucky with its "leadership." [...]

Do you go April next to the Congress, in Jerusalem? It is very sad to see how a great movement, of very great merit, goes from failure to failure, down and down – and just a few years after its great triumph of fulfillment of its vision. The movement loses rapidly its status at home, and is weakened vis-à-vis the world outside. That Switzerland should bar a Zionist conference!...What was granted to a few *individuals* in 1897 etc. is being denied to a *movement* after it has given birth to a State. This is one of the many, many symptoms of the "metamorphosis" in Jewish and general affairs in recent years. [...]

Here – during the session of the University work is much, no time for "speculation," while in summer, during the vacation, it is too hot to "speculate" (nachdenken)....My wife and son – Gott sie Dank. Both drive a second-hand Chevrolet – I shall always remain a pedestrian....Gehe zu Fuss....I "changed" in one minor point....You told me a few times, you were sorry I did not "drink".... – so I began to drink, a small "glesele" of whiskey before going to bed, sometimes into a sleepless night – by doctor's orders....I drink and drink – and have not discovered the *taam* yet....But Gott wet helfen...."

Epilogue

In the hot humid summer days of July 1957, as he was starting a one semester sabbatical leave, Rawidowicz did not feel well and upon his doctor's advice, entered the hospital for tests. With him he took a shoe-box full of paper slips containing entries for the index to *Babylon and Jerusalem*, which he hoped to prepare there. However, on the next day, July 20, at the age of 60, he suffered a fatal heart attack. Alexander Margulies, his nephew William (the son of his late brother Ben-Zion), and the family of Rawidowicz supervised the final stages of the publication of *Babylon and Jerusalem*. Thus, after slightly over fifteen years, the Ararat Publication Society came to an abrupt end.[17]

---

[17]However the name was revived once, in 1961, when Rawidowicz's family published, on the basis of an outline found in his Nachlass, a slightly expanded second edition of his *Kitve Ranak* (Berlin, 1924), which had been out of print for years.

Index

Brown Judaic Studies

Brown Studies on Jews and Their Societies

Brown Studies in Religion